A sheet of the MS of *The Siege of Malta* corresponding to pp. 148–49 of this book, which relate the dialogue between the two Turkish leaders, Mustapha and Piali, about the siege of Fort St Elmo. The sheet was numbered 23 by Scott (top left-hand corner) and renumbered 72 in Edinburgh (top right-hand corner) on delivery of the MS from Naples.

THE SIEGE OF MALTA REDISCOVERED

By the same author:

Samuel Taylor Coleridge in Malta and Italy: 1804-1806

Benjamin Disraeli in Spain, Malta and Albania: 1830-1832

Sir Walter Scott in his study at Abbotsford in March 1831 after his second stroke and a few months before his journey to the Mediterranean.

From a painting by Francis Grant

THE SIEGE OF MALTA REDISCOVERED

An Account of
Sir Walter Scott's Mediterranean Journey
and his Last Novel

DONALD E. SULTANA

Senior Lecturer in English Literature
University of Edinburgh

1977

SCOTTISH ACADEMIC PRESS

Published by
Scottish Academic Press Ltd.
33 Montgomery Street, Edinburgh EH7 5JX

ISBN 0 7073 0131 9

Printed in Great Britain by
R. & R. Clark Ltd., Edinburgh

Contents

Maps

List of Illustrations

Principal Abbreviations and References

COLE   'A Last Memory of Sir Walter Scott' by B. Owen Cole in *Cornhill Magazine*, September 1923, 257-267.

Journal   *The Journal of Sir Walter Scott*, ed. W. E. K. Anderson, 1972.

FRERE   *Memoir of John Hookham Frere* by Sir Bartle Frere, 1874.

Frere Family Letters. Family Letters of John Hookham Frere and Susan Frere relating to Scott's visit to Malta, October 1831–January 1832 (MS letters in possession of Frere family).

GELL   *Reminiscences of Sir Walter Scott's Residence in Italy* by Sir William Gell, ed. J. C. Corson, 1957.

HALL   *Fragments of Voyages and Travels* by Captain B. Hall, 3rd Series, 1833.

Letters   *The Letters of Sir Walter Scott*, ed. H. Grierson, 1932-35.

LOCKHART   *The Life of Sir Walter Scott* by J. G. Lockhart, 1839.

MADDEN   *The Literary Life and Correspondence of the Countess of Blessington*, 1890.

SKENE   *Memories of Sir Walter Scott* by J. Skene, 1909.

Preface

Although Scott's last journey has been related by many of his biographers, no one has so far attempted to present it in the context of *The Siege of Malta*, which was the novel that he conceived at Portsmouth, started in Malta, and completed at Naples. This novel, although it was the central literary feature of his last journey, has so far gone comparatively unnoticed by his biographers, because the manuscript itself has not only remained unpublished but is virtually unknown. It was written in an apoplectic hand, and Lockhart, to whom Scott sent it from Naples for publication in Edinburgh a few months before his death, failed to read it through, and contented himself with a mere sentence about it in *The Life of Scott*. Moreover, in this same sentence, he gave out to the world that it was unfinished, and that it would damage Scott's reputation if it were published.

Although the world has come to learn that, notwithstanding his distinction as a writer of biography, Lockhart was hardly a model of accuracy, his information about *The Siege of Malta* has remained substantially unchallenged. Only two persons have attempted to read the manuscript. The first, who was anonymous, made a copy, in a highly edited form, in 1878 without publishing it. The second, who was a Maltese journalist living in New York, made a typescript of the copy in 1932, again without publishing it. The copy and typescript were read independently by Sir Herbert Grierson and S. Fowler Wright, neither of whom saw any reason to dissent from Lockhart's opinion. Indeed, Fowler Wright constructed a theory that Scott had merely written 'a historical skeleton' with the intention of dictating a romance to an amanuensis, after his return home from the Mediterranean, for incorporation into the 'skeleton'. Grierson, for his part, regretted that the manuscript had not been burned. Grierson, moreover, in his laudable concern to forestall a possible charge of plagiarism against Scott from his French source, the historian Vertot, not only took no account at all of the many original elements in *The Siege of Malta* but subordinated fact to fantasy in determining how much Scott used his memory in writing the novel and how much he used Vertot.

In the pages that follow, therefore, it has been my task to dispel these misunderstandings and to explain how they came to arise with special reference to the documents relating to *The Siege of Malta*, which have hitherto been either treated perfunctorily or misinterpreted. I have sought to do this in two ways: first, by describing Scott's last journey, principally, although not exclusively, from the viewpoint of *The Siege of Malta*. For it seemed to me that there was scope for a fuller and more accurate account of the voyage, especially one written from an approach not hitherto available to his biographers. In attempting to trace the genesis of *The Siege of Malta* in detail in the developing action of Scott's journey, I not only specify and comment on the various stages of its composition but also show how the journey itself, particularly in Malta, contributed to the novel with hints, images and names for scenes, incidents and characters. At the same time I have explained how Scott put something of himself into one character, and I have related the theme of the novel or parts of its dialogue to the broader historical background of the Reform Bill as the principal political issue of Scott's last years. Indeed, bearing in mind Scott's great knowledge of history, I have tried to do him at least some justice by putting the journey for the first time in its proper historical setting, particularly in regard to the Mediterranean.

These aims I have endeavoured to accomplish in the first five chapters of this book, after which, in the last chapter, devoted exclusively to *The Siege of Malta*, I describe the manuscript with special reference to its alleged incompleteness and to its existing pagination, which is peculiar. Then I survey its later history briefly before revealing its contents in full in a narrative of the whole novel interspersed with extensive quotation, including *literatim* passages from those parts of the text that are well written and call for no editing. In the narrative itself I draw attention to the parts in which Scott departed from his source, and indicate the manner in which he did so. The last chapter, therefore, explains and justifies, I trust, the title of the book, which is intended to underline that *The Siege of Malta* is being presented as a 'new novel' by Scott. In it will be found a range of original and swift-moving scenes, marked by heroism, tenderness, drama and intrigue in an action compared by Scott himself to *Ivanhoe* but perhaps more reminiscent in setting of the oriental atmosphere of *Tales of the Crusaders*. Ideally I should have wished to have been able to publish the entire *Siege of Malta* on its own in a separate edition, but I am persuaded that the form in which I am presenting the novel is the only practicable and readable version in which it can come to light. For the purpose of quick readability, in fact, I have not scrupled to supply the necessary punctuation to the text, even though I do say, in the introductory part of the last chapter, that the manuscript, as it has come down to us, is largely without punctuation. I have also modernised the spelling in a few of the quotations.

My obligations, which I now gratefully acknowledge, are various, if not many: foremost to the New York Public Library, Astor, Lenox and Tilden Foundations, for a photocopy of the manuscript and 1932 typescript of *The Siege of Malta* in the Henry W. and Albert A. Berg Collection, and for permission to quote from them, at very great length in the case of the manuscript, and to a much less extent in the case of the typescript. I am particularly indebted to Professor D. V. Erdman, the Editor of Publications of the New York Public Library, for information about the manuscript, 1878 copy, and 1932 typescript. Permission to quote from the manuscript has also been kindly given by Mrs P. Maxwell-Scott, while the Trustees of the National Library of Scotland have given permission to quote from manuscript and printed material relating to Scott, to which I had quick access, together with useful information, thanks to the staff, particularly Mr Alan Bell. My book would certainly not have seen the light without the encouragement and extremely valuable practical help I received from Principal J. Steven Watson of the University of St Andrews as Chairman of the Scottish Academic Press, who, on the initiative of Principal Lionel Butler of Royal Holloway College, first persuaded me to embark on this research, and afterwards read my typescript. Mr W. E. K. Anderson, the editor of *The Journal of Sir Walter Scott*, also encouraged me with his warm response to my first draft of *The Siege of Malta*. Finally, I am grateful to the Postgraduate Studies Committee of the Faculty of Arts of the University of Edinburgh for a generous grant towards the typing cost of the book, and to Dr James C. Corson, the Honorary Librarian of Abbotsford, for the informative replies I invariably received from him.

University of Edinburgh   D. E. S.

We are pilgrims for a season, the evening is necessarily the weariest and the most overclouded portion of our march, but while the purpose is firm and the will good the journey may be endured, and in God's good time we shall reach its end foot-sore and heart-sore perhaps but neither disheartened nor dishonoured.

(Scott to John Morritt, Dec. 14, 1827)

The time is gone of sages who travelled to collect wisdom as well as heroes to reap honour. Men think and fight for money.

(Scott, *Journal*, Oct. 18, 1831)

I

Introduction and Journey from Abbotsford to London

It was in the late summer of 1831 that Sir Walter Scott, on making a partial recovery from a series of strokes, at last yielded to medical advice that he should spend the coming winter at Naples. His younger son, Charles, was a junior *attaché* in the British legation at Naples, which was then the capital of a separate kingdom called the Two Sicilies. Although a newcomer to Italy, he was enjoying the climate, as he suffered from rheumatism. His father, in fact, had used his influence with the late King George IV to have him transferred from the Foreign Office in London to Naples. Before his appointment to the Foreign Office he had graduated from Oxford without distinction, perhaps because, according to his father, he was 'somewhat indolent', although 'a good boy and clever'.[1] He was a bachelor aged twenty-five.

Scott had lately completed two novels entitled *Count Robert of Paris* and *Castle Dangerous*, the latter written, or rather, *dictated* very rapidly, for his hand had become almost illegible after his third stroke; and his speech and movement were also affected. He was therefore dependent on an amanuensis in the person of William Laidlaw, officially the manager of his estate but in fact more of an old and trusted friend. Good-natured and well-read, Laidlaw wrote a good hand. In contrast to *Castle Dangerous*, *Count Robert of Paris* had been composed slowly and with painful suspensions between the strokes. It was laid in Constantinople at the time of the First Crusaders, whereas *Castle Dangerous*, which was much shorter, had an entirely Scottish subject and was laid in Lanarkshire. Scott had lately revisited that county to refresh his memory of some of its scenery and antiquities in the company of John Gibson Lockhart, his son-in-law and future biographer.

He preferred *Castle Dangerous* to *Count Robert of Paris*, although both were markedly inferior to his earlier novels. He was now providing his publisher, Robert Cadell, with a long series of Introductions and Notes to a new edition of all his novels in forty-eight volumes, which had been appearing for the last two years at the rate of a volume a month from 'the author of Waverley'. For he still continued to be known to the public by that soubriquet, although he had at last, two years before the new edition's appearance, openly acknowledged his authorship of *The Waverley Novels*.[2] Both he and Cadell commonly referred to the new edition as 'the magnum'. Cadell's 'judicious management' of it and 'extreme exertions' to promote it had earned him Scott's entire confidence.[3] It had met with such unprecedented success that the profit from its sales promised to enable Scott to repay the balance of a debt of £120,000, with which he had found himself saddled on the failure of his publishers in the Great Crash of 1825 on the London Stock Market. His creditors had lately received a second dividend from him in settlement of the debt, more than half of which was now paid. It was a point of honour with him to achieve financial independence with his pen and to leave his children as heirs unburdened with debt.

For that purpose he had laboured heroically for the last five and a half years, turning out, before the publication of 'the magnum', a prodigious volume of writing. It included three novels, several histories and chronicles, and countless reviews and articles, mainly in *The Quarterly Review*, edited by Lockhart. The heroism of his labours stemmed from his having turned out all this volume in the intervals between his regular attendance at Edinburgh as a Principal Clerk to the Court of Session. His official profession, in other words, had not been that of an author but of a legal civil servant. It had kept him 'in the course and stream of actual life, which is a great advantage to a literary man'.[4] He had retired, in fact, from the Court of Session on a reduced salary after twenty-four years' service only the year before he agreed to travel to Naples. The determining cause of his retirement had been his first stroke as a climax to increasingly painful walking, particularly in the leg that had been lame since childhood.

Thanks to the second dividend lately paid to his creditors he was again in possession of the library, furniture and antiquities of the Scottish baronial mansion that he had created over several years from a mere cottage on the river Tweed at Abbotsford. His creditors had presented them to him in appreciation of his labours. The mansion itself, however, had been bequeathed by him, before the bankruptcy, to his eldest son, Walter, who was still its heir as well as future owner of the adjoining large estate. It included some 1200 acres of woodland, reared by Scott from pasture land with most loving care, thereby explaining why he had referred in his journal to 'the laying out of ground and plantation' as among 'my favourite themes' of conversation.[5] He could now survey or show the woods to his visitors only by riding on a pony at a foot-pace, accompanied by his forester or by Laidlaw, who had to lift him on the saddle.

His journal was—and will undoubtedly remain—the best and most moving record of his endeavours to honour his obligations to his creditors. He had started it, only a few months before the bankruptcy, partly in imitation of the diary that Byron, an old friend of his, had kept in self-exile in Italy, and partly in imitation of the newly discovered diary of Pepys, about which Scott had afterwards written a long article in *The Quarterly Review*.[6] For the greater part of his five and a half years of labour he had made up his journal with method and resolution, again in the intervals between his hours of duty at the Court of Session, filling it with his Shakespearean range of interests and observations, but focussing it, in the main, on the inner drama of his struggle against misfortune, bereavement, suspense, and creeping ill-health as part of what, in a carping mood, he had called 'the necessity which makes me drudge like a very hack of Grub Street'.[7] Lately his journal had been marked by gaps between the strokes and by 'a cloudiness of words and arrangement', as Lockhart was to put it in *The Life of Scott*. It corresponded to his own lament that 'there is a wavering in my composition sadly visible'.[8]

He was aged sixty and a widower, Lady Scott having died after a long, wearying illness a few months after his financial ruin. He had mourned her loss and recorded his first feelings of desolation in the most moving entries in his journal.[9] She had borne him, besides Walter and Charles, two daughters, Sophia and Anne. Sophia was married to Lockhart. She was Scott's favourite. Natural, engaging and resourceful, she was widely considered to have inherited his gentle manners, although his straitened circumstances after the bankruptcy and, lately, his illness made him betray occasional impatience and irritableness, particularly when his younger, unmarried daughter, Anne, allowed the house-accounts to go beyond the retrenchment on which he insisted.[10] Anne had taken over the domestic duties of Abbotsford after Lady Scott's death. Barring her accountancy, he had come to appreciate her worth as 'an honest, downright good Scotch lass'. Her only other weakness, in his eyes, was 'a spirit of satire', which he had attempted, not very successfully, to check, having always himself tried to avoid personal satire as 'an odious accomplishment'.[11]

In keeping with his resolution, after his bankruptcy, that 'I must not let Anne forgo the custom of well-bred society', she fully indulged her love of balls, plays and concerts as part of the social season of the gentry and aristocracy of Edinburgh as well as of the country-houses around Abbotsford. As his constant companion after Lady Scott's death and after Sophia's removal to London on Lockhart's appointment to *The Quarterly Review*, she had benefited, before his retirement and illness, from his extensive intercourse with the *élite* of Scotland as well as with the *beau monde* of London on his journeys to the south connected with his writing. He, in turn, as a judge of character, had given her credit for her 'good-humour and alacrity' as travelling companion. He took pleasure in quoting her wit in his journal and family correspondence.[12] Her health, however, was delicate. Her nerves, in particular, had been permanently injured, first, by the strain of her mother's long illness, followed by recurrent incidents of suspense from his financial ruin, and lately by frightening experiences from his strokes.

Sophia was a mother of three children, including little Walter, who was named after Scott, to his grandfather's pleasure. The eldest, Johnnie, named after Lockhart, was a doomed invalid with a tuberculous affection of the spine. Scott had addressed him tenderly as 'Hugh Littlejohn' in the extremely popular History of Scotland written for him under the title of *Tales of a Grandfather*. He was now resigned that Johnnie 'was not formed to be long with us'.[13] It was also regrettable to him that Walter, as heir of Abbotsford, had no children by Jane Jobson, a rich, though rather dull, heiress of an estate at Lochore in Fife, which Walter had no intention of making his permanent residence in preference to Abbotsford. He was a major in a hussar-regiment, and excelled in field sports and manly games without sharing his father's literary interests. Scott, for his part, took pride in Walter's handsome figure and physical prowess, especially now that his own strength was decaying. The affection between them was strong.

Walter's regiment was stationed at Sheffield in the centre of the manufacturing counties, which were the strongholds of the Whigs, who had lately come to power amid riots throughout the country over the Reform Bill, which had passed the House of Commons by one vote before its rejection by the predominantly Tory House of Lords. A general election having been held soon after Scott's third stroke, he had gone with Lockhart to Jedburgh to vote for the re-election of his Tory kinsman despite pleas to remain indoors from his daughters and in defiance of abuse and stones at his carriage from a Whig rabble.[14] The Whig government of Lord Grey was now back in power with an increased majority in the House of Commons, determined to force the Reform Bill through parliament despite the opposition of the Lords, led by Scott's old friend, the Duke of Wellington, whose party, after years of unbroken rule, had split and fallen, mainly over the issue of Catholic Emancipation. Scott as a Scottish Episcopalian and a Tory gentleman of the old school had first opposed Emancipation but later had come to consider it as necessary, and in the end had approved its passing.[15] Only his third stroke, however, had made him, on second thoughts, retreat from an open intervention with a political essay against the Reform Bill. Cadell, moreover, had warned him that, if he 'meddled' in politics, he would damage his extraordinary popularity as a novelist and reduce the sales of 'the magnum', on which his ultimate freedom from his creditors depended. It was not in his character, finally, to disregard the possible effect that such intervention might have on the future prospects of Charles as an *attaché* on a very small salary under a Whig Foreign Secretary.[16]

His principal listening-post for London was Lockhart in the centre of the political storm as editor of *The Quarterly Review*, the leading Tory journal in opposition to *The Edinburgh Review* of the Whigs. Scott had played an active part in founding it. Thanks to Lockhart its circulation was on the increase, surpassing that of all other journals.[17] Lockhart's ultimate ambition was to enter parliament, but as an independent member. Scott highly approved of this ambition, knowing as he did that parliament 'is the broad turnpike to importance and consequence'.[18] He looked to Lockhart to continue 'the magnum' in the event of his death from another stroke at home or abroad. He also looked to Lockhart 'to write some sort of life or biographical sketch' within a year or two of his death;[19] for Lockhart's talents as a biographer had been tried and proved in a recent *Life of Burns* (1828). It was Lockhart who was to draw the best picture of Scott in the late summer of 1831 before his departure for Naples, quietly convalescing in the dearly loved setting of Abbotsford and in the congenial company of his family and a few close friends without in any way neglecting the remaining Introductions and Notes to 'the magnum' for Cadell.

It was Lockhart too who was to stress that Scott had dictated *Count Robert of Paris* to Laidlaw between three strokes and *Castle Dangerous* soon after the third one, so that Laidlaw's 'prevalent feeling', as he had listened to Scott, must have been admiration.[20]

Scott's intention, as he had already informed Charles, was to go to Naples after a journey by sea from Leith to Rotterdam for the Rhine and across the Alps. Walter and Jane would accompany him, but his principal companion, as in the past, would be Anne. Sophia and Lockhart might join them in the spring for the return journey if the political situation and Johnnie's health allowed it. At Weimar in Germany Scott would have an opportunity of meeting Goethe, the Grand Old Man of European Letters. They were great admirers of each other and had corresponded a few years previously on an equal footing.[21] Scott's literary career as a poet, well before the years of fame on the success of *Lay of the Last Minstrel*, had opened with a translation of a tragedy by Goethe. More recently he had again drawn on the same tragedy for one of the best descriptions in *Anne of Geierstein*, one of the novels written in those five and a half years of labour before 'the magnum'. In his library was a pair of medals struck with Goethe's own profile and sent as a present for delivery by Thomas Carlyle. It was one of several presents from literary friends, including a handsome silver urn from Byron.

Lockhart as editor of *The Quarterly Review* was in touch with John Wilson Croker, an old friend of Scott and formerly a First Secretary to the Admiralty in the Tory administration before the advent of Lord Grey. On hearing of Scott's intention to go to Naples overland, Croker wrote to Lockhart discouraging the idea in favour of a journey by sea, and expressing confidence that the navy would feel honoured to take Scott as a guest. He promised that he would inquire at the Admiralty about warships for the Mediterranean, and let Lockhart know. As an alternative he suggested that, if Scott 'does not go *all the way by sea*, he should at least go from Marseilles to Naples by the steamboat'.[22] Lockhart passed Croker's letter to Anne, who in turn forwarded it to Cadell with a note that she thought Scott would accept the offer of a passage in a warship, if it were made to him, but, as there was a chance that he might not accept, she suggested that Cadell might write him a letter urging him to do so. It was an advantage that he 'is never sick' at sea, and 'the accommodation is so capital'. She also asked Cadell to advise Scott against drinking wine, 'as I do most seriously think papa will bring on another attack which may prove fatal'. Perhaps Dr Abercrombie, Scott's physician, might write to him about it. She trusted that Walter would obtain leave of absence from his regiment in a fortnight.[23]

Cadell wrote to London to a retired naval officer, Captain Basil Hall, who was an old friend of Scott, asking him confidentially to find out how a passage in a warship going to the Mediterranean might be obtained. Hall walked straight to the Admiralty long after office hours, and requested an interview with

Sir James Graham, the First Lord. On being told that Sir James had gone to his room to dress for dinner, he sent up a note that he had just received a letter about Scott, which he was anxious to communicate at once. Sir James received him instantly, and even before Hall had time to read half through Cadell's letter, he assured him that whatever was considered likely to promote Scott's recovery would undoubtedly be granted by the government, and that, as a warship was shortly to sail for Malta, a passage in her might be considered as certain. Therefore to give Scott as much leisure to prepare as possible, he urged Hall to write back at once. Hall put a letter in the post for Cadell immediately.[24] It was couched 'cut and dry sans phrase in the regular Basil Hall style', which Cadell knew well enough, for Hall was the author of a popular series of travel-books interspersed with autobiography published by Cadell. 'Lo! The Captain', Cadell wrote to Scott, 'goes smack to the First Lord and settles the whole affair in a trice.' It was delightful that 'you are to receive a passage on board a man-of-war to Naples—it will be the very thing of all things for you, and I hope you will not hesitate to take advantage of it'. Cadell also entreated Scott 'to avoid wine as you would the evil one'. The last time Cadell had met Dr Abercrombie he had felt obliged to own the truth, that Scott was fond of 'a weall sma' wine'. ' "Poison," said he, "every glass of wine causes Sir Walter to step two paces back for one he makes in advance." '[25]

Scott blamed Abercrombie's prescription of 'severe diet and constant purgation' for a return of 'the spasms to which I have been so long a martyr'. Otherwise he claimed that 'I am getting better every day'. He hesitated about a passage in a warship, even though he admitted at once that it was difficult to refuse such a handsome offer. Moreover, 'Malta is a place I have always longed to see'. But he doubted whether he could be 'so greedy as to ask a passage to Malta for Walter and his wife' in addition to Anne and himself. He was ready, however, to set off at short notice, and had written to Walter to wait for them at Sheffield if the journey were settled. 'You have now a fair field before you,' he wrote to Cadell, on sending him the remaining Introductions to 'the magnum', including *Woodstock*. Only the *envoi* or concluding paragraph rounding off the whole series at the end of *Castle Dangerous* remained to be written. 'It should be a clever thing,' he added to Cadell with an eye to his final bow to the public.[26]

Failing a warship, they could travel via Marseilles, as suggested not only by Croker to Lockhart but also by Charles in a letter from Naples, urging Scott to make an early start before the rainy season in the belief that they still intended to travel overland. Bearing in mind that Scott, in the tradition of eighteenth-century men of letters, also cultivated an interest in science as a sideline, and that he was President of the Royal Society of Edinburgh in virtue of his eminence in Scottish society, Charles informed him of a new volcano that had just appeared as an island between Malta and Sicily.[27] Graham Island, as it had been called in honour of the First Lord of the Admiralty, was *the* sensation of the year in the

Mediterranean. It lay in the direct sea-route to Malta.

Graham wrote privately to Scott not only confirming the offer already made through Captain Hall but representing it as a command from the King to the Admiralty in proof of 'his regard for Sir Walter Scott and the importance he attaches to whatever may contribute to his welfare and satisfaction'. The command was for a *free* passage for Scott and Anne in the *Barham*, which would be sailing from Portsmouth in three weeks' time. In cases such as this, where the passage would be met from the public purse, the practice was to secure royal approval first. In this way Scott would be absolved from any personal obligation to Captain Pigot of the *Barham*, who as yet was a stranger to him. Captain Pigot, for his part, was debarred by the etiquette of the service from receiving compensation from his guests. As a descendant of an ancient and distinguished family bordering on Scotland Graham expressed great pleasure at this 'opportunity of evincing that respect which in common with the nation I feel, and which from me, as a Borderer, is due to the Wizard of my native hills'.[28]

In his reply Scott explained his difficulty over a passage for Walter and Jane before expressing his deep sense of obligation to Graham and the King in a separate letter to Cadell. 'I shall know my destination in two or three days.' He would rather stay than go, but 'for the sake of my family I am willing to make an exertion for experiment's sake'.[29] His family now prepared to move with him. Lockhart expressed gratitude to Croker for the original suggestion of a sea-voyage. 'Sir Walter is quite unfit for a long land journey, and the annoyances innumerable of continental inns, and above all, he will have a good surgeon, in case of need.'[30] Graham relieved them of their last uncertainty by promptly replying that he would undertake to provide a passage for Walter and Jane. As to Scott's scruples at receiving 'financial favours', Graham dispelled them with the compliment that 'the public will remain deeply in debt to you for ages to come'. The *Barham* would not be sailing from Spithead until 12th October, so that Scott would have time to prepare for the journey.[31]

Accordingly, after sending a formal acceptance, he applied for £500 as travelling expenses from John Gibson, the secretary of the trust that had been formed for payment of the creditors. Gibson in turn gave notice of his departure to the three insurance companies with whom Scott's life had been insured for a very substantial sum, and inquired if an additional premium would be charged for the hazards of the journey. Scott resumed his journal after another gap of several months with a view to keeping a diary of the journey in response to an earlier offer of £1000 from Cadell for its eventual publication. 'He is determined to try the journal,' Laidlaw as his amanuensis confirmed to Cadell.[32] He had no financial fears provided *Count Robert of Paris* and *Castle Dangerous* had 'a sale equal to their predecessors', but as 'apoplectic books' they did not 'deserve the same countenance'.[33] He was anxious to hear how he stood in his accounts with Cadell, who had become his banker as well as publisher. Above all, 'I shall like to see your views on clearing out my affairs about 1832 or 1833 at furthest, which would be a blessed prospect'.[34] Cadell had a scheme to pay off the creditors within a few years and thus prevent the heavy interest from accumulating on the balance of Scott's debt.[35]

Laidlaw also wrote to Cadell that 'Sir Walter is talking of Malta and Italy and of meeting Goethe in Germany on the return'.[36] A large party of guests had arrived at Abbotsford to bid him goodbye. So he asked Cadell to see to the proofs of *Castle Dangerous*. Walter was also come from Sheffield with news that he had obtained leave of absence from his regiment. The guests included the painter, William (later Sir William) Allan, an old friend of Scott, for whom he had painted the fine, full-length portrait of Walter, in hussar uniform, that adorned —as it still does—the mantelpiece in the library. Allan, according to Anne, 'is so quiet and agreeable that he is a great addition'.[37] He made a beautiful drawing for her, which, she suggested to Cadell, 'would do handsomely for the poems' in allusion to a new edition of Scott's poetical works that it was intended to bring out in twelve volumes after 'the magnum' with illustrations by Turner.

Allan had come for the party from Edinburgh, whereas Wordsworth, the last of the guests to arrive, came from his home at Rydal Mount on the first stage of a tour of Scotland. He was suffering from an eye-complaint, and could scarcely lift his eye to the light, but he was the guest whom Scott, as a fellow-poet, had been wanting most to see.[38] His presence was also welcome to Lockhart both as a spur to Scott's morale before his departure and on his own account as a great poet whom Lockhart had been among the first to hail in the teeth of widespread detraction from the critics, especially those of *The Edinburgh Review*. He was accompanied by his daughter, Dora, who had lately come to take the place of her aunt—the famous but ailing Dorothy—as her father's companion on his travels. Scott described her in his journal as 'a fine girl',[39] as she certainly was, although at twenty-seven she was really an elegant young lady of the same age as Anne. Both she and Wordsworth had last seen Scott in London before his illness. They now found him sadly changed, so much so that Wordsworth, as 'a philosophical poet', could not help recalling, in proof of the instability of human life, that Scott had once told him that 'I mean to live till I am eighty'.[40] Lately, however, he had made repeated predictions in his journal that he would not live beyond sixty.[41] His family assured Wordsworth that he was much better since his last attack.

As the family and guests assembled for dinner, the old splendid scene inside Abbotsford was revived for the last time. Scott took delight at hearing Sophia sing old Scottish ballads to her harp, followed by impromptu acting of humorous stories by Allan. Wordsworth and Dora admired Walter's patience at some ill-tempered expressions from Anne.[42] Wordsworth and Lockhart accompanied Scott and Allan to the library, where Scott said how singular it was that Fielding and Smollett—'the fathers', as he usually called them, of the English novel— had both been driven abroad by declining health, and had never returned. Lockhart, to give the conversation a more cheerful turn, referred to the last journey of Cervantes to Madrid in a coach with a student, who was later enraptured at discovering that he had been riding with the author of *Don Quixote*. Scott, who had unbounded admiration for Cervantes, could not remember the incident, and asked Lockhart to find it for him in a *Life of Cervantes* in his library. Lockhart translated the passage for him, and he listened with lively but pensive interest.[43]

Lockhart had meant to make a quick run into Lanarkshire to his relatives' home, taking little Walter with him in the stage-coach, and leaving Johnnie with Sophia as too delicate for travel. But Anne was not feeling well from her late exertion; so he remained at Abbotsford and let Sophia depart alone with the children by steamer from Leith to prepare for Scott's reception at their home in London.[44] Before Sophia left, they agreed that she would inform him of their safe arrival, and particularly of Johnnie's health, by means of a letter directed to Sheffield, where Scott meant to make a short halt on the journey to London. Scott made a point of asking Sophia to make his impending arrival in London known to his dear friend, Lady Louisa Stuart, whom he was anxious to see before going abroad. She was a daughter of Lord Bute, the favourite of George III in his early manhood. Some of Scott's best letters had been written to Lady Stuart in reply to admirable ones from her.

Scott took his guests in carriages for sight-seeing to Newark Castle on the river Yarrow, the beauties of which both he and Wordsworth had celebrated in several poems. Wordsworth noticed Scott's pleasure in revisiting his favourite haunts, and he was himself stirred by Scott's presence with him in such a romantic spot. A few days later Wordsworth caught the feeling of the excursion in *Yarrow Revisited*. He was more deeply stirred on crossing the Tweed on the return to Abbotsford in sight of the Eildon Hills, which Allan had lately used as background for a striking portrait of Scott. Thinking it probable that it might be the last time that Scott would cross the stream, Wordsworth, in an impulse of esteem for one of the great spirits of his generation, saluted Scott in a noble sonnet, invoking 'blessings and prayers' on his journey mixed with 'the whole world's good wishes' for his recovery.[45]

This was more than Scott himself expected, for he had openly written that 'I feel no great certainty of ever returning again' in a letter to the secretary of the Bannatyne Club,[46] which he had founded to promote the publication of works of Scottish history and antiquities on the model of the Roxburghe Club of London. Despite this foreboding, however, he was in high spirits on the morning of Wordsworth's departure with Dora, who asked him, as was then the fashion, to write something in her album. He attempted a few verses 'for your father's sake', probably the last he would ever write, but he made 'an ill favoured botch' of them, so that Wordsworth saw how much his mind was impaired.[47] At breakfast (a long and late meal in those days) they were joined by Laidlaw and by Scott's good-humoured neighbour, Sir Adam Ferguson, a friend of long-standing. At table Scott faced John Ballantyne, a nephew of James

Ballantyne, who had been his partner in ruin, although he was still his printer under contract for Cadell despite a recent estrangement over the Reform Bill. Scott enlightened the conversation with touches of humour, and an occasional flash of wit lit up his face.[48]

On retiring to the library for a serious conversation with Wordsworth—their last together—'he spoke with gratitude of the happy life which upon the whole he had led'.[49] In the evening, before the party broke up, he asked John Ballantyne, with his usual kindness towards youngsters, if he had seen his collection of antiquities—his 'curiosities', as he called them—and on John's answering in the negative, he led him into the room where his most treasured relics were, and pointed out lovingly to him his especial favourites, among them Rob Roy's gun and the keys of Edinburgh's old jail, the Tolbooth, as he had described it in *The Heart of Midlothian*. Then, seating himself by the window in the fading light with his hands crossed on his stout walking-stick, he told John various anecdotes and legends called up by the antiquarian treasures. When the hour came for the guests to leave, he accompanied them to the hall, and dismissed John with a kindly pat on the shoulder. As they were going out, John heard Ferguson say to his father that he had 'never heard Sir Walter more brilliant in his palmiest days'.[50]

Before retiring early to bed, as was his practice since his illness, he left orders that he was to be wakened when Cadell arrived, since he was expecting him from Edinburgh with important news about the purchase of the copyright of his *Miscellaneous Essays* from one of his former publishers. Both he and Cadell were anxious to add the *Essays* to 'the magnum'. When Cadell arrived, he cheered Scott with the news that the copyright had been purchased, and despite the late hour Scott talked at length and with glee of the long line of books that would follow the novels. The conversation was continued early on the morning of 23rd September, the day fixed for his departure for London. He sought Cadell in the library, and indicated his intention of writing a preface in London for *Count Robert of Paris* and *Castle Dangerous*. He then mentioned the idea of a series of Letters from Malta, based on the diary that he intended to keep, 'with some account of the Knights of St John, and the last great battle they fought' in allusion to the Great Siege of 1565 against the Turks. He said an honest penny could be turned out of this to meet expenses. Laidlaw had not seen him in such high spirits for some months, and he rejoiced to see little or no impediment in Scott's speech.[51]

He then directed Laidlaw to take from the shelves the standard history of the Knights by the French historian, Vertot, to go with him to Malta. He had last used Vertot for *Count Robert of Paris*[52] and, before that, for *Ivanhoe* and *Tales of the Crusaders*. It was a book—to quote his own words—'which, as it hovered between history and romance, was exceedingly dear to me'.[53] He had two copies of Vertot, both of which Laidlaw put aside to go with him, in the mistaken belief, however, that one was 'Vertot's Knights of Malta' and the other a

'History of Malta'.[54] The truth was that one copy was an *English* translation of
Vertot, magnificently printed in two large folio volumes, with some seventy
plates of Grand Masters of the Order of St John, while the other copy was a
French version of Vertot in five small volumes with the title of *Histoire de
Malthe*. This title misled Laidlaw into thinking that he had taken down a
'History of Malta' besides Vertot's History of the Knights. Laidlaw put the two
copies of Vertot in a box to go to Cadell in Edinburgh for forwarding to Scott
in London.

All the silver plate of Abbotsford had already been dispatched to Cadell for
safe keeping, so that there was much fun and laughter at their all having to use
kitchen metal spoons and a copper kettle, and to drink coffee from a jug. As
Sheriff of his county of Selkirkshire Scott gave Laidlaw a letter of authority to
represent him at county meetings, and a paper of instructions as to keeping the
house, the library and the plantations in order. In particular, the 'dogs to be
taken care of'.[55] Laidlaw avoided taking leave of Scott, 'as I knew he relished
it as little as I did myself', but before they saw the last of each other Laidlaw
met him in the entrance hall, and Scott told him that he had just been to say
goodbye to Mary Purdie, the widow of his beloved factotum. Bearing in mind
the hostile attitude of the ruling school of political economists called Utilitarians
to the type of Tory squire represented by himself, Scott told Laidlaw that
'political economists may say as they like, but I maintain that much good is
done by the residence of gentlemen in the country and much comfort added to
the condition of the poor and the dependants of a family'.[56] The comment
underlined his ideal of a benevolent feudal order of society, such as had prevailed in many ways at his birth in the eighteenth century, and which the
Reform Bill was designed to overthrow. 'It has fallen easily, the old Constitution,' he had written with grief in his journal at the passing of the Reform Bill for the first time by the House of Commons.[57] The House of
Commons had voted for it again only the day before he made the comment
to Laidlaw.

His departure was reported in all the Edinburgh newspapers, as was the news
of the late purchase of the copyright: the latter not so much for its own sake as
to draw attention to the fact—without parallel in literary history—that Scott,
as 'the most voluminous author this country has produced', was now 'the proprietor of all his own writings, poetry as well as prose, extending to something
near 100 volumes'.[58] In other words, he had bought back or acquired all the
copyrights that he had sold to various publishers in the course of a long writing
career. Irrespective of political colour, all the newspapers wished him well.
Naturally *The Scotsman*, a Whig newspaper, made a point of explaining that the
offer of a passage in the *Barham* to Scott reflected honour on the government of
Lord Grey, 'whose political sentiments are different from those of our illustrious
countryman'. Scott's merits, however, were of 'an order which are calculated to
extinguish, if it existed, every feeling that is inconsistent with kindness and

respect'.[59] The sentiment was fully echoed in *The Caledonian Mercury*, which catered for the more affluent and cultured classes. It disclosed, moreover, on information presumably from Cadell as part of his publicity campaign for 'the magnum', that before leaving Abbotsford, Scott 'finished the whole notes and introductions to his celebrated novels now in the course of so successful a career'.[60]

The first stage of his journey to London was marred to some extent by very wet weather and by Anne's spitting blood in one of her chronic stomach attacks. For these reasons they travelled by easy stages, Scott preferring to rise early in the morning to avoid travel by night and also to have a fresh look at familiar objects of antiquity.[61] Anne was attended by her maid, Celia Street, a young woman of trust and tact. Scott, besides Lockhart and Walter, had his faithful and efficient John Nicolson to look after him: a servant attached to the household since childhood, so that, according to Lockhart, he now regarded Scott 'with the love and reverence of a son'.[62] Calm and dexterous, he had been trained in the use of the lancet—and indeed had already applied it several times—to forestall attacks of apoplexy. Fortunately he was not called upon to use it on the journey, for Scott—barring a slight attack of dizziness—bore the exertion well as far as Rokeby in Yorkshire, where they spent a day on a farewell call on John Morritt, the traveller and classical scholar, one of Scott's earliest friends. His long poem, *Rokeby*, had been dedicated to Morritt.

They 'were all so happy to see us', Anne later wrote to Laidlaw about their reception at Morritt's, where Scott found a reply from Lady Stuart, warmly thanking him for wishing to see her in London and assuring him that she was cutting short a visit to the country to meet him.[63] He intended to consult her about a fictitious series of *Seventeenth-Century Letters* that they had projected together many years previously. He wished to revive the project. So before leaving Morritt's 'hospitable mansion', he wrote to Cadell for a copy of the printed fragment of *Seventeenth-Century Letters*, 'which I will soon finish abroad', as 'I am now certain of meeting' Lady Stuart in London. Besides confirming his intention of sending Cadell an Introduction to *Count Robert of Paris*, he asked him for the Introduction to *Woodstock* that he had lately sent him for 'the magnum'. There was a point of antiquarian scholarship in it that he meant to follow up in London at the British Museum for a fresh Introduction.[64]

Unwilling to put literary work behind him, as Dr Abercrombie had urged him to do, he mentioned another project to Cadell, namely, to add a volume to his very successful *Lives of the Novelists*. It would include not only his favourite novelist, Jane Austen, about whom he had written a well-known article for Lockhart in *The Quarterly Review*, but also Fanny Burney, 'the celebrated authoress of *Evelina* and *Cecilia*'.[65] Bearing in mind the vast literary work and correspondence that had passed across the continent between Byron and his publisher, John Murray, Scott suggested to Cadell that 'Byron and Murray kept their machine going abroad and why should not we?'[66] Yet he confessed in a journal entry that he was not 'the Walter Scott I once was', for 'the change is great'. Besides 'a total prostration of bodily strength' when he attempted to walk, there was 'some mental confusion', the extent of which was beyond his power to determine. Like Fielding and Smollett, 'I am perhaps setting'. What he feared, in view of his father's medical history, was that 'I should linger on, "an idiot and a show" '.[67]

Walter parted temporarily from him at Rokeby to go to Sheffield for his leave and to fetch Jane. 'I suppose Jane has made up her mind for three weeks on board the *Barham*,' he wrote to a relative in uncertainty as to how she would be reacting to the prospect of a sea voyage in lieu of a land journey.[68] Scott altered his route by giving up Sheffield and went to London direct by the Great North Road, best known in his novels for the epic journey of Jeanie Deans in *The Heart of Midlothian*. No place on the road, he observed for later information to Laidlaw, seemed to have trees better attended to than the plantations at Abbotsford.[69] Anne wrote confidently to Laidlaw about the best places to sleep at on the road in the light of her experience on former journeys with her father. 'Papa feels himself as comfortable as he does at home,' but 'Lockhart seems most anxious about Johnny' in the absence of news from Sophia, whose promised letter they would not now be collecting from Jane at Sheffield.[70]

Sophia informed a kinsman at Raeburn near Abbotsford that Scott had arrived at her house in Regent's Park, 'very little fatigued', unlike Anne, who was still unwell but expected to improve by quiet and change of air. 'Johnny is much the same, very unwell, but did not suffer from the voyage' to London.[71] Scott wrote to Cadell that 'a very civil letter' from Sir James Graham had awaited him to tell him that the *Barham* had postponed her departure for a week, and would now be sailing towards the end of October. A reply had also come from Gibson assenting to the £500 requested by Scott from the trust for travelling expenses. Two of the three insurance companies had answered Gibson that they stipulated an additional premium for the hazards of Scott's journey, while the third, in 'a very handsome letter', made no charge. On the other hand, a sister-in-law had unexpectedly applied for £150 that Scott had pledged for a nephew in India. He trusted for Cadell's help in this matter, in return for which he repeated that he would be writing 'Letters from Malta'.[72]

In proof that he had not been fatigued by the journey he felt able, the day after his arrival, to drive in Sophia's carriage to the city to ask Whittaker, Cadell's London agent, for a travel-book for use in the Mediterranean. Inevitably from what he was offered he chose Patrick Brydone's *Tour through Sicily and Malta*. It was, as he remarked to a kinsman on returning to Regent's Park, 'still as good a companion as any' that Whittaker could recommend. The kinsman was John Scott, commonly known by his territorial name of Gala. He had come to bid Scott goodbye, and was pleased to see that, although he had been prepared for a change in Scott's appearance, he was not struck with so great a one as he had expected. Scott had certainly lost strength, but 'his eye was good'. Scott confirmed that 'weakness was his principal complaint' before he digressed to 'the state of the nation' on the eve of the opening of the debate in the House of Lords, for the second time, on the Reform Bill. In the language of the day, 'the democrats', now clamouring for the passing of the Reform Bill, had been 'flattered and courted', in Scott's and Gala's view, by the ruling Whig aristocrats, so that now 'their appetite for power won't be easily satisfied'.[73]

Scott then spoke 'of as strange a tale as any traveller could imagine' in allusion to the new volcano between Malta and Sicily. He seemed anxious to see Graham Island, 'if it will *wait* for me'.[74] As president of the Royal Society of Edinburgh he was under a moral obligation to transmit to it any information of a scientific nature that he might come across. Gala, whom Scott had long esteemed as 'one of the best informed men whom I know',[75] drew an immediate response from him with a remark that Malta would interest him much with its Knights of St John and their fine library at Valletta, full of treasures of chivalry. Scott feared that 'I shall not be able to appreciate Italy as it deserves, as I understand little of painting and nothing of music' other than Scottish airs. 'But there are many other subjects of interest,' Gala replied, 'to you in particular' as historian and antiquary, and he listed Naples with its mediaeval castle of St Elmo, followed by Paestum, Pompeii and Herculaneum. Gala had himself seen Naples at the peace after the war with Bonaparte; so he mentioned to Scott that he would probably be seeing there a sister of one of Scott's earliest friends, Matthew Lewis, better known as 'Monk' Lewis. She was married to the English consul at Naples, Sir Henry Lushington, and Gala had been introduced to them by Lewis, who had collaborated with Scott over ballads, and had negotiated for the publication of Scott's translation of Goethe after his own outstanding success with *The Monk*. Gala was sure that Scott would enjoy meeting so 'pleasant' a couple as the Lushingtons. As to Lewis, 'Ah, poor Mat!' Scott remarked, 'he never wrote anything so good as *The Monk*.'[76]

Cadell sent him the Introduction to *Woodstock* with a friendly remark that he need not give himself too much trouble over it in the British Museum. 'I most cordially agree with you that, if Byron carried on the war abroad, you may and ought certainly to do so as well.' Gibson having informed Cadell that a credit of £500 had been established for Scott for travelling expenses at Coutts, the bankers in the Strand, Cadell explained that Coutts would provide Scott with the foreign currency that he would be needing. 'When you find the £500 getting low, you may acquaint me, and a fresh supply will be provided.' A box was on the way to Scott from Cadell, containing the two copies of Vertot together with a trunk for Walter, who wrote from Sheffield that he 'doubted whether Jane will be prevailed on to venture' in the *Barham*, 'as she suffers so much at sea'.[77] Like Laidlaw, Cadell believed that one of the copies of Vertot was a 'History of Malta'.

Anne had originally fretted at the *Barham*'s delay, but she had ceased to do so by the time that Scott had the pleasure of seeing Lady Stuart, to whom he mentioned *Seventeenth-Century Letters*. She had so 'totally forgotten the whole transaction that I faced him down he was mistaken'. Scott convinced her by showing her a copy of the printed fragment of *Seventeenth-Century Letters* that Cadell had sent him with the Introduction to *Woodstock*. It was 'not at all pleasant at a certain age'—Lady Stuart was seventy-four—'to be confronted with such a staring proof of forgetfulness'. To please Scott she agreed to write a few more letters provided she remained anonymous.[78] Scott received a call from Captain Basil Hall, 'that curious fellow', as he had already described him to Gala, 'who takes charge of everyone's business without neglecting his own'.[79] Hall admittedly had done a great deal over the *Barham*, and Scott expressed his personal gratitude. Hall now wished to do more, and offered to accompany Scott's party to Portsmouth to assist in the embarkation. Scott declined on the ground that he had already given Hall and his friends of the Admiralty too much trouble, although he gladly accepted an offer from his old friend, Lord Melville, formerly the First Lord of the Admiralty, to recommend him to Sir Henry Hotham, the Commander-in-Chief of the Mediterranean fleet stationed at Malta.[80]

Scott was taking a letter to a midshipman in Hotham's flagship, whom he had been instrumental in placing in the navy. The midshipman was a young kinsman, Francis Scott, and the letter was from his father. 'It will be such a feather in his cap if, from a recollection of former days, you should take the trouble of showing my younger son any countenance.'[81] The *Barham* was due back at Portsmouth from a visit to Ireland, and, according to Anne, 'has caused quite a sensation, many applying to go' in her. She assured Cadell that 'papa cannot be at a better place', as Lockhart 'is so *kind* and judicious'. Although he still complained that Dr Abercrombie's *régime* was making him feel weaker, he was thankful that he had no pain, and even speculated about the 'too happy' possibility of euthanasia. Tom Purdie had died by easy and painless decay. 'I should wish, if it pleased God, to sleep off in such a quiet way. But we must take what fate sends. I have not warm hopes of being myself again.'[82]

Nevertheless the eminent doctors, who were called in for a consultation on his case by Dr Robert Ferguson, a brother of his neighbour at Abbotsford, held out a prospect that the incipient disease of the brain might be arrested if he obeyed their directions regarding diet and repose, and refrained from literary labour. They agreed with Scott that Abercrombie had put him on too severe a system of diet and medicines, and approved highly of the sea-voyage. Their verdict greatly relieved him. Indeed he did not conceal that he had 'feared insanity and feared *them*'.[83] Sophia reported this 'very comforting result' to her kinsman of Raeburn. Anne, on the other hand, was vexed that the doctors had allowed Scott 'three glasses of wine' in flat contradiction of Abercrombie's prescription. Since one of the doctors was the King's physician, Sir Henry

Halford, and the other was a high-society consultant, Dr (later Sir) Henry Holland, Anne represented them to Cadell as 'such *courtiers*; they will let papa do anything he wished'. Cadell could have no idea, however, 'what a deal of good it has done papa coming here'. She had herself had no recurrence of her stomach complaint since their arrival. They never dined out, but 'have one or two friends at breakfast and never more than two at dinner, and he seems to enjoy it so much'.[84]

His improved spirits were reflected in a long letter to Laidlaw after a little work in the morning on the Introduction to *Count Robert of Paris*. 'I think I can defy the disease, but am not quite so sure of escaping the doctor.' It was not without alarm that he considered 'the state of inactivity, to which I must be reduced' on board the *Barham*. 'But I trust I will be able to crawl about and visit what is remarkable in Malta.' In the meantime he was anxious to hear from Laidlaw how the dogs went on at Abbotsford, and he had fresh advice for him about the plantations. Although Laidlaw was a Whig—as was Cadell—Scott had long been in the habit of venting his Tory politics upon them without the slightest injury to their personal relationship. On the contrary, he had enjoyed debating with Laidlaw not only about politics but also about religion in contrast to his recent quarrel with James Ballantyne, who had originally championed the Tory cause in his *Weekly Journal* but had now turned Whig over the Reform Bill. Scott predicted to both Laidlaw and Cadell that the Reform Bill would be defeated and that a prorogation of parliament would follow.[85]

Lockhart went almost every night to the House of Commons to collect material for *The Quarterly Review*, and to be within ear-shot of the Tory leaders. Even the Duke of Buccleuch, the chief of Scott's clan, was come all the way from Dalkeith near Edinburgh to take part in the crucial vote at the end of the debate. Anne gave the news to Cadell in a letter acknowledging a draft on Whittaker for the £150 that Scott had requested for his sister-in-law. 'There is nothing talked of but the Bill,' she added. She had gone to Montagu House in Whitehall, where the Duke and Duchess of Buccleuch were staying with their uncle and aunt, Lord and Lady Montagu, who were old friends of Scott and on the most cordial terms with Sophia. At Montagu House Anne had seen the newly born son and heir of the Buccleuchs. The King had offered to stand godfather to it, somewhat to the parents' annoyance, as 'both King and Queen and all the royal family must be at the christening'.[86]

Lockhart's employer, John Murray, was not only an old friend of Scott but had originally published *Old Mortality* as the first of the series of *Tales of my Landlord*. Scott honoured Murray by making his house in Albemarle Street his first visit, but Murray was out at a meeting with Croker,[87] who was one of the principal Tory spokesmen against the Scottish Reform Bill, also under discussion, but for the first time, in the House of Commons. Scott drove to the city for another call on Whittaker for the £150 that he needed for his sister-in-law. Whittaker informed him that 'my traps', as he called his luggage, had not yet come from Edinburgh, and he appears to have gathered that the new edition of his poetical works ornamented with plates by Turner 'will be a successful speculation',[88] thereby reducing the balance of his debt still further and hastening the day of his ultimate freedom from his creditors. Murray was in when he called again with Anne and Sophia. Murray received them in the celebrated drawing-room where the meeting—equally, if not more, celebrated—between Byron and Scott had taken place more than fifteen years previously.

Murray had published at the time of that meeting the humorous poem popularly known as 'Whistlecraft' by John Hookham Frere, on which Byron had modelled the metre of *Beppo*. Scott knew and admired both the poem and its author, who was now living in retirement in Malta. He was therefore looking forward to seeing Frere as well as his other old friend, Sir John Stoddart, who was also living in Malta as Chief Justice. 'I should like much to see if they can show me any remains of the memorable siege,' he wrote to Charles at Naples in happy expectation of seeing him soon.[89] In view of his 'pitiable want of strength' he also gave Charles notice that, when settled at Naples, 'I will be obliged to see about an open carriage and a couple of stout horses'. As to assistants, John Nicolson and Celia Street were enough, particularly as 'I may get up a little of the language myself', of which he had acquired a reading knowledge in his youth in view of the importance of Italian for romances of chivalry, especially for Tasso and Ariosto.[90] Byron, in fact, had called Scott 'the Ariosto of the North'.[91]

Although he had not sent Frere advance notice of his impending call at Malta, Frere had come to know of his intended residence in Naples. So he wrote Scott an affectionate letter to persuade him that Malta, not Naples, 'is the true climate for a sexagenarian'. It had everything he needed: excellent medical advice from British doctors attached to the garrison; comfortable accommodation at cheaper charges than in Naples, and monthly steam-packets for communication with England. Moreover, if Scott wished to visit Naples from Malta, he could promise him that the Governor's yacht would 'certainly be at your service'.[92] In keeping with his self-effacing nature Frere omitted to inform Scott that he had commissioned a traveller to England from Malta called Hope to present Scott with a copy of his translation of Aristophanes, which was about to be published. Hope had himself known Scott many years before in Edinburgh, as he lost no time in informing him on reaching London before the delivery of Frere's letter. After referring to the presentation-copy, he assured Scott that 'you will find Mr. Frere there; I should think your meeting would be a mutual pleasure'. He then ventured to explain, in the light of his own recent experience at Naples from Malta, that the custom-house officials in Italy 'ask more particularly about books than anything else', and 'numbers with these fools always creates suspicion'.[93] As Charles was later to confirm to Sophia, books 'are certainly seized for custom and censure'.[94]

This information reached Scott almost at the same time that he received his 'traps' from Cadell through Whittaker, including the box containing the two copies of Vertot. 'I understand they are absurdly strict about contraband books,' he wrote to Cadell. Therefore he was sending back 'the folio copy of the Knights of Malta, which I would not like lost; the small one must take its chance'. In other words, he sent back the valuable *English* translation of Vertot, but kept the French version in five small volumes. Pleased with his 'traps', he remarked to Cadell that 'I shall be very fine, having nothing less than the uniform of a brigadier-general' of the Royal Archers, the ancient body-guard of Scotland. It was intended as a court-dress for Italy, where he expected to be presented to the King, Ferdinand II of Naples. Whittaker had offered him 'any further supply' in addition to the money for his sister-in-law, but 'I shall have no occasion'. Everything was now ready for their departure except the *Barham*, 'which I have not yet heard of, but which is spoken of as daily expected' from Ireland. He was 'now eager to cast to sea', unlike Jane, who 'seems to have taken fright and will stay with her mother' until Walter returned from Italy.[95]

Inevitably the disturbed political situation had caused a slump in business, particularly in the city, so that Scott wrote confidentially to Cadell, whose own business was inextricably connected with the London market, that 'in this town people say, and knowing ones, that money matters are certain to be as bad as in 1825', the year of the Great Crash on the Stock Exchange, which had precipitated the bankruptcy of Scott's publishers. Even Murray 'is not so sure as I wish'. If he were to fail, 'Lockhart and Sophia might be ruined, which God avert'.[96] As yet Scott had had no time for his own research in the British Museum for the Introduction to *Woodstock*, but he would be going there again before meeting Captain Hall for advice about the proper etiquette to be observed on board the *Barham*, particularly in regard to Captain Pigot as their host. In the meantime he sent Cadell the Introduction to *Count Robert of Paris*, complete with the *envoi* for the closure of 'the magnum' at the end of *Castle Dangerous*.[97] In it he made telling use of Cervantes' last journey to Madrid, as he had come to know about it from Lockhart. Recalling the many 'venial errors of the inimitable Cervantes', who might have pleaded 'the apology of indifferent health' when labouring to finish the second part of *Don Quixote*, he freely admitted such 'discrepancies and inaccuracies' in *Count Robert of Paris* 'as are apt to cloud the progress . . . of a mind . . . when the evening is closing around it'. Yet he had no intention, as he explained in the *envoi*, to complain of the usual 'shadows and storms' of old age, for he was one, as he had already said to Wordsworth, 'who has enjoyed on the whole an uncommon share of the most inestimable of worldly blessings'. Not the least of this was his popularity as 'the author of Waverley'. He was now 'on the eve of visiting foreign parts for his health', and although *Count Robert of Paris* and *Castle Dangerous* were 'the last child of mine old age', his great hope was that his mind might be spared him abroad. In that event he might again appear before the public in some form of literature other than the novel, such as the projected Letters from Malta about the Knights of

St John. Thus it might not be said of him, as Dr Johnson had said of Swift in *The Vanity of Human Wishes*, that

Superfluous lags the veteran on the stage.

Cadell calmed his fears about the book trade by assuring him that he had not accepted credit from the booksellers for his novels. 'I dictated cash to them as the terms.'[98] In other words, he had learned his lesson by being no party to the widespread system of 'accommodation bills', which had involved Scott's publishers and Scott himself in ruin. 'The magnum', according to Cadell, was selling far better—at 30,000 volumes a month—than its nearest rival: the poetical works of Byron published by Murray. 'The magnum is a grand quarry to hawk at, and I have no doubt of the public requiring me to act as quarryman for many a long day—my main wish is that the grand ore-maker may live to see the smelting go on to good purpose.'[99] The main purpose being to liquidate the balance of Scott's debt, Cadell again encouraged him that 'matters will come smooth some day', before he received further encouragement in an answer from Laidlaw about the plantations, which were benefiting from the unusually mild October weather. Laidlaw was delighted with Anne's account of Scott's health, and bearing in mind that Scott looked well 'when I saw you leave your own door', he confidently expected 'to hail your return as at any former time I ever saw you depart'.[100]

Scott urged Laidlaw not to hesitate to apply to Cadell not only for the household expenses of Abbotsford but for 'any reasonable sum for yourself on me'. Owing to the 'devilish poor way' of the book-trade in general even Murray was retrenching, or rather, was cutting down his more ambitious projects into a series of editions 'like our magnum'. Scott trusted to Cadell that, having got possession of the market with 'the magnum', they would keep it despite Murray's attempt at imitation, 'which I look upon as a great compliment to your bookselling ingenuity'. He was looking at the new books modelled on *The Waverley Novels* in order to see how they bore comparison as competitors for public favour. In the meantime he was waiting for a transcript from a tract that he had traced in the British Museum. On collecting it, he would send Cadell the Introduction to *Woodstock*.[101] Captain Hall was indisposed, but Scott would be seeing him at a breakfast-party in the house of Lady Gifford, the widow of the former Chief Justice. He assured Cadell that he had not been out once to dinner, 'nor exceeded three glasses of wine or rather half glasses'. The Duchess of Buccleuch had sent 'a profusion of game' for their voyage. Even the Duke had called to ask Scott to attend the christening of his son in the presence of the King as godfather. It was singular that Scott had stood godfather to the Duke himself. He appreciated the compliment of 'being asked as an ally and friend of the family'. At the ceremony he would have an opportunity of 'trying on my braws', as he called his fine clothes to Cadell in one of the homely Scottish expressions that they both enjoyed injecting into their correspondence. Besides trying his 'braws', he would also have an opportunity of thanking the King personally for the interest he had taken in his voyage.[102] He knew William IV much less well than George IV, to whom 'the magnum' had been dedicated.

Sophia held a small dinner party for him, to which she invited Lady Stuart and Croker, who later delivered, on information from Scott, a brilliant speech in parliament against the Scottish Reform Bill.[103] The town, as Scott put it in his journal, had become 'afoam with politics', and on 8th October the Lords threw out the Reform Bill—'quoited downstairs', in his jubilant language, partly derived, as so often, from Shakespeare, 'like a shovel-board shilling, with a plague to it'. The Bill, as the Tory press had argued, was 'the most uncalled-for attack upon a free constitution under which men lived happily'.[104] He would have wished 'to have had some share in so great a victory'; nevertheless 'I am glad I have been quiet' in not publishing the political essay that he had written at Abbotsford against the Bill.

Its rejection led to a resurgence of the earlier riots, but this time much more violent, particularly against the Tory leaders. The rioters became increasingly active in window-breaking, so that Scott 'passed several glorious specimens' of their feats on the way to Roehampton for breakfast at Lady Gifford's. The house of the Duke of Newcastle—one of the most notorious opponents of the Reform Bill—had been 'very sufficiently broken'. On hearing that 'the maidens' of the Duke's house had 'greatly embarrassed the assailants' by flinging coals on them from the roof-top, Scott, as master of mediaeval sieges, notably that of Torquil-stone in *Ivanhoe*, argued that in view of the rioters' determination to use a right so questionable without corresponding counteraction from the government, surely 'some modes of resistance' other than firearms might be resorted to, such as 'coals, scalding oil, boiling water, or some other mode of defence against a sudden attack'.[105] The remark was a pointer to what he could do with the 'modes of resistance' of the Knights of St John in the Great Siege of 1565. The counter-parts of the rioters in Nottingham had burned to the ground the same Duke of Newcastle's country mansion, but Scott was not yet aware that the rioting had spread to the Midlands.

On meeting Captain Hall at Lady Gifford's, he asked, in some perplexity, if it was proper for him, as some well-intentioned friend had suggested, to make Captain Pigot of the *Barham* some present at the end of the voyage. Hall replied that such a thing was unusual and might cause offence. 'But may I not give the captain a copy of *The Waverley Novels*, for instance, with an autograph inscription?' Hall assured him that he might do this with perfect propriety, and took advantage of the opportunity to repeat his offer to accompany him to Portsmouth, were it only to escort back those ladies of his party, such as Jane and Sophia, who would not be embarking. This time Scott consented.[106] At the same pleasant party he was delighted to meet his old acquaintance, Lord Sidmouth, formerly the Prime Minister, Henry Addington, a survivor, like himself, of the French Revolution and the Napoleonic War: 'at 75, he tells me, as much in health and spirits as at 60'.[107] Sidmouth had figured in Scott's *Life of Bonaparte* (1827), which had sold thousands of copies before 'the magnum'. In that history Scott had related how Malta had first been captured from the Order of St John by Bonaparte, and how in turn the French had capitulated to the English, who, after making peace with Bonaparte under a treaty signed by Addington, had gone to war with him again over Malta until finally it had been confirmed as a British possession after Waterloo.[108] Scott had two reasons, therefore, for always wanting to see Malta: first, for the siege of 1565 under the Knights, and second, for the siege, or rather, blockade from 1798 to 1800, which had led to its capture by the English from the French.

On driving to Lambeth Palace from Lady Gifford's, he was pleased, as a great lover of the Gothic, to see 'this splendour of church architecture returning again' under the able direction of Edward Blore, the designer of the original plan of Abbotsford. Blore took him round the hall, chapel and library—all in process of restoration in 'the best gothick taste', which was then going through a great revival. Abbotsford itself, as a Scottish imitation of that style, was a contribution to the revival. Blore explained to Scott how the high cost of the work was being met before he found a message at Sophia's from Sir James Graham that the *Barham* 'is come to the Downs' and would be sailing at the earliest in eight days, certainly in ten.[109] 'The time now approaches near,' he wrote to Cadell after quoting to him one of his own sea-songs in *The Pirate* about 'a ship of fame', bound, like the *Barham*, 'to High Barbary etc'. Cadell had sent him a proof of *Count Robert of Paris* and *Castle Dangerous*, which he had corrected for dispatch to Edinburgh before the Introduction to *Woodstock* with the transcript from the British Museum.[110] Cadell had already informed *The Caledonian Mercury* of Scott's intended attendance at the christening ceremony of the Buccleuchs with the King as godfather. Although the news was published with a notice of Scott's impending departure from London, the ceremony was postponed by command of the King on account of the riots. Anne and Sophia, who had taken pains over their dresses, were disappointed, but Scott professed indifference at the postponement on the ground that he had 'no taste for a banquet of stones'.[111]

Anne's stomach complaint had recurred, but Sir Henry Halford and Dr Holland 'give her much comfort'. Scott gave Cadell to understand that 'I think my speech gets more distinct than it was', but, on attempting to walk to Lady Stuart's, he felt a little vertigo and turned back. 'I am promised fair weather in Malta,' he wrote to Cadell after a call on him from Captain Duncan of the Admiralty to brief him about the embarkation.[112] Walter distressed him with news that, after serious riots in Derby and Nottingham, he had gone north on a dangerous service with inadequate force. Moreover he might be unable to join them in time at Portsmouth, and his leave might be suspended. 'Pray come up the instant your duty will permit,' for which purpose he sent him a cheque for £30 for travelling expenses as 'a sort of marching money'.

'Every day has mended matters' in London. Strong bodies of the police were stationed in all the squares, supported by troops in still greater numbers. He was therefore hopeful that 'your leave will go on'. In any event, if there should be a repetition of the riot scenes that had culminated in the burning of the Duke of Newcastle's mansion, 'I trust you will study to draw lost souls out of the body of one weaver, for in such cases severity is mercy'.[113] The weaver quotation was again from Shakespeare.

In a long note in his journal he speculated on the constitutional *impasse* created by the defeat of the Reform Bill. As a Tory of the old school he had long championed 'the doctrine' that 'the King can do no wrong'. But William IV was now sheltering, by authority of that doctrine, the defeated Whig ministers, who were keeping their places instead of resigning. There was a rumour, moreover, that the Whigs might secure the countenance of the King by an attempt 'to legitimate the Fitz Clarences', his illegitimate offspring by Mrs Jordan, at the expense of Princess Victoria, the legitimate heiress to the throne.[114] 'God forbid!' Scott exclaimed in horror, as that would result in an *elected* instead of a *hereditary* monarch in violation of a fundamental principle of the British constitution. He had already defended that principle as far back as 1818 in a letter from Paris published in his travel-book called *Paul's Letters to his Kinsfolk.*[115] But the July Revolution of 1830 in Paris had put an elected monarch, Louis-Philippe, on the throne in lieu of Charles X, the hereditary monarch. 'It may end in that, even in England,' Scott therefore feared. Against such a contingency he conceived 'a remedy' worthy of the boldest exploits of Ivanhoe and Rob Roy: 'seize on the person of the Princess Victoria, carrying her north and setting up the banner of England with the Duke of Wellington as dictator'.[116] Wellington had long been, in Scott's eyes, the only man who could yet save England.

Paris, as he wrote to Laidlaw, was not the 'only object of our imitation'.[117] There was also the revolution that had broken out in Brussels against the union between Holland and Belgium formed by the victorious allies after Waterloo. He had already expressed misgivings in *Paul's Letters to his Kinsfolk* about the ultimate success of the union,[118] and now they seemed to have come true in the rebellion of the Belgians against the Dutch. There was a rumour, moreover, that the British fleet, including the *Barham*, was being diverted to the coast of Holland 'to bully the King' of that country, but, on inquiring at the Admiralty, Scott was reassured that the berths of his party were all getting ready. 'I saw the order go down to Captain Pigot,' he informed Walter, who cheered him with better news, as he had 'come off with advantage' in an encounter with the rioters.[119]

Sophia held another small dinner-party for him, and invited his old friend, Tom Moore, who, like Wordsworth, had last seen Scott before his illness; so, on entering with Murray, he was rather shocked at Scott's look and utterance. At dinner Scott took little part in the conversation, and Moore could follow him only with difficulty. 'The great object in sending Scott abroad', Lockhart told him, 'is to disengage his mind from the strong wish to *write* by which he is haunted.'[120] The motive for the wish, however, remained unexplained to Moore, namely, to pay off the balance of Scott's debt, which Cadell had given him to understand could be done in the foreseeable future. On going upstairs after dinner, Moore found a large party, all Scots, including Lady Louisa Stuart, who had long shared Scott's pleasure in Sophia's singing. Since Moore was as famous for his singing as for his poems, he was persuaded to sing to the company after Sophia, who sang a wild Scottish song such as her father, assisted by Laidlaw, had collected at the start of his career for the popular *Minstrelsy of the Scottish Border*. Moore called again on Scott, and in talking of a novel, which might well have been one of the imitations of *The Waverley Novels* that Scott was looking at to see how they compared for public favour, Lockhart told Moore that no matter how bad a book was, if it had but a story in it, Scott would read every word, 'and to this Sir Walter pleaded guilty very amusingly'.[121]

Moore was charmed to see 'how Scott's good temper and good nature remained unchanged' despite his illness, contrary to the impression of another old friend, Mrs Hughes, the wife of a canon of St Paul's Cathedral, who saw him almost every day, frequently accompanying him in his drives round Regent's Park or to different parts of the town. 'With me he was always kind and gentle, but I remember that often to his daughters and servants he had a fierce impatience so wholly different from his nature.' Scott had stood godfather to Mrs Hughes's son, who had been named after him. On going to breakfast at her house with Anne and Sophia, he took a copy of *Tales of a Grandfather* as a present to little Walter, but on inscribing it for him, he suffered another lapse of memory. For a while he seemed to feel it deeply before he became cheerful at breakfast and ate heartily, being particularly pleased with some Yarmouth bloaters, so much so that Sophia asked Mrs Hughes if she could obtain a supply for him. On going to Billingsgate herself for them, Mrs Hughes was first answered that they could not be sent to Sophia's. 'I am sorry,' she involuntarily said, 'the order was for Sir Walter Scott.' 'Sir Walter Scott—did you say, Madam!' the rough fishmonger cried loudly, 'He shall have them directly if I carry them myself. They say he has been ill; how is he?' He kept his word, and Scott, on hearing of the incident from Mrs Hughes, laughed heartily and said, 'I do not think my works ever produced an effect so much to my taste before.'[122]

London, he wrote in his journal, 'seems pretty secure', and Edinburgh, according to Cadell, was 'all peace and quietness and resignation to the LORD's will'.[123] 'The magnum' had continued to sell well. Scott learned with pleasure that one of the many people who, according to Anne's information, had applied to go in the *Barham* as fellow-passengers, was Captain John Forbes, 'the son of my old and early friend Lord Forbes', the premier baron of Scotland. On calling on Scott, Forbes gave him news of his father before Scott wrote his last letter to Laidlaw from London. He thought the crisis caused by the rioters was over. On going to the British Museum, he was seen there by Frederick (later Sir Frederick) Madden, who had made a name for himself by discovering the famous manuscript of *Havelock the Dane*, which had been published by the Roxburghe Club. Madden was struck by Scott's 'uncouth' appearance and 'broad Scottish accent'.[124] Scott loved to hear 'the broad accents of my native land' when in London in a Scottish party.[125] There was no dearth of them at a 'small but lively party' at Sophia's after he had collected the transcript from the British Museum for the Introduction to *Woodstock*. The party included, besides Lady Stuart, Samuel Rogers, the poet, who had always delighted in Scott's company in response to 'the charm', as he later put it to Lockhart, 'which Scott always threw around him wherever he came'.[126]

This was the last of the dinner-parties, for Captain Duncan called to introduce Captain Pigot, who announced that the *Barham* would be sailing on 23rd October. He offered to call at Lisbon, Cadiz, Gibraltar, wherever the wind permitted; so Scott wrote confidently to Cadell that 'I have little doubt to get stuff for our work' in repayment not only for the earlier advances by Cadell but for a fresh loan through Whittaker for doctors and druggists. He also drew on Cadell for a modest monument he had promised to erect to a Helen Walker, the prototype of Jeanie Deans in *The Heart of Midlothian*, about whom he wrote a touching inscription and sent it to Edinburgh with the Introduction to *Woodstock*, based on the tract that he had traced in the British Museum.[127] The tract reflected his antiquarian interest in witchcraft and demonology, about which he had written a book besides filling his novels with incidents and figures of folklore and magic. Egypt was traditionally the land of magic, as he had lately recalled in *Count Robert of Paris*.[128] In London a well-known traveller, Lord Prudhoe, had recently introduced a leading magician from Egypt to English notice. Scott was disposed to believe 'a strange tale of ghost-seeing', which was going about town on Prudhoe's authority. He wrote a long account of it in his journal in the hope of meeting other English travellers in Malta from Egypt, who might help him to go deeper into it.[129]

Walter came to town from his regiment on leave for four months and accompanied by Jane, who confirmed that she would be remaining with her mother at Brighton. Anne wrote to Cadell that Scott's physicians 'think there is decided improvement'. She liked Captain Pigot very much. It was '*just as well*' that Jane was not going with them as she would be 'rather heavy on hand when Walter leaves us', for Walter feared that his leave might be recalled while he was abroad, in which case, as Scott explained to an old friend, Jane 'might be a check on the necessary rapidity of his motions'. The old friend was William Adam, the Lord Chief Commissioner of the Jury Court of Edinburgh, whose son, Sir Frederick Adam, was Governor of the Ionian Isles, which as a British Protectorate had close links with Malta. 'I am uncertain if I shall fail in my hope of finding benefit from my travels, but they tell me that I may recover a part of my strength,' Scott wrote to Adam after prolonged leave-taking, including a call on Lady Stafford, who had long earned his gratitude for many kindnesses to himself and Anne on previous visits to London.[130] She now showed Anne a batch of newspapers containing alarming reports of cholera on the continent. Lady Stafford promised to let Anne have some of the newspapers for Laidlaw.[131]

Scott authorised Cadell to 'correct what is grossly wrong' in the proofs of *Castle Dangerous* and *Count Robert of Paris* besides pressing for a competent person to go through the preface containing his valedictory to the public, since 'Mr. Ballantyne', their printer and proof-reader, 'makes deplorable errors'. Captain Hall had hastened in advance to Portsmouth to engage rooms for Scott's party before the embarkation. Scott called on Coutts, the bankers in the Strand, in the belief that '£50 will clear me', whereas Coutts had paid bills to the amount of £130 out of the £500 allowed Scott from the trust for travelling expenses. He expressed confidence at this stage that the balance would be adequate for Gibraltar and Malta. Walter had a separate credit with Coutts for £200 on Malta.[132] Lockhart remained in London to look over *The Quarterly Review* and to see to the proofs of *Count Robert of Paris* and *Castle Dangerous*, to which he made substantial cuts and corrections on receiving them from Cadell. Johnnie was unfit to travel to Portsmouth with Sophia, who wrote to Naples informing Charles of their father's impending departure in ignorance for the time being that Charles had received a hint from the Foreign Office that his presence was likely to be required in London. A letter from him, in fact, was on the way to Downing Street asking for an extension of his stay at Naples not only on his father's account but on his own behalf on the grounds that as a rheumatic 'I should run great risk in quitting this mild climate so late in the year'. He had no doubt of a favourable answer.[133]

Cadell passed the news of Scott's departure to *The Caledonian Mercury*,[134] which also informed its readers of 'the strong hopes' of his ultimate recovery entertained by his physicians. The hopes were ardently shared by an anonymous admirer of Scott, who made his way to Sophia's house on the chance of his having a view of her father before their departure. After standing in front of the house 'with beating heart', wondering if Scott was within, the admirer suddenly saw the door open,

A moment more
And there he stood—he came—he passed before mine eye.

Without dwelling at all on Scott's faded strength the onlooker, in a spirit of rapture, gave expression to his feelings in verse, and sent the poem to Lockhart.[135]

References for Chapter 1

1. *Journal* 386.
2. Ibid 282.
3. Ibid 576–77, 592; *Letters* XI, 258.
4. *Journal* 396.
5. Ibid 304.
6. Ibid 49.
7. Ibid 550.
8. Ibid 618.
9. Ibid 146–51.
10. Ibid 508, 511, 592.
11. Ibid 29, 75, 236.
12. Ibid 211, 270; *Letters* X, 499; XI, 214.
13. *Journal* 492.
14. Ibid 656; Lockhart X, 72–74.
15. *Journal* 530–31, 544.
16. Ibid 621–22, 644.
17. *Letters* X, 414.
18. Ibid XI, 346–47.
19. Ibid 275, 450; Lockhart X, 70.
20. Lockhart X, 67–68, 90–96.
21. *Letters* X, 249–52; *Journal* 278.
22. MS Acc. 5131, ff. 183–84.
23. Ibid f. 180.
24. Hall 283–85.
25. MS 1752, p. 395; MS 3919, f. 139.
26. MS 1752, pp. 368–84.
27. MS 917, Aug. 29, 1831.
28. MS 5317, f. 150; MS 1752, p. 385.
29. MS 1752, pp. 384–85.
30. S. Smiles, *A Publisher and his Friends*, 1890, p. 290.
31. MS 5317, f. 156.
32. MS 1752, p. 387.
33. *Journal* 659.
34. MS 1752, p. 376.
35. Cf. Acc. 5188, June 4, 1832.
36. MS 1752, p. 386.
37. MS Acc. 5131, f. 180.
38. *Poetical Works of Wordsworth*, ed. E. de Selincourt, 1954, V, 524; *Letters of W. and D. Wordsworth: The Later Years*, ed. E. de Selincourt, 1939, pp. 575–79; Lockhart X, 104.
39. *Journal* 661.
40. *Poetical Works of Wordsworth*, ed. E. de Selincourt, 1954, V, 525; *Letters of W. and D. Wordsworth: The Later Years*, ed. E. de Selincourt, 1939, p. 579.
41. *Journal* 529, 592, 651.
42. *Poetical Works of Wordsworth*, ed. E. de Selincourt, 1954, V, 525.
43. Lockhart X, 104.
44. Ibid 100, 103–4; S. Smiles, *A Publisher and his Friends*, 1890, p. 290.
45. *Poetical Works of Wordsworth*, ed. E. de Selincourt, 1954, V, 525–26; *Letters of W. and D. Wordsworth: The Later Years*, ed. E. de Selincourt, 1939, p. 579; *Letters* X, 104–6.
46. *Letters* XII, 32.
47. John Ballantyne, 'The Last Days of Sir W. Scott' in *Edinburgh Evening Courant*, Aug. 16, 1871, p. 8, col. 5; *Journal* 661; *Poetical Works of Wordsworth*, ed. E. de Selincourt, 1954, V, p. 526.
48. John Ballantyne, 'The Last Days of Sir W. Scott' in *Edinburgh Evening Courant*, Aug. 16, 1871, p. 8, col. 5; *Journal* 616–17; Lockhart X, 20–23.
49. *Poetical Works of Wordsworth*, ed. E. de Selincourt, 1954, V, 526.
50. John Ballantyne, 'The Last Days of Sir W. Scott' in *Edinburgh Evening Courant*, Aug. 16, 1871, p. 8, col. 5.
51. MS 921, p. 210.
52. Cf. *Letters* XI, 373.
53. Lockhart I, 66.
54. *Catalogue of the Abbotsford Library*, ed. J. B. Cochrane, Edinburgh, 1838, pp. 41, 401; MS 921, p. 210.
55. MS 921, p. 210; R. Chambers, *Life of Sir W. Scott, with Abbotsford Notanda by R. Carruthers*, 1871, p. 181; Lockhart X, 104.
56. MS 921, p. 210.
57. *Journal* 641.
58. *The Scotsman*, Sept. 24, 1831; *Caledonian Mercury*, Sept. 24, 1831.
59. *The Scotsman*, Sept. 24, 1831.
60. *Caledonian Mercury*, Sept. 26, 1831.
61. MS 1752, pp. 389, 397; MS 3009, f. 31; MS 860, p. 37; Lockhart X, 107.
62. Lockhart X, 3–4.
63. MS 860, p. 37; MS 5317, f. 162.
64. MS 1752, pp. 389–90.

65. Ibid; *Journal* 240.
66. MS 1752, p. 389.
67. *Journal* 659, 615. See also 621, 653.
68. MS 3009, f. 31.
69. MS 1752, p. 397.
70. MS 860, p. 37.
71. MS 2890, Oct. 3, 1831.
72. MS 1752, p. 393.
73. Lockhart x, 109–11.
74. Ibid 110.
75. *Journal* 425.
76. Lockhart x, 110–11.
77. MS 5317, ff. 105–6; MS 1752, p. 400.
78. *Lady Louisa Stuart*, ed. J. A. Home, 1891, pp. 270, 272; MS 1752, p. 490.
79. Lockhart x, 110.
80. Hall 291; cf. MS 1553, f. 239.
81. MS 5317, f. 166.
82. MS Acc. 5131, f. 212; *Journal* 660.
83. Lockhart x, 113; MS Acc. 5131, f. 211.
84. MS 2890, Oct. 3, 1831; MS Acc. 5131, ff. 211–12.
85. MS 1752, pp. 397–99.
86. MS Acc. 5131, f. 212.
87. W. Peck, 'A Publisher's Friendship for Scott' in *Sir W. Scott Quarterly*, Jan. 1928, vol. 1, No. 4, p. 203.
88. MS 1752, pp. 394–99.
89. MS 1752, p. 400; G. Festing, *J. H. Frere and his Friends*, 1899, p. 343.
90. MS 1752, p. 400; Lockhart I, 63–64.
91. *Childe Harold*, Canto IV, St. 40.
92. MS 5317, p. 187.
93. Ibid, p. 172.
94. MS 917, Oct. 10, 1831.
95. MS 1752, p. 401.
96. Ibid; *Journal* 662.
97. MS 1752, p. 401; Lockhart x, 118–119.
98. MS 5317, f. 112.
99. Ibid.
100. Ibid, f. 199.
101. MS 1752, pp. 403–4, 413.
102. Ibid, pp. 404–5; *Journal* 661.
103. *Journal* 663; Lockhart x, 117.
104. *Journal* 661.
105. Ibid 662.
106. Hall 291–92; *Journal* 662.

107. *Journal* 662.
108. *Miscellaneous Prose Works of Sir W. Scott*, Edinburgh 1841, II, pp. 258, 261–62, 318, 332, 341–45.
109. *Journal* 663; MS 1752, p. 406.
110. MS 1752, p. 406; *Letters* XII, 34.
111. *Caledonian Mercury*, Oct. 20, 1831; *Journal* 664; MS 1752, pp. 406, 413.
112. MS 1752, pp. 405–6; *Journal* 665; MS 5317, f. 195.
113. *Journal* 665; MS 1752, pp. 408–9.
114. *Journal* 664.
115. Edinburgh, 1816, p. 441.
116. *Journal* 664.
117. MS 1752, p. 412.
118. Edinburgh, 1816, pp. 228–29.
119. *Journal* 665; MS 1752, p. 408.
120. *Memoirs, Journal and Correspondence of Tom Moore*, ed. Lord John Russell, VI, pp. 226–27.
121. Ibid 229–31.
122. *Letters and Recollections of Sir W. Scott by Mrs Hughes*, ed. H. G. Hutchinson, n.d., 375–80.
123. *Journal* 665; MS 5317, f. 114.
124. *Journal* 667 & nn$^{2-3}$; MS 1752, pp. 412–414.
125. *Journal* 470.
126. Ibid 668; S. Rogers, *Recollections*, 1859, pp. 171–73; Lockhart I, 127–29.
127. *Journal* 668–69; MS 1752, pp. 415–16; *Letters* XII, 33; Lockhart x, 118.
128. Edinburgh ed. of 1874, Ch. VII, p. 107.
129. *Journal* 665–67.
130. MS 1752, pp. 416–17; MS Acc. 5131, f. 239; A. Aspinal, 'Some New Scott Letters III' in *Times Literary Supplement*, April 24, 1948, p. 240; cf. *Journal* 42, 541.
131. MS 860, p. 39.
132. MS 1752, p. 419; *Journal* 669; MS 5317, p. 203.
133. W. Peck, 'A Publisher's Friendship for Scott' in *Sir W. Scott Quarterly*, Jan. 1928, vol. 1, No. 4; MS 917, Oct. 10, 1831.
134. Oct. 29, 1831.
135. MS 5317, ff. 201–2.

2

Portsmouth and Passage to Malta

The anonymous poem was written on the eve of the prorogation of parliament for a month to enable the Whig government to bring in a third Reform Bill. Scott and his party were then on their way to Portsmouth by coach, stopping briefly at Guildford, where he escaped with a bruise on being thrown to the ground by a coach-horse. He related the incident with his usual humour to Captain Hall on arriving at the Fountain Inn. The *Barham*, he learned, would not be sailing immediately. The port-admiral, Sir Thomas Foley, was giving an entertainment to the Lords of the Admiralty, who were on a visit of inspection to the fleet, which, except for the *Barham*, was sailing after all to the coast of Holland. Foley sent an invitation to Scott, but he pleaded bad health and remained indoors, unlike his daughters and Walter, who gladly accepted the offers of naval officers to show them the sights. Captain Pigot called on him 'with an offer of all manner of civilities', followed by the Lieutenant-Governor of Portsmouth and the other local authorities, who, in Hall's words, 'placed at his disposal all the means in their power to make his stay pleasant'.[1]

'I think my head clearer than it was but my body much frailer,' he wrote to Cadell. As 'my eyes and power of writing are better since I left Scotland', he had 'an idea in my head which is worth entertaining'. It was 'a novel called the Knight of Malta' in the style of *Ivanhoe*, which would have 'much description and some real history'. Unless he grew worse, 'it shall be one of the best which I have written'; but first he wanted to *finish* it before he would print a word of it in order to avoid 'the errors of last season', when Cadell and Ballantyne, who served as critic as well as printer, had objected to parts of *Count Robert of Paris* and *Castle Dangerous* with the result that the proofs had had to be cancelled and the objectionable parts rewritten.[2] Ballantyne, in particular, had deeply wounded him with his criticisms, thereby laying the ground for their subsequent quarrel over the Reform Bill.[3] The projected novel, he added, would not 'supersede other plans', such as the *Seventeenth-Century Letters* and the diary of his tour, but rather postpone them. The novel was 'the result of three weeks' deliberate reflection' in London after a reading of many of the imitations of *The Waverley Novels* as competitors for public favour. He could still keep his hold on his readers with the 'Knight of Malta', which would not be 'a hurried business', so that Cadell 'will have time to settle the best mode of publication'.[4]

Anne and Sophia made him a little uneasy with their 'senseless custom of talking politics at all weathers and in all sorts of company' without considering that they were among strangers, who might take offence as Whigs. His own

more outspoken views, particularly against the rioters of London and the
Midlands, were reserved for the journal, which he wrote in Captain Hall's
presence after rising from bed between six and seven. Hall took care to be up
and dressed before him in order to give him his arm. 'It is rather hard,' he told
Hall, 'that just at the moment . . . that I can call myself free to go anywhere or
do anything I pleased, I should be knocked up in this style.'[5] He was not really
'free', as Cadell had not told him that all the debt had been paid. None the less
he repeated this remark to the wife of his old friend, John Schetky, the artist
who had illustrated *The Lay of the Last Minstrel*. The Schetkys called on him
from their house near Portsmouth as the inn began to overflow with visitors
during the *Barham*'s detention by a contrary wind.[6]

Hall noticed 'a lurking sort of hope' in Scott that the *Barham* might be ordered
away with the rest of the fleet to Holland, that he might thus have an excuse
for not leaving the country. The moment, however, that he was informed that
the *Barham* would not be diverted from her original destination, he made up his
mind to the necessity of leaving home, and his spirits appeared to recover their
usual elasticity. He told Hall, for instance, the story of the fishmonger in
London, who had walked all the way with the Yarmouth bloaters from Billingsgate to Sophia's house on Mrs Hughes's instructions, and he held that gesture
to have been 'the greatest honour yet to have been paid to my celebrity'. Mrs
Schetky was enchanted with his urbanity of manners, which were also publicly
extolled in the newspapers, including *The Caledonian Mercury*, in an account of
how he had received a delegation of the local literary and scientific society.[7]

'Our good Samaritan, Basil Hall, still sticks by us,' he wrote to Cadell after
the fleet had sailed for Holland. Anne watched the sailing from the ramparts
with Walter, Jane and Sophia, and wrote about it in a farewell letter to Laidlaw.
'Papa continues as well as we could expect. The change even from London has
done him good, but we are getting quite anxious to get away, since we are to
go.' If Laidlaw addressed his letters to Sophia, Anne would receive them in Malta
by the monthly steam-packets from Falmouth. 'By the bye I can't tell you the
dread I have of the cholera coming to England; it seems *so sure* that it will be
here.'[8] Lady Stafford having sent the promised newspapers about it, Anne
informed Laidlaw that she would make Sophia send them to him in apparent
unawareness that the newspapers in Scotland were already reprinting the London
reports about the epidemic.

On 29th October the weather at last changed, and in anticipation of their
sailing the admiral sent Captain Forbes, their fellow-passenger, to Scott with
an offer of his barge to convey them to the *Barham*. Captain Pigot soon called
to summon the party on board. Scott made good-humoured remarks at the
tardy women in the style of his Antiquary in Hall's hearing. The signal having
been made for the admiral's barge, they were rowed, on a beautiful day, over a
smooth surface. Scott put nautical questions to Hall, who observed that 'nothing
escaped him' until they reached the *Barham*, 'a beautiful ship' of seventy-four

guns reduced to fifty for speed. Although an accommodation ladder had been fitted, the officers had slung an arm-chair, so that he might have the option of walking up or being hoisted in. He preferred the chair as less fatiguing. After inspecting the cabins and declaring himself highly pleased with them, he went again on deck for conversation with his family till it was time to take leave, as a breeze had sprung up and the ship was getting under way. 'I shall not soon forget', wrote Hall, 'the great man's last look, while he held his friends successively by the hand as he sat on the deck of the frigate, and wished us goodbye, one after another, in a tone which showed that he at least knew all hope was over.'[9]

The vessel glided along by the Isle of Wight, but 'we landfolk', he remarked in his journal after a full meal, 'feel that queerish sensation, when, without being in the least sick, we are not quite well'. Both he and Walter were unwell on gaining Plymouth against a contrary wind. Anne was frightened for a night or two with the 'terrible tossing'. Scott attended Sunday service with her and Walter on deck in daylight, though it was bitter cold. A squall drove them back to Falmouth. Captain Pigot told Anne that the ship's boat was going off with letters; so she scribbled a note to Cadell that, although sea-sick, Scott was in 'very high spirits' and in excellent medical hands, as Dr (later Sir) John Liddell, the head of the naval hospital in Malta, was travelling with them. 'Nothing can be kinder than our reception here.'[10] As they stood for Cape Finisterre, the sea-sickness began to leave them. The *Barham* pitched a great deal in the Bay of Biscay. There was no object so far to look at on the water.[11] They lay—in the words of Coleridge's *Ancient Mariner*—

> As idle as a painted ship
> Upon a painted ocean.

Scott knew large parts of *The Ancient Mariner* by heart. He was particularly fond of quoting from Coleridge's *Knight's Tomb*,[12] an unpublished poem originally recited to him in London by John Hookham Frere,[13] who belonged, like himself, to the old tradition of the oral transmission of literature.

Everybody was ready to assist him, however helpless he felt on rising to get about on deck. Around him the sailors were on training in exercising the great guns on a new sort of carriage. At rest in the after-cabin he read Byron's poems, and afterwards remarked in a letter to Cadell that it was good both for himself and his publisher that Byron had not turned from 'tale telling' in verse to prose, as Scott had himself done, for 'he would have endangered our supremacy in that department'.[14] Meanwhile the appetite of the passengers returned, and they indulged it on their sea-stock of game, cold beef and biscuits. Anne rejoiced on her father's account that, although Captain Pigot lived most comfortably, there was no drinking of wine and no smoking of cigars. The wind became decidedly favourable when they passed the Bay of Biscay, and on getting southward at full speed, they began to feel a milder and more pleasing temperature.[15] On 10th November, on passing the north-west tip of Spain, they skirted Corunna, where Sir John Moore, as Scott had related in *The Life of Bonaparte*,[16] had died in a gallant rearguard action in the Peninsular War. Scott saw a wild cluster of naked rocks rising out of the sea, and he likened them at once to the skerries called Macleod's Maidens in the Isle of Skye.[17]

The *Barham* passed Oporto and Lisbon at night, so that he had no opportunity of seeing—as so many sea-voyagers used to do—the heights of Torres Vedras, where Wellington had thrown up the famous fortified lines in the Peninsular War. Instead, on watching the sword exercises of the sailors, he relished the recollections of his own training in the yeomanry in the old days of the war with Bonaparte. In the distance the coast of Portugal appeared bare and wild, The wind changed to sirocco, 'abominated for its debilitating qualities', but Scott did not really feel them except for some 'obscure dreams' attributed to it. As they neared Gibraltar on one side and Tangier on the other, he was reminded of a loud-voiced antiquarian friend, who was then at Tangier as British consul. Scott had attended the farewell dinner of the Antiquarian Society of Edinburgh for him, and he now recalled him, 'speaking against thirty members of a drunken company and maintaining the predominance'.[18] Scott's heart beat faster when the *Barham* came in sight of Capes St Vincent and Trafalgar— 'spirit-stirring sounds' for their naval associations, which he had celebrated in his poems and in *The Life of Bonaparte*.

It was too soon for him to say whether he was getting any benefit from the climate, 'which is delicious', and whether he could in reason expect that the failure of his limbs in a year's bad weather could be remedied by a few mild and serene days. But he thought there was some change for the better. 'I certainly write easier and my spirits are better.' The officers complimented him on this, including Dr Liddell, whom he liked very much as an obliging gentleman and as skilful professionally. The difficulty, he admitted in his journal, 'will be to abstain from working hard', especially as 'I often think of my Maltese tale' in reference to the projected 'Knight of Malta'. He intended 'to put together a specimen of it' when he got to Malta for transmission to Cadell, who would then 'judge what is to be made of it'. In Laidlaw's absence as amanuensis he would take pains to write whatever he had for Cadell 'in as good a hand as possible'. Lockhart would correct anything Cadell wished to publish.[19] He hoped the new novel 'may be a step forward at least, not backward'; in other words, that it would be better than *Count Robert of Paris* and *Castle Dangerous*, though he supposed Cadell would 'think the first effect of my sea voyage is to make me abominably conceited'. As he was still sensitive to the objections that Cadell and Ballantyne had made of the earlier novels, he again suggested that such criticism 'does more ill than it does good, however well it is meant'. Cadell could rest assured that 'I shall observe your advice in not being in a hurry to work hard but make it my chief business to get into trim if I can'. He would put the letter to Cadell ashore for Edinburgh. In return a letter from

Cadell would be most welcome in view of his anxiety to hear whether *Count Robert of Paris* and *Castle Dangerous* were out, and, if so, how the public had received them. It was *private* news he wanted, not public, as he would be learning about the progress of the Reform Bill from the newspapers. In fact, he gently warned Cadell that 'much politics will not make letters very safe'. A few days would bring them to Malta, 'where I will take up my abode for six weeks or two months, as I have a notion that the climate will suit me, and I am sure that the tumult of Naples would drive me mad'. Besides he cared very little for *classical* antiquities whereas Malta was full of relics of the Knights of St John.[20]

The *Barham* passed the Straits of Gibraltar on 14th November in a picturesque setting of evening light and colour. Scott's aesthetic sense was drawn out by the landscape of Andalusia, formed of a chain of distant mountains. The sun gave brilliance to the sharp points, while the shade conveyed 'an effect of softness equally beautiful'. The wild variety of mountain scenery reminded him of the Highlands. Even its geology 'seemed to be of the first formation, liker, in other words, to the highlands than those of the south of Scotland'. His great interest in military architecture and his feeling for battle-scenes were immediately engaged by 'the celebrated fortress', which he was pleased to find corresponded fairly closely to the idea that he had formed of it from the prints that had become very fashionable through such publishers as Murray and Ackermann. He wrote a fairly detailed description of the fortress in his journal with special reference to the Spanish lines and British defences in the famous Siege of Gibraltar in the American War.[21] As one of the most notable events of his childhood that siege was still fresh in his memory, including the heroic part played by Sir George Elliot, the Governor of Gibraltar, who had hailed from a town near Abbotsford.

The earlier battle-scenes between the Moors and the Christians in Spain—treated by him in *The Vision of Don Roderick*—were associated in his mind with the old Moorish town of Algeciras beyond the caverns and towers of Gibraltar —themselves formerly 'the habitation or refuge of the Moors', who had overrun Spain from Andalusia until they had been pushed back by, among others, the Cid. Scott was familiar with the *Poema del Cid* as Spain's national epic of chivalry from the popular *Chronicle of the Cid* (1808) published by his old friend, Robert Southey, the poet laureate. He was even more familiar with Lockhart's *Ancient Spanish Ballads* (1822), dealing with the exploits not only of the Cid but also of the Knights against the Moors, of whom he was again reminded on catching sight of vantage-points on the mountains of Andalusia, 'occasionally garnished with an old watch tower to afford protection against a corsair'. The corsairs had operated from the opposite coast of Barbary, marked by a similar chain of hills but more lofty and much more distant. For that reason he could not identify Ceuta, on the African side of the Straits, forming, with Gibraltar, the two pillars of Hercules.[22]

The *Barham* was refused communication with Gibraltar on account of the spread of the cholera epidemic to England from Germany a few days after their departure. No passenger was permitted to send letters ashore, including the one that Scott had meant to dispatch to Cadell. Therefore he kept it for transmission from Malta. The only news that reached them was that there had been another riot, this time at Bristol, 'in which the mob have got the worst', so that Scott interpreted the information as not unpleasing.[23] On the other hand, if the rioting continued or spread, Walter might have his leave of absence cancelled. Much depended on developments at Westminster, where parliament was summoned for the beginning of December for the third Reform Bill. Scott was confident that Cadell was making great exertions to bring *Count Robert of Paris* and *Castle Dangerous* out before the commons and peers reassembled.[24]

A breeze and the current always running at Gibraltar carried the *Barham* to the African side of the Straits in sight of Ceuta, which was dominated by 'the celebrated ridge of Atlas', varied in form like the mountains of Spain but lighter and wilder. Only one or two turbaned men carrying long pikes could be seen, apparently ploughing, after Scott had looked in vain for cattle and flocks of sheep in 'this mockery of cultivation'. The calm that set in at night reinforced the general impression that he had already formed of the Mediterranean Sea as 'a gentle element'.[25] 'We had nothing to do', he later wrote to Lockhart from Malta, 'but sit on the deck and enjoy the climate, which since we entered the Mediterranean has been something more delicious than I could have conceived.' Captain Pigot obliged him by sailing close to Algiers, where the French had landed the year before to colonise North Africa. In a long entry in his journal he recalled the whole French operation leading to the daring capture of Algiers, and compared their success with the failure of the Spaniards under the Emperor Charles V in the earlier war against the Moors after their expulsion from Spain.[26] The harbour of Algiers was protected by the famous mole built by Barbarossa, the renowned corsair, who had a long record of actions against the galleys of the Knights of St John as the allies of the Spaniards. Scott read his history in his copy of Vertot's *Knights of Malta* in preparation for the projected new novel. 'I felt it unsafe to walk on deck,' he wrote to Lockhart in the same letter from Malta, 'but delightful to sit and read there. I travelled through the history of the Knights.'[27]

Thanks to 'the immense batteries' mounted on Barbarossa's mole Algiers had been considered impregnable until a British squadron under Lord Exmouth had bombarded it before the landing of the French. It was a wonder, Scott recalled, 'that Lord Exmouth's fleet was not altogether cut to pieces'.[28] The French were said to hold Algiers very precariously, and 'wish themselves well clear of their bargain', since they had found themselves involved in a war with all the rulers of North Africa. Their situation reminded Scott of the Roman Emperor Julian,[29] who, as Gibbon had related in one of the best-known chapters in *The Decline and Fall of the Roman Empire*,[30] had been destroyed by the Persians under similar desert conditions. Scott had last used Gibbon as a source for *Count*

Robert of Paris. Like Oran, Algiers had 'a singular oriental look' with its closely packed, populous, white houses without windows and with terraced roofs.[31] The look was 'very dear to the imagination' in view of the exciting oriental scenery created by Scott in his novels, notably in *The Talisman.*

   The weather continued fine as the *Barham* glided along the coast towards Tunis in sight of barren hills with an occasional fort at the mouth of a river or sheltering bay. Dr Liddell enlightened Scott about the islands they passed, including Galitha, formerly the scene of bitter fighting between the Christians and the Moors, and now inhabited only by wild goats as 'a species of deer park free to everyone for shooting upon'.[32] As such the island was of interest to Scott, formerly a keen hunter at home. Besides, he had long made a point of describing wild animals on high ground as constituting—with ruins, vaults, gibbets and dimly lit chapels—the more 'Gothic' element in his novels. Galitha and the neighbouring islands were the counterparts of the havens that he had been reading about in Byron's poems as hide-outs of the pirates, notably of Conrad in *The Corsair.* The most formidable corsair after Barbarossa had been a buccaneer called Dragut, who had operated from Tunis and Tripoli as well as from Algiers. Lockhart had a poem about him in *Ancient Spanish Ballads.*[33] Scott was even more interested in him than in Barbarossa for his projected novel, since Dragut had been the most colourful Turkish leader against the Knights in the Siege of Malta. On reading about him in Vertot, he appears to have conceived Dragut as not unlike his own Cleveland in *The Pirate,* bent on settling old scores with his enemies, many of whom had been Spanish knights owning castles and estates along the coast that the *Barham* had skirted. One of these was intended by Scott to be *the* 'Knight of Malta' as the hero of the new novel in keeping with the title that he had already announced to Cadell from Portsmouth. The Knight was to be summoned to Malta from his castle in Spain near Gibraltar to defend the island in the siege against Dragut as part of the old scores to be settled between them.[34]

   It was easy for Scott to make the transition from the *Barham* to the Knights and the corsairs even without the help of Vertot, for there was 'a general exercise' on board the *Barham* off Tunis with the great guns as well as with the small arms of the sailors and marines.[35] It included a boarding attack from the ship's yards, complete with pistols and cutlasses, in the manner of the assaults of the Knights from their galleys against the corsairs. Scott was so impressed with 'the awful pause when a vessel armed for war is stript to action' that he later inserted it in the new novel, as the best image he could think of for the tension before 'the shock of battle' in the Siege of Malta.[36] It was highly entertaining to him to watch the crew's discipline—'the men take to their quarters with the unanimity of an individual'—before the firing of 'our fifty 36 pounders'. The noise was 'loud enough to have alarmed the shores', so much so that he fancied that the Tunisians might have imputed the firing to 'an opportune quarrel between the French and the British', and have shouted 'Allah

Kerim—God is merciful!' for delivering them from the war with the French.[37]
He had a stock of these Arabic exclamations and war-cries for the more oriental
scenes in his novels as the counterparts of the traditional Highland cries in
Gaelic.

The *Barham* was overtaken off Tunis by the steamship from Falmouth to
Malta, which he had seen at Portsmouth before their departure. He would have
wished to have gone ashore to see the ruins of Carthage, but this was impossible
owing to the plague at Tunis. There was much talk around him about the exact
situation of Carthage, including the ancient lake adjoining the famous port of
Tunis, which was called La Goletta.[38] Having read in Vertot that Charles V
had besieged and taken La Goletta before the Siege of Malta, he conceived the
hero of the new novel, the Spanish 'Knight of Malta', as first distinguishing
himself by 'cleaving Dragut's helm in the siege of Goletta'.[39] Beyond Tunis lay
Cape Bon, the prominent headland below the west coast of Sicily, which the
Barham passed at night. The French occupied Cape Bon as a coral fishery, and
the bombardment of Algiers by Lord Exmouth had arisen as a reprisal against
the Algerians seizing many Neapolitans who had been fishing for coral off the
cape. The sea beyond the cape was dotted with islets and rocks, which again
reminded Scott of the skerries at home as the weather, having turned squally,
played on the sea in varying rays of light and shade to a background of hills on
the coast, surmounted by 'a smoky umbrella' of clouds resembling a volcano.[40]

The squall dropped as rapidly as it had arisen, and a fair wind carried the
Barham past Pantelleria, which Scott described as 'a species of Botany Bay',
since the Sicilians used it as a state prison. Everybody on board watched expect-
antly for the new volcano called Graham Island. The officer who knew most
about it was the first lieutenant, 'our friend Mr Walker', as Scott later called
him. He had seen it on an earlier voyage when his ship had received a shock
from some part of it encountering the island in its ascent in a sensation greatly
resembling an earthquake. On sighting it, they formed the impression that it
had considerably diminished since the last accounts. Scott went out in one of
the ship's boats to 'survey this new production of the earth' with great interest.
Anne and Walter went with him together with Captain Pigot's clerk as amanuensis to make a sketch of the volcano, with notes, for transmission from Malta
to the Royal Society of Edinburgh.[41] Anne's shoes were burnt through with the
heat, and she later wrote to Sophia that 'it was a horrid landing place where one
might expect to meet the devil'.[42] However, far from associating Graham Island
with the devil, Scott conceived 'the notion of a magician of the old romance':[43]
in other words, of a latter-day Prospero on a magic island. Finding it impossible
for his infirm feet to walk on sinking earth, he mounted on the back of a strong
sailor, who carried him nearly to the top of the island in full view of a fellow-
sailor called Woodrow, who had a brother living at Kelso, not far from
Abbotsford. Woodrow observed him enjoying his ride on the sailor's back in
remembrance of 'my old talents for horsemanship'.[44] After collecting the largest

blocks of lava he could find together with shells for the Royal Society, he returned to the *Barham* for dinner, contented with enough information to fill a letter to 'our friends at Edinburgh'.[45]

In the mess they enjoyed the company of the officers, benefiting, in particular, from Dr Liddell's knowledge of Malta as well as of Walker's recent experiences in Greece during the War of Independence from Turkey. Walter appears to have made Walker and another officer called Maitland his best companions during the voyage. Even Anne, as Scott later informed Lockhart, 'was for once pleased with the number and quality of her beaux'.[46] They included Captain Pigot, who was a bachelor. Scott passed an indifferent night before he sighted Gozo, the sister-island of Malta, on the morning of 21st November. The stone walls intersecting its fields at once reminded him of the same material used in his own Selkirkshire, and the likeness was increased by the appearance of old square towers similar to those he had already observed in Spain.[47] The towers had been put up by the Knights as observation posts against marauding Moors, and had therefore served the same purpose as that of the beacons that he had described in *The Antiquary* as scattered on the east coast of Scotland and in Northumberland against the threatened invasion by Bonaparte.[48]

Gozo was of especial interest to him for the new novel, as it had been sacked before the Siege of Malta on Dragut's advice in an episode marked by acts of courage, cowardice and treachery that could be turned to profit in varied narrative.[49] Gozo, moreover, was traditionally the island of Calypso. He had read about it as such either in Brydone's *Tour through Sicily and Malta* or in Byron's *Childe Harold*.[50] On being shown from the deck the entrance to Calypso's reputed cave—'as rude a cavern as ever opened out of a granite rock' —he was inclined to disbelieve not only the authority for her legend but also for St Paul's shipwreck in one of the rocky bays that appeared after Gozo.[51] The bay, with its neighbouring creeks, suggested another action for the new novel, complete with the traditional craft that used to ply between Malta and Sicily, as described by Brydone and other travellers. The action would involve his hero, the Spanish 'Knight of Malta', whom he conceived as threatened with capture by the galleys of Dragut on attempting to go ashore to take part in the Siege.[52]

References for Chapter 2

1. Hall 293–94, 297–98; MS 1752, pp. 421–22; *Journal* 669–70.

2. MS 1752, pp. 421–22; *Journal* 652–53, 659.

3. Lockhart X, 10–17, 21–25, 70, 77.

4. MS 1752, p. 422.

5. *Journal* 671; Hall 305–6, 312.

6. J. H. Schetky, *Sketches*, ed. by his daughter, 1877, pp. 163–65; Hall 303.

7. Hall 299–300, 304–5; J. H. Schetky,

Sketches, ed. by his daughter, 1877, p. 164 n; *Edinburgh Evening Courant*, Nov. 3, 1831, See also Hall 302–3.

8. MS 1752, p. 424; MS 860, p. 39.
9. Hall 317–21; *Journal* 673.
10. *Journal* 673–74; MS 1553, f. 238; MS Acc. 5131, ff. 245–46.
11. *Journal* 674–75.
12. Cf. *Ivanhoe*, Ch. VIII; *Castle Dangerous*, Ch. IX.
13. *Collected Letters of S. T. Coleridge*, ed. E. L. Griggs, 1956–57, vol. V, 379–81.
14. MS 1752, pp. 426–27; *Journal* 674.
15. *Journal* 675; MS 1553, f. 238.
16. *Miscellaneous Prose Works of Sir W. Scott*, Edinburgh, 1841, II, p. 490.
17. *Journal* 675.
18. Ibid 676.
19. *Journal* 676; MS 1752, pp. 426–27.
20. MS 1752, pp. 427–28.
21. *Journal* 677; cf. *Siege of Malta*, f. 1.
22. *Journal* 678.
23. Ibid 677–78; MS 1752, p. 428.
24. Cf. MS 1752, p. 423.
25. *Journal* 678–79; cf. *Siege of Malta*, f. 1.
26. MS 1752, p. 421; *Journal* 680.
27. Ibid.
28. *Journal* 680.
29. Ibid; MS 1752, p. 431.
30. Ch. XXIV.
31. *Journal* 680.
32. Ibid 681.
33. 'Dragut' in *Ancient Spanish Ballads*, 1875, p. 165.
34. *Siege of Malta*, ff. 7, 23, 69, 87.
35. *Journal* 681.
36. *Siege of Malta*, f. 41.
37. *Journal* 681–82.
38. Ibid 682; MS 1752, p. 431.
39. *Siege of Malta*, f. 50.
40. *Journal* 682.
41. Ibid 682–83; Skene 197–99.
42. MS 1553, f. 240.
43. Dr J. Davy, 'Some Remarks in reply to Dr Daubeny's note . . . over the Site of the Recent Volcano in the Mediterranean' in *Philosophical Transactions of the Royal Society of London for 1834*, vol. 124, part I, p. 552.
44. *Caledonian Mercury*, Jan. 2, 1832; Skene 197–98.
45. Skene 197; *Journal* 682–83.
46. MS 1752, pp. 430–31; MS 1554, f. 49.
47. *Journal* 683.
48. Ch. 45, para. 3.
49. Cf. *Siege of Malta*, ff. 13, 22–23.
50. Canto II, St. 29.
51. *Journal* 683.
52. *Siege of Malta*, ff. 58–62.

3

Malta and Beginning of Composition of 'The Siege of Malta'

'At last we opened Malta,' Scott wrote in his journal as 'the famous Valetta' spread out before the *Barham*. It was the city built by and named after the hero of the Knights, the French Grand Master, La Valette. Under a chivalric impulse Scott called it 'a city like no other in the world', guarded at the harbour's entrance by the historic Fort St Elmo, which immediately called up from his memory the heroic defence of it by the Knights before its eventual fall to the Turks under Dragut and other leaders.[1]

The Governor of Malta was General Sir Frederick Cavendish-Ponsonby, a brother of Lady Caroline Lamb. Although he was in England on leave, he had left orders that every possible attention should be paid to Scott and his party, who could also use his yacht, if necessary, for Naples, as Scott had already been informed in London by Frere's letter. The health regulations of Malta, however, required a quarantine for all ships from England on account of the epidemic of cholera. Fortunately, as the *Barham* had sailed from England before the first cases had been confirmed, the quarantine was reduced from thirty days to ten. Scott was allowed the privilege of performing it not in the ordinary lazaretto but in a suite of rooms specially prepared for him in a large old fort in the second harbour of Valletta commonly called the Quarantine Harbour.[2] He was already familiar with it from Vertot as the haven used by the Turkish fleet for the attack on Fort St Elmo. On entering it, he had an opportunity of observing the strictness of the quarantine in Malta when a sailor fell into the sea from a yard-arm of the *Barham*, and the Maltese boats backed away for fear of the regulations, while an English boat, which picked him up, was condemned to ten days' quarantine.[3]

The place assigned them was called Fort Manoel, and on going to it in the *Barham*'s boat, Scott found it 'spacious and splendid, but not comfortable', since the apartments were only kept as barracks or lazaretto. Having long prided himself as the builder of Abbotsford in a fantastic style of architecture and decoration but with 'all the comforts of a commodious habitation', he claimed that, if he were to live in Fort Manoel a sufficient time, he would make its apartments handsome.[4] In deference to Spain as the traditional home of chivalry he imagined the fort to have been built by 'a Spanish don' as 'a palace for himself and his retinue', whereas it had been built as an additional protection to the fortifications of Valletta by a Portuguese grand master called Manuel de Vilhena. Vertot had dedicated his history to him. Scott took his name and adapted it for the hero of his new novel, whom he called 'Don Manuel de Vilheyna'. In view of the fort's 'decayed grandeur' he described it as 'a world too wide for the shrunk shanks' of Vilhena.[5] The quotation was again from Shakespeare. A part of the fort was occupied as barracks by a Captain and Mrs Dawson. She was the daughter of William Erskine, one of Scott's earliest friends. He had known her as a toddler, and had last seen her on her wedding day. The Dawsons chose to remain with Scott's party in quarantine; so did Dr Liddell, contrary to Walter's wishes but to Anne's delight. 'He has been so useful, always attending upon papa,' Anne afterwards reported of him to Sophia.[6]

Captain Pigot, on hearing an exaggerated report of their being uncomfortably situated, went himself in his barge to reclaim them. 'We returned our cordial thanks, but felt we had already troubled him sufficiently.' In their rooms they found books and flowers from Lady Hotham, the wife of the commander-in-chief of the Mediterranean fleet, to whom Scott had been recommended by Lord Melville. He also found an affectionate letter from Sir John Stoddart, the Chief Justice, reminding him that 'I am the oldest friend you have at Malta', since they had known each other as young advocates when 'we heard Henry Brougham (now the Lord Chancellor!) make his first motion at the Circuit Court at Jedburgh'. Stoddart offered Scott the use of his splendid house in Valletta overlooking Fort Manoel or of his country-house in St Julian's Bay when his quarantine would be over. 'Lady Stoddart you know is an old Scotch woman, and will know how to prepare for you the comforts to which you have been used.'[7] She was a daughter of Sir Henry Moncrieff, a leading Edinburgh preacher. Stoddart had married her on securing an earlier appointment in Malta, when the Governor's secretary had been Coleridge. He, therefore, explained to Scott that 'if you take up your lodgings at my house, as Coleridge did some 25 years ago or more, you would afford me infinite delight'.[8]

Stoddart anticipated that Scott would be 'harassed' with visitors, for his arrival had caused something of a sensation, and the landing-place of Fort Manoel was taken up with boats and parties. The visitors were forbidden to approach more than a yard to him by the quarantine guardians.[9] Among the first callers was John Hookham Frere: a tall, distinguished-looking man, older than Scott by two years, but in much better health. Although Scott had not seen him for more than ten years, he had mentioned him in *The Life of Bonaparte* as the former British Minister to Spain during the Peninsular War.[10] They were delighted to see each other again, particularly as Frere did not find Scott so much altered by his illness as those who had known him more closely. Frere's heart was set on accommodating Scott and his party in the splendid country-palace of the Governor at San Antonio, a few miles from Valletta, which Frere was temporarily occupying with his sister, Susan, while repairs were being made to his house at La Pietà on the waterfront of the Quarantine Harbour. Scott left it to Anne and Walter to decide about their eventual accommodation, but he later wrote to Lockhart that the English 'inhabitants abound in every kind of civility, and when our confinement is ended, we have the office of twenty *palazzos* if one will serve'.[11]

Frere was joined at the bar separating him from Scott by Colonel and Mrs Bathurst. Colonel Bathurst was the acting Governor, while his wife—commonly called Mrs Seymour-Bathurst—was a leading society figure, first, in Malta and, later, in London. Her husband had first met Scott in the house of his father, Lord Bathurst, a minister in Pitt's government and a visitor to Abbotsford.[12] They were accompanied by Mrs Davy, a sister-in-law of Sir Humphry, one of Scott's close friends. She had lived almost next door to Scott in Edinburgh, and kept a diary of his visit, which Lockhart later used as the main source for Malta in his *Life of Scott*. At seeing her and the Bathursts, Scott rose, but with difficulty, the paralytic look of his face being most distressing to Mrs Davy, who had last seen him in health in Edinburgh. To their formal speech that he would stay at Malta as long as possible he replied courteously in his natural manner but with thickened articulation. He wore Lowland trews. Anne and Walter stood behind him, and as he sat with his hands crossed over his walking-stick, he reminded Mrs Davy of the well-known portrait of him by the American artist, Charles Leslie, which had been engraved for one of the fashionable annuals.[13]

After dining with the Dawsons, they slept uncomfortably in their new quarters before he entered a curious note in his journal on reading of a super-stition in Malta exactly similar to one in Scotland. The Maltese, he read, never married in the month of May because of the many misfortunes they associated with it. He had himself believed so strongly in this ancient superstition that, when Sophia had married Lockhart, he had set out from London to Scotland with all possible speed to ensure that the wedding would be held in April and not in May.[14] The book in which he read of the Maltese superstition was in French, so that it was either Vertot or, more likely, one of the books sent to his apartment by Lady Hotham. He read it in his room overlooking the ditch of Fort Manoel, in which was an old gallows of the Knights, 'menacing death', as he later put it to Lockhart, 'to anyone who shall infringe the quarantine laws'.[15] The comment had a touch of 'Gothic horror' about it, so often associated with gallows in his novels.

The Hothams had put a boat at his disposal for himself and his party to be rowed round the two harbours during their confinement, while the officers of the *Barham* spent most of their quarantine time with them. On having a closer look at Valletta from the boat, he again called it 'a splendid town' not only for its deep creeks and fortifications but also for the picturesque effect of its streets of unequal height, which the Knights had never been able to level on account of fresh threats of attack from the Turks after the siege. 'The greatest variety' resulted from these streets.[16] The sounds heard in the distance from the belfries scattered through the town and echoing over the water from the nearby villages suggested a devotional scene to him for the new novel to contrast with the war-cries that he intended to put in the mouths of Dragut's followers during the siege.[17] In particular, the watch-towers on the bastions in warm stone drew out his building instinct, so that he formed some ideas for adding a screen to one of the fronts of the old barn at Abbotsford. It would not involve much expense, he explained in a letter to his old friend, James Skene, to whom he enclosed the information about Graham Island, with the specimens, for the Royal Society of Edinburgh. Skene was the society's secretary. His son was serving in Malta as a lieutenant in a regiment, and had called on Scott, but, like the ghost of Hamlet's father, 'he vanished like a guilty thing when, forgetting that I was a contraband commodity, I went to shake him by the hand, which would have cost him ten days' imprisonment'. Scott expected to see young Skene again at more leisure on release from quarantine. 'I am in my usual spirits, and look so well that I believe my Malta friends think that I am shamming Abraham.'[18]

He hoped to bring 'a thumping journal' with him for publication by Cadell, to whom he wrote in the continuation of the letter that he had been prevented from sending from Gibraltar. In proof of 'my own incapacity of lying still' he confirmed 'my purpose of writing the Siege of Malta', which now became the the title of the new novel in lieu of 'The Knight of Malta'. He would have time and books for it in Fort Manoel, and on his release he would have 'the freedom of two fine libraries' in Valletta and all manner of information from Frere, Stoddart and others. Confident that he would finish *The Siege of Malta* in two or three months, he left it to Cadell to settle whether to publish it as part of 'the magnum' or separately like *Count Robert of Paris* and *Castle Dangerous*. The money from it might conveniently go into his bank-account at Coutts in London, although there was no need for it at the moment, as 'my cash has had few demands' without apparently taking account of his considerable London bills, which he had miscalculated, and the unforeseen expenditure at Portsmouth owing to their delayed departure.[19]

They were all looking for letters with great anxiety on account of bad reports about the cholera in England. Moreover they were now in possession of fuller news of the riots in Bristol, in which more atrocities had been committed by the mobs than in any of the scenes that Scott and Walter had witnessed in London and the Midlands respectively. 'If Bristol does not bring people to their senses, nothing will,' Scott wrote to Lockhart as if in confirmation of his belief that even the Whig rulers would come to see the violence as a threat to property from the masses, to whom the Reform Bill had pandered. Anne was inclined to take a more gloomy view: 'there seems everything going wrong in England'. The most anxious, however, was Charles at Naples, who feared that the health authorities there might insist on a long quarantine for vessels from Malta. Besides, he had just heard from London that the Foreign Office had granted his request for an extension of his stay at Naples but only until the beginning of February. So he wrote to his father 'to beg you not to delay at Malta, because, if you do not come quickly, I shall have but little time to see you'.[20]

Unaware of Charles's solicitude, Scott was inclined, from his experience of the delightful climate of Malta, to remain rather than to proceed to Naples, and to send for Charles to come and see him in Malta. Whether the weather 'will do my bodily complaints any good I cannot as yet say', but he was feeling, as he had stated to Skene, decidedly better in spirit, and 'I am getting on well with this Siege of Malta'.[21] His intention was to use it as a test 'to satisfy myself in the important question whether I am Giles* or not'. Accordingly, on finishing a part of it, he would send it to Lockhart for an opinion. 'I will either bring it to a good conclusion,' he wrote to Lockhart, 'or give up the Muses for ever.' In the meantime Lockhart could see from 'an animated and hopeful account of myself' in a long letter packed with information about his journey that 'I am thinking and much disposed to act like the man again'. Although he had certainly brought the printed copy of *Seventeenth-Century Letters* with him—the same copy, in other words, that he had shown Lady Louisa Stuart in London on persuading her to complete her share of it—he made no mention of it again for the time being either in his letter to Lockhart or to Cadell. He merely authorised Lockhart to show Lady Stuart any portion of his own letter to him if she wished to read it. He hoped Johnnie Lockhart was better.[22]

Anne and Walter were both very well, and had gone out with Captain Pigot to take an airing in one of his boats. Unfortunately they were hampering Scott by not being 'desirous to follow my amusements', such as visiting the site where Dragut had been killed by splinters from a rock in one of the assaults on Fort St Elmo. The site—called Dragut's Point—was very close to their apartments. In view of Lockhart's description of Dragut in *Ancient Spanish Ballads* as 'a celebrated corsair of Algiers', Scott explained Dragut's death to him in some detail before adding that there was a good deal that he wished to see in Valletta, including 'a splendid armoury' and the great cathedral of St John, 'where the Knights of the Order lie buried'. He could see its towers from Fort Manoel besides hearing about its treasures from Frere, who came to see him every day and passed more of his quarantine time with him than anyone else. 'Frere is one of the greatest prizes,' he wrote to Lockhart, 'Sir John Stoddart is another.'[23] Stoddart's son—a young advocate whom Scott had first met at a dinner in Edinburgh—had a good knowledge of Arabic, and had travelled in Egypt. By means of him Scott claimed to Lockhart that 'I have got a key' to the 'strange tale of ghost-seeing' at Cairo that he had heard in London from Lord Prudhoe and other travellers. Without wishing 'to mingle in the controversy' over the tale's credibility he would question young Stoddart further when he would next have a chance of seeing him.[24] The tale itself was a form of *séance* conducted by the most renowned magician of Egypt, who claimed that he could read his clients' minds through his hirelings, usually slaves or children.[25]

The *Barham* had shifted her berth from the Quarantine to Grand Harbour, where all the warships anchored. Scott was rowed to see 'a formidable spectacle'.

* 'Giles' = Scotticism for 'sane'. Cf. *Letters* x, 192.

including Sir Henry Hotham's flagship, H.M.S. *St Vincent*, in which his kinsman, Francis Scott, was serving as a midshipman. Scott could not yet meet him and hand him his father's letter on account of the quarantine. The beauty of the warships' build, rigging and tapering masts made him recall a description in *The Red Rover* by his American friend, James Fenimore Cooper, at that time a very popular novelist. The warships were reported to be under orders 'to go up the Levant' in defence of British interests against Greek pirates and Russian diplomacy in the Balkans as a centre of unrest and intrigue after the Greek War of Independence. They seemed to Scott 'a formidable weight in the bucket' of power politics. It was with pride that they looked at the *Barham*, 'once in a particular manner our own abode'.[26] She rode in sight of the largest and most historic fortress in Malta called Fort St Angelo, which the Turks had failed to capture after the fall of Fort St Elmo, and in consequence they had raised the Siege.[27]

It was difficult for Scott, as he confessed in a strikingly personal passage in *The Siege of Malta*, to visualise the original fortifications as they had existed during the Siege, and to distinguish them from the later additions, which had become 'so extensive as to take 30,000 men to garrison them'. Nevertheless, 'whether willing or not, I must needs make an attempt' to describe them for his readers, although 'I feel somewhat dubious in its issue', mainly from 'total want of the powers of the draughtsman'.[28] He had therefore lately written in his letter to Skene, whom he regarded as 'the first amateur draughtsman in Scotland', that 'I would have given a great deal for you, my friend', as 'the frequent and willing supplier of my defects' with his sketch-book.[29] Despite his diffidence he grappled tenaciously, in several passages, with the fortifications, summing them up as bearing 'a strong resemblance to those used in the Middle Ages when the style of defence against gunpower began to be adopted and improved upon'.[30] The most celebrated 'improvement' had been a system of huge mortars known to him from Brydone's *Tour through Sicily and Malta*.[31] One or two surviving mortars could still be seen on the coast near Fort Manoel. He inserted them in *The Siege of Malta* in the action that he had conceived for his hero against the galleys of Dragut in the bay off Gozo. Bearing Graham Island in mind, he likened the mortars' effect to 'those volcanic eruptions which occur frequently' in Sicily and the nearby islands.[32] On being rowed to Dragut's Point, he observed that the corsair's death 'would be a fine subject for a poem'. Although he did not write it, he gave Dragut a hero's death in *The Siege of Malta*.[33] On hearing that the quarantine guardians 'tell some stories of this famous corsair', he approached them as if, like Edie Ochiltree in *The Antiquary*,[34] they were 'oracles of the district'. 'But I can scarce follow their Arabic.'[35]

Captain Pigot and some of his officers left the *Barham* to dine with him and his party before they heard with joy that their quarantine had been shortened by a day. Anne tried unsuccessfully, with Dr Liddell, to make him regulate his diet, particularly to abstain from drink, as he had done on the voyage.[36] Frere took his sister to see him after setting young men to write Latin verses in his honour. She confirmed her recollection of his character as marked by simplicity and sweetness. 'There is not the play of features and vivacity which appeared formerly when he was conversing, but there is much gentle expression.' He won her heart by telling her how gratified he was to find her brother looking so well. Anne also pleased her with her appearance, particularly her 'good dark eyes', a legacy of her French mother. Walter, on the other hand, 'is tall, thin and whiskered; neither of them have any resemblance to their father', on whose account, as Anne explained to Susan Frere, they had decided, in view of his infirmity, to engage apartments for him in a hotel at Valletta for quick medical assistance, which was not available at Frere's temporary residence at San Antonio.[37] Moreover it was convenient to be within easy reach of the monthly steam-packets in Valletta for letters to Sophia and Cadell and for news from Edinburgh about *Count Robert of Paris* and *Castle Dangerous*. Lockhart was also expected to write about the reception of those novels.

The hotel that they chose was an old converted *palazzo* of the Knights, lately renamed Beverley's Hotel after the English proprietor who managed it. Scott was delighted to move into it from 'the dreary fort of Don Manuel', which had become 'ghastly' to Anne with its mosquitoes and lizards. 'It is unpleasant', Scott remarked about quarantine, 'to be thought so very unclean and capable of poisoning a whole city.' The Inspector of Quarantine—himself a Scot called Greig—accompanied Scott's party in the boat to the waiting carriage of Lady Hotham, which took them to the hotel opposite the house of Mrs Davy. Her husband was the head of the medical staff, so that Anne was relieved to have a doctor so near. On hearing the sound of Scott's voice as he chatted sociably to Greig, Mrs Davy was touched with sentiment at its home-bred quality. She had last heard it, five or six years before, in North Castle Street at Edinburgh before her marriage as Miss Fletcher to Dr Davy. Her father had been one of Scott's brother-advocates. Now, as she saw him leaning on Greig's arm while walking from the carriage to the hotel-door, she heard her English maid remark: 'Poor old gentleman, how ill he looks.'[38]

Nevertheless, soon after he was installed in the 'very excellent apartments' of the hotel, he went with Anne and Walter to the *Barham* for 'a most handsome dinner' with the wardroom officers. Anne wrote to Sophia that Dr Liddell had despaired of getting him to give up drink, and that she dreaded his going out to dinners, which he would do, instead of remaining quietly at home with two or three friends, as he had done at Sophia's in London. Yet he was certainly better than when Sophia had last seen him, though not so much as on board ship. In view of Malta's healthy climate and their comfortable rooms in Beverley's Hotel she hoped they would stay till the end of January. Captain Pigot wanted to take Scott to Naples in two months' time, which would be 'the very thing for him'. Walter, however, wished to leave immediately on account of uncertainty about his leave of absence, particularly after the Bristol riots. Even if he *did* leave, she would have no fear of want of friends: Mrs Davy was a very nice neighbour, and Lady Hotham and Mrs Seymour-Bathurst were also very close. In keeping with her 'spirit of satire' she criticised Walter to Sophia for his 'dissipation' in going to a ball after the dinner on board the *Barham*. She was most anxious for *accurate* news of the cholera from Sophia or Lockhart, for their initial bad reports of it had been succeeded by information from a newly arrived captain from Marseilles that 'it has not yet come to England'.

Mrs Seymour-Bathurst took Scott in her carriage to St John's Cathedral, the principal church and burial-place of the Knights. He described it as 'the most magnificent place I ever saw in my life' in a journal entry charged with the 'Gothic' imagination and enthusiasm of a poet and antiquary. Even the 'dim religious light' of Milton's *Penseroso* was pressed into the picture of 'the huge and ample vaults' bending over 'this scene of death' as represented in the drawings and inscriptions on the marble pavement.[39] The scene evoked his favourite lines from Coleridge's *Knight's Tomb*, which he later inserted in *The Siege of Malta*.[40] Having promised himself a second visit to the cathedral—for he had still to see La Valette's tomb in the crypt, for which he would need assistance—he drove to Frere's house at La Pietà in Frere's carriage before making the longer journey to San Antonio, 'a beautiful place with a splendid garden, which Mr. Frere will never tire of, unless some of his family come to carry him home by force'. Scott's remark was prophetic; for Frere was never to return to England, although he was to outlive Scott by many years and to see Lockhart, in fact, echoing Scott's remark in the *Life of Scott*.[41]

Although Frere had become a little indolent, Scott was much gratified to see him, as he had always known him, 'a good Tory as ever, when the love of many is waxed cold'. Scott had long resented the defection of many Tories of eminence, who had joined the cry of reform at the coming of the Whigs to power. Frere had taken less long than Scott to make up his mind in favour of Catholic Emancipation, since he had served as junior minister at the passing of the Act of Union with Ireland as a prelude to Emancipation. Both of them had been close friends of George Canning, the prime minister associated with Emancipation. Scott referred to the Emancipation Act on revisiting St John's Cathedral, accompanied by Captain Pigot and several officers. The Maltese subjects of William IV 'now pray for the King etc since the Catholic Bill'. Captain Pigot and the officers helped him to go down into the crypt, and 'greatly to my joy I found La Valette most splendidly provided with a superb sepulchre of bronze, on which he reclines in the full armour of a knight of chivalrie'.[42]

He had already accepted an invitation to a grand ball in his honour by the garrison. 'An odd kind of honour', wrote Mrs Davy in her diary, 'to bestow on a man suffering from paralytic illness.' But he appears to have appreciated it, for he noted it in his journal with evident satisfaction at the large attendance—'about 400 gentlemen and ladies'—the *élite*, in fact, of the army, navy and civil service. A deputation of Malta's dignitaries met him at the door to the sound of

Scots' music, followed by reels in the great hall of the Union Club, formerly the *auberge* of the Knights of Provence. He stayed for three hours, and, according to Susan Frere, left 'a general persuasion that he was very much amused'.[43]

Lady Hotham calmed Anne's fears with an assurance that there would be no more balls for him, although Anne herself was invited to another one by Lady Hankey, the wife of the Chief Secretary, with whom Charles corresponded from time to time on official business from Naples. At the ball she had an opportunity of watching Maltese ladies of her own class. They were ill used, she afterwards wrote to Sophia, by their English counterparts,[44] whereas Scott represented their ancestors as in a state of happy relationship as 'vassals' of the Knights in *The Siege of Malta*. Indeed he took advantage of a mere hint in Vertot to write them up, in an original scene of dramatic quality, as faithful 'feudal dependants' in keeping with his own partiality for that system of the Middle Ages. Nor was he at all displeased as a Protestant to find that several English soldiers had crossed from Sicily to Malta as volunteers during the Siege 'notwithstanding the quarrel between our distant Island and the See of Rome'. Accordingly he took pains to name them in *The Siege of Malta* after he had explained that the English branch of the Order had been suppressed by Henry VIII during the Reformation.[45]

The more he saw of the Knights the more he was astonished, he wrote to Skene, 'at what a gorgeous generation the Order must have been of old'. He also informed Skene that he had seen his son repeatedly since his release from quarantine; and in his subsequent *Memories of Sir Walter Scott* Skene referred to his son's receiving a note from Scott to ask him if he would accompany him on a tour of Valletta and the fortifications, which he wished to see leisurely and without being 'gazed at as a lion'.[46] Skene had himself visited Malta many years previously after its capture by the English, and, as he was soon to write to Scott, 'two of the old knightly triremes were still floating in the harbour when I was there'. So before Scott set off on his tour with Lieutenant Skene, 'he had the goodness to say, "the first place you are to take me to, is the house your father inhabited at Malta; it will do my heart good just to see it and be able to tell him so, if it should be God's will that we meet again" '.[47] It was not to be God's will.

Skene also referred to Scott's passing a good deal of time in the library of the Knights, working on *The Siege of Malta* in the intervals between the drives and the dinners. He finished, as he wrote to Cadell on 4th December, '30 close pages' of manuscript amounting to 'half a volume of the usual size'. His intention was to publish it, as was customary, in three small volumes, and he left it to Cadell to judge whether they should change James Ballantyne, their printer and reader, for it, 'because I shall have the advantage of Lockhart's opinion, where it is necessary, and besides I have quite recovered the power of thinking for myself, and must after all be my own best critic'.[48] He had real reasons for preferring Andrew Shortreed, the young printer and son of his old friend, Robert, the Sheriff-Substitute of Roxburghshire, to Ballantyne. In fact, he had already—

long before—recommended Shortreed to Cadell 'for a printing job now and then when Ballantyne is overloaded'. On the other hand, Ballantyne, whose 'taste' as a critic he still respected despite his wounding remarks about *Count Robert of Paris* and *Castle Dangerous*, 'has been so long in the habit of printing these things' that 'for reasons applicable to ourselves' it was perhaps better to retain him for the new novel.[49] 'Before I leave Malta I shall send you full copy for the Siege of Malta volume 1st', which contained an 'original story' about his hero, the Spanish 'Knight of Malta', after his arrival in the island to take part in the Siege. It was 'an inestimable advantage' to Scott to have the use of the library of the Knights as well as of the equally good lending library of the garrison, both in the same building, and close to the armoury of the Knights, to which, surprisingly, he made no reference in his journal, although he was to enlarge, in *The Siege of Malta*, on the armour not only of the Knights but also of the mercenary soldiers in their pay.[49a] Moreover, he had a splendid field before him in the novel for those 'modes of resistance'—coals, burning oil, boiling water and so forth—that he had spelt out in London during the Reform Bill riots as ancient forms of defence against sudden attack.

Anne also confirmed to Sophia that 'papa never tires of the tombs of the Knights of Malta, and then there is such a good library, to say nothing of Mr Frere with whom he swears eternal friendship'.[50] Scott himself held up Frere to Cadell in the same letter of 4th December as the most accomplished man he had met in Malta. He valued a set of engravings from Frere as illustrations to *The Siege of Malta*. Dr Davy was also accomplished, besides being a member of the Royal Society of London, to which he had lately sent an authoritative account of Graham Island.[51] Mrs Davy referred to it and to much else about Scott in her diary in keeping with her literary interests as the daughter of Mrs Fletcher, a well-known blue-stocking, who had already written Scott a letter inquiring if he had any material to give her for a biography that Dr Davy was writing of his brother.[52] Anne invited Mrs Davy to a quiet dinner with Scott and one or two officers of the *Barham*. It was very much a homely Scottish occasion, particularly as they were joined by Francis Scott from H.M.S. *St Vincent*. Scott was in his old manner of raconteur and table-minstrel. After the dinner he looked very animated and recited a long passage to the ladies from Frere's translation of the *Poema del Cid* after he had himself inserted the Cid in *The Siege of Malta*. Anne told Mrs Davy that she had never seen him so like himself since he had come to Malta, and wrote to Sophia that 'he is better without champagne'.[53]

Captain Pigot wished to take them to Naples sooner than he had originally suggested, since he was afterwards to go to Tunis on government service. Walter was pressing Scott, as Charles had already done from Naples, to leave Malta immediately. Scott was uncertain what he had best do. On the one hand, Captain Pigot's offer was not to be 'despised'; on the other hand, if he were to remove to Naples before the arrival of the December packet from Falmouth, it would be 'at the expense of protracting the news from Scotland' about the sales of *Count Robert of Paris* and *Castle Dangerous*. For he had become really anxious to hear from Cadell about them in consequence of a small overdraft on his London bankers after paying two bills for board and lodging at Beverley's Hotel. Although he was confident that he would clear the overdraft with *The Siege of Malta*, which would also earn him money for the winter in Naples, he feared that his letters to Cadell might be delayed by the uncertain post owing to the cholera epidemic, and that Cadell might be prevented from settling the overdraft with Coutts, the bankers. In that event his draft on Coutts might not be honoured with the result that he might find himself in the same situation as that of the year of his financial ruin.[54]

Fortunately Dr Liddell declined 'a handsome fee' for his services, and Walter drew on his separate credit with Coutts for his bills. Anne claimed to Sophia that she was observing strict economy, resisting even the temptation of buying her a *faldetta*, the pretty Maltese head-dress worn as a national costume. Walter was taking one with him for his wife, 'but I was determined that he never shall have it to say that I spend money'.[55] It was Scott who in the past had complained of her accountancy. Whether Walter was also doing so now is impossible to tell in the absence of extant letters to his wife or Sophia from Malta. As to Scott himself, he even meditated, in one or two gloomy entries in his journal, on 'a sad purpose', apparently self-destruction, 'in case of my being disgraced' by the bankers or by the reading public. Similar thoughts of suicide had floated once or twice in his mind since his financial ruin and apoplexy, but he had fought them off gallantly even without considering, as he did in this instance, that his life had been insured for as high a figure as £20,000, which would have been lost 'if I had been guilty of a crime of that nature'.[56]

All his fears, in fact, were unfounded, for *Count Robert of Paris* and *Castle Dangerous* were 'selling capitally' according to information from Lockhart in a letter *en route* to Malta by the December packet. 'All the literary gazettes London and Edinburgh treat them with courteous words.'[57] If not equal to their predecessors in quality, they were at least superior to the majority of the many imitations of *The Waverley Novels*. All the reviewers had drawn attention to the 'affecting' valedictory that Scott had appended at the end of *Castle Dangerous* after announcing that the two novels would be the last that he would write. *The Caledonian Mercury*[58] had refused to believe 'these gloomy anticipations of the mighty enchanter'. Scott 'may yet live to earn fresh laurels'. *The Scotsman*,[59] on the other hand, had taken him at his word, and had turned its review of the two novels into an eloquent leave-taking of him despite the political differences that divided him from that Whig newspaper: 'we were never blind to the transcendent literary talents which belonged to our political opponent'. Lockhart for his part seemed to prefer *Castle Dangerous* to *Count Robert of Paris*: 'I think if you had had leisure to work *Castle Dangerous* to three volumes, it might have been one of your very finest things.' Cadell had done

An artist's re-creation of H.M.S. *Barham* carrying Sir Walter Scott to Malta in November 1831. From a painting by Horace Vernet. (By courtesy of the Malta Union Club)

3
John Hookham Frere (1769–1846), translator, poet and diplomat: Scott's principal host in Malta.

From a painting by John Hoppner

4. Fort Manoel and Quarantine Harbour, Malta. Scott performed quarantine in Fort Manoel, where he began to write *The Siege of Malta.*

well to get the novels out a week before parliament reassembled for the
Reform Bill.[60]

Even 'the magnum' was continuing to sell very well, as Cadell himself
informed Scott in a letter sent to Lockhart for forwarding by the same packet.
'In fact I have nothing but good to speak of' not only on matters of sales but
also about domestic affairs at Abbotsford. He had paid all the bills for wages and
other expenses received from Laidlaw. 'Glad indeed shall I be that the first
tidings from Malta bring good accounts of you and all with you.'[61] For neither
Cadell nor Lockhart was yet in receipt of Scott's letter from Fort Manoel.
'Day after day we now look and languish for some tidings from the *Barham*,'
Lockhart added before confirming that 'the cholera has now been for a month
at Sunderland, and appeared within these few days at Newcastle'. Hitherto it
had touched but few of the upper classes, and the original alarm that it had
created appeared to be diminishing. He could give Scott no definite news about
the Reform Bill, 'for tomorrow parliament meets and we shall begin to understand where things are and have been'. All Scott's old friends were poised for a
last-ditch stand against the Bill, in face of the overwhelming majority for it in
the House of Commons. It remained to be seen whether it would again 'stick
in the Lords'.[62]

Scott could read about politics at home and on the continent in *The Malta
Gazette*. He was delighted to meet a veteran of the Napoleonic Wars in the
person of the Bishop of Malta, who had been one of the leaders of the Maltese
insurgents against the French in the capture of Malta by the English. On that
account this 'fine old gentleman' soon came to loom in Scott's romantic
imagination as 'my fighting Bishop of Malta'. He was a brother in the
flesh, in other words, of the Bishop of Tyre in *The Talisman*. Scott was taken to
him by Colonel Bathurst as Acting-Governor. On hearing that the Bishop had a
journal of the blockade of the French by the Maltese and English similar to the
documents he had used for *The Life of Bonaparte*, Scott pressed him to publish
it and offered his assistance 'for the benefit of the poor of the diocese'. Although
the Bishop seemed pleased with the proposal, he does not appear to have taken
the journal with him on returning Scott's call in full state exactly answering to
Scott's love of pageantry.[63] He was 'superbly dressed in costume' as fine, if
not finer, than Scott's own uniform of a brigadier-general of the Royal Archers
of Scotland, that he had brought out with him as a court-dress for Naples.

Frere—laconic as a correspondent compared with his sister—wrote to London
that Scott 'is much benefited by the climate and will I hope do well if we do not
kill him with dining'. He appears to have come near to that state after dining
with Sir John Stoddart and partaking too freely of port and champagne. Anne
had to call Dr Davy in out of fear of an impending stroke on seeing Scott in a
stupor and unable to form a letter on paper in reply to a note from Admiral
Hotham. Yet, on seeing Mrs Davy with her husband, he asked her courteously
if she had recovered from a little illness she had complained of the day before,

and, turning to Dr Davy, began to talk to him about the biography of his brother. 'I hope, Dr Davy, your mother lived to see the scientific distinction attained by Sir Humphry.' The kindly observation dropped from him naturally, and Mrs Davy rightly perceived his sense of the worth of the domestic affections.[64]

Dr Davy applied leeches to his head, and within twenty-four hours he felt fit for a drive in Mrs Davy's carriage and company as far as San Antonio for an impromptu call on Frere. It was a beautiful day, and he rose to the occasion with cheerful talk and anecdote interspersed with literary comment. 'This town is really quite like a dream,' he first said, on driving through the streets of Valletta in sight of carved stone balconies associated in his mind with picturesque 'belvederes', as he called them in *The Siege of Malta*. When the carriage reached the open country, he recalled his days of long walks over moss and moor with a gun on a shoulder. San Antonio was thick with new oranges, which he snuffed with delight. On failing to find Frere at home, they drove back without waiting, and he talked about the women novelists in fashion with readers of Mrs Davy's culture. Foremost among them was Jane Austen: 'There's a finishing off in some of her scenes that is really quite above everybody else.' The praise was a variant of his earlier remarks about her in his journal and in *The Quarterly Review*.[65] Good writers, he observed, again repeating a view often expressed in the journal, were not very good company owing to a want of tact. The exception was his friend Tom Moore. 'He's a charming fellow—a perfect gentleman in society; to use a sporting phrase, "there's no kick in his gallop".' Mrs Davy's carriage drove on without Scott saying anything else on account of fatigue, but she never forgot 'the kindly good humour with which he said, in getting out of his hotel-door, "Thank ye for your kindness—your charity, I may say—to an old lame man—Farewell" '.[66]

It was not strictly farewell for good. They were to see each other again when Frere took Scott to see the old capital of Malta called Città Vecchia, and when Dr Davy accompanied him to the street in Valletta where he had been told that the young Knights had fought their duels. Although he seemed pleased with what Frere showed him at Città Vecchia, he did not look animated to Mrs Davy, especially in comparison with his active response to the duels in the street of Valletta. It was the *only* street where the Knights had been allowed to have their duels, and in quitting it, he looked round him earnestly and said, 'It will be hard if I cannot make something of this.'[67] In the event he did not work it into *The Siege of Malta*, as calls of a more practical nature pressed upon him on consenting that same day to Walter's wish that they leave Malta for Naples in the *Barham* in the hope that he might find letters and money there from Cadell to the care of Charles; for his overdraft on Coutts had now risen to £70 after payment of a third bill to Beverley's Hotel, and his cash credit was exhausted.[68]

Anne disapproved of their hasty move, especially before the arrival of the December packet from England. Even Dr Liddell and Dr Davy were most anxious that he should remain in Malta. Despite the limited society of Valletta 'one could have made it agreeable to papa'. Although she had never left his side, 'Walter was out all day long and *all night*, dining at messes; and the swearing *at waiters* and bills in the morning was too much for one's patience'. Her maid, Celia Street, and Scott's servant, John Nicolson, 'have both nearly given up their places'.[69] Even Susan Frere referred rather coldly to Walter before their departure on 13th December, which was preceded by 'a rude shock of an earthquake'. It alarmed Scott, who was inclined to associate it with the reported disappearance of Graham Island. 'By all accounts it has vanished altogether,' he afterwards wrote to Skene, rounding off the information, appropriately, with a phrase from *The Tempest*: 'leaving not a wrack behind'.[70]

His departure nearly coincided with the arrival in Edinburgh of his letter to Cadell from Fort Manoel. After expressing great delight at reading of his 'good heart and spirits', Cadell, in an immediate reply, enlarged on Lockhart's earlier information about the excellent sales of *Count Robert of Paris* and *Castle Dangerous*. 'The number printed is nearly sold off.' He could not 'recollect anything in my trade as a bookseller that has been more cheering than this success of Count Robert and Company, always excepting the magnum', which continued to sell 'capitally'. As to Scott's new novel, 'most gladly shall I see the Siege of Malta, I shall print it the moment it arrives, and bring it out as soon as ready, and most cheerfully place its value at your command as you express'. When added to 'the magnum', it would reduce the balance of Scott's debt still further. In keeping with his earlier promise to supply Scott with cash abroad, but in ignorance of his present urgent need for it, Cadell hoped that 'you will allow yourself to suffer no inconvenience for money while I can honour your drafts.'[71] In ignorance also that Scott was on the way to Naples, he trusted that 'the climate of Malta will give you additional vigour', which was precisely the impression that he communicated to readers of *The Caledonian Mercury*[72] in an edited extract from Scott's letter containing an allusion to his experiences in the *Barham* and on Graham Island, and forecasting that 'we shall remain in Malta six weeks or two months', whereas in point of fact they had only remained three weeks. For that reason he had not yet sent Cadell 'full copy for Siege of Malta volume 1st', as he had said on 4th December that he would be doing.

His visit to Malta was reported by Mrs Davy to her mother in a letter praising 'the cheerful variety' of his conversation flavoured with 'happy allusion and quotation'. What she liked still better was 'the pleasant old man's benevolence of his manners'. Her letter was afterwards transcribed by her mother for his friend, Allan Cunningham, the poet.[73] Scott had already declared in his journal that he looked upon Cunningham's famous sea-song, 'A wet sheet and a flowing sea', as 'among the best songs going', and he knew it by heart.[74]

References for Chapter 3

1. *Journal* 683.
2. Lockhart x, 132–33; *Journal* 683.
3. Skene 220; MS 1752, p. 435.
4. *Journal* 683–84; cf. Ibid 411.
5. Skene 200; *Journal* 683; MS 1752, p. 429; *Siege of Malta*, f. 20.
6. *Journal* 684, 508; MS 1553, f. 239.
7. *Journal* 684; MS 1553, f. 239; MS 5317, f. 207.
8. MS 5317, f. 208; D. E. Sultana, *S. T. Coleridge in Malta and Italy*, 1969, pp. 18, 142, 159.
9. Lockhart x, 132–33; *Journal* 684; MS 1553, f. 239; MS 1752, p. 430.
10. *Miscellaneous Prose Works of Sir W. Scott*, Edinburgh, 1841, II, Ch. 46, p. 488.
11. *Frere Family Letters*, Oct. 31, Nov. 29, 1831; Frere 331; MS 1752, p. 430.
12. *Journal* 364, 469.
13. Lockhart x, 133–34.
14. *Journal* 684; Lockhart VI, 208–9; *Letters* VI, 159.
15. MS 1752, p. 433.
16. MS 1553, f. 239; *Journal* 684; MS 1752, p. 433.
17. *Siege of Malta*, ff. 38–40.
18. Skene 196–202; MS 1752, pp. 429, 433; MS 1553, f. 240.
19. MS 1752, p. 429. Cf. Ibid 437.
20. MS 1553, f. 238; MS 1752, p. 425; MS 917, Nov. 24, 1831.
21. *Frere Family Letters*, Nov. 29, Dec. 3, 1831; MS 1752, p. 433; *Journal* 685.
22. MS 1752, pp. 433–35.
23. Ibid 431–33.
24. Ibid 431–32.
25. Cf. Eliot Warburton, *Crescent and the Cross*, 16th ed., n.d., Ch. VIII, p. 69.
26. *Journal* 685.
27. Cf. Ibid 683.
28. *Siege of Malta*, f. 63; MS 1752, p. 437.
29. Skene 198. Cf. ibid vi.
30. *Siege of Malta*, f. 30.
31. ed. of 1774, vol. I, p. 360.
32. *Siege of Malta*, f. 61.
33. Ibid, ff. 113–14; *Journal* 685.
34. Ch. XXXVI.
35. *Journal* 685.
36. *Journal* 685; MS 1553, f. 239.
37. G. Festing, *J. H. Frere and his Friends*, 1899, p. 345; *Frere Family Letters*, Nov. 26, 1831.
38. *Journal* 685–86; MS 1553, ff. 238–40.
39. *Journal* 686; MS 1553, ff. 238–40.
40. f. 81.
41. *Journal* 687–88; Lockhart x, 130.
42. *Journal* 687–88.
43. MS 1553, f. 240; Lockhart x, 136; *Journal* 687–88; *Frere Family Letters*, Dec. 3, 1831.
44. MS 1553, ff. 240, 242, 246; MS 917, Nov. 24, 1831.
45. *Siege of Malta*, ff. 80, 83–85, 117 n.
46. Skene 193–94, 201.
47. MS 5317, p. 212; Skene 195.
48. Skene 196; MS 1752, p. 442. This letter has no date and has been placed after another letter by Scott from Naples, but it was certainly written in Malta, and judging by MS 1553, its date appears to be Dec. 4, 1831.
49. MS 1752, p. 442; *Journal* 576.
49a. Cf. 1932 typescript of *Siege of Malta* (Berg 64B4878), p. 100.
50. MS 1553, f. 242.
51. *Journal* 688; MS 1752, p. 442; Dr J. Davy, 'Some Account of a New Volcano in the Mediterranean' in *Philosophical Transactions of the Royal Society for 1832*, pp. 237–49.
52. *Letters* XI, 441–42.
53. Lockhart x, 136–38; *Siege of Malta*, f. 52; MS 1553, f. 241.
54. MS 1553, ff. 240–43; *Journal* 689; Skene 203–4.
55. *Journal* 688–89; Skene 203; MS 1553; ff. 245–46; MS 1554, f. 71.
56. *Journal* 690, 698; Skene 204. Cf. *Journal* 653.
57. MS 5317, f. 90.
58. Dec. 8, 1831.
59. Dec. 28, 1831.
60. MS 5317, f. 90.
61. Ibid, f. 116.
62. Ibid, f. 117.
63. *Journal* 690, 692, 694; Skene 204–5.

64. *Frere Family Letters*, Dec. 11, 1831, Lockhart x, 139–40.
65. Lockhart x, 141–43. Cf. *Journal* 353.
66. Lockhart x, 144. Lockhart suppressed the passage in Mrs Davy's Malta diary (MS 3389, f. 444) containing Scott's remark on the alleged 'defect of tact' of some good writers. Cf. *Journal* 461, 467.
67. Lockhart x, 144–45. Cf. P. Brydone, *Tour through Sicily and Malta*, 1774, i, 362.
68. *Journal* 690; MS 1752, p. 437.
69. MS 1553, ff. 244–45.
70. *Frere Family Letters*, Dec. 3, 1831; *Journal* 690; MS 1553, f. 245; Skene 201.
71. MS 5317, f. 118.
72. Dec. 19, 1831.
73. MS 2617, f. 73.
74. *Journal* 238.

4

Naples and Completion of 'The Siege of Malta'

Scott did not describe the passage in the *Barham* from Malta to Naples in detail. He merely entered it in his journal as 'a picturesque voyage' of five days, although several weeks later he recalled in a letter to Skene 'the splendid beauties' of the east coast of Sicily, to which, according to Anne, the *Barham* ran quite close before sailing up the Straits of Messina to skirt all the landscape of Calabria.[1] Anne herself thought that Sicily 'seems to be the most beautiful country possible', even though Mount Etna disappointed her by not throwing out lava when they passed it, contrary to Stromboli, which was 'very grand' with a brilliant flame at night as well as lava running down into the sea. Altogether they were treated to 'scenes as various as the heart of man can conceive' until they anchored in the Bay of Naples late on the evening of 17th December in rather cold and misty weather. For that reason the celebrated view of Naples fell a little short of their expectations before Anne was seized with one of her chronic stomach attacks, aggravated by a fear that 'I was in for the cholera'. The ship's doctor bled her, 'and after one horrid night of suffering I got better'.[2] Her plight, which was partly nervous, drew silent sympathy from the sailor named Woodrow, who had accompanied them in the landing on Graham Island. 'She lay helpless to all appearance,' he afterwards wrote to his brother at Kelso in a letter describing the passage to Naples, which to him had culminated in a view of Vesuvius throwing out flashes of fire at night.[3]

Scott had no sooner admired the beauty of the Bay of Naples in daylight than he wrote an anxious letter to Cadell explaining the circumstances of his overdraft on Coutts and urging him to settle it as soon as possible. He also requested a fresh supply of money 'for our necessary expenses, including occasionally that of a little caleche', which was the open carriage that he had first explained to Charles from London that he would be needing, 'with two stout horses', so that John Nicolson might drive him round Naples. In return for the money he repledged *The Siege of Malta* to Cadell. It was about 'one fourth finished', and he thought it 'one of the best I have written and mean it for immediate publication' together with *Seventeenth-Century Letters*, which he now mentioned for the first time since he had last given Cadell to understand from Portsmouth that he would defer completing it until he had finished *The Siege of Malta*. He meant it as 'a little quiz' of about one hundred pages without indicating if he had received the promised contribution to it from Lady Louisa Stuart. 'My health is very good,' he added, and had been even better thanks to 'the blest climate of Malta'. The knowing officers of the *Barham* 'tell me I must look to find' the weather colder at Naples, which had 'a less comfortable' lazaretto, for 'we expect the confinement of the quarantine as we had at Malta'. In consequence he feared that, much as he wished to hear from Cadell, it might be long before he did so in the absence of communication with the shore.[4]

Nevertheless Charles managed to get alongside the *Barham* and look at his father through the window of his cabin. He had not seen him for two years. 'Certainly papa is a great deal changed, which I had been prepared for,' he afterwards wrote to Sophia, 'but he was in good spirits', as was Walter, whereas Anne was fatigued, and had gone to sleep. Charles saw her, however, on going again alongside the *Barham* after he had approached the magistrate of the board of health about their quarantine. She looked 'rather delicate', but he expected her to get over her fatigue when they were settled. The magistrate had been very civil, and Charles was hoping that in consequence of letters that the *Barham* had brought from Malta, testifying to a clean bill of health all the way from England, their quarantine might be lessened, 'in which case they will remain on board'. Even if they were to move into the lazaretto, his chief, Mr Hill—the future Lord Berwick—had promised him anything in the way of comforts, on hearing that 'another English family were in possession of all the pest-house furniture'.[5]

Although he had letters for Walter from his wife, he had none for Scott from Cadell, who, nevertheless, was about to follow up his last jubilant letter to Malta with another one, answering Scott's question about his proposed method of publication of *The Siege of Malta*. He would put it in print the moment he received it in an edition of four to five thousand copies before adding it, in a separate edition, to 'the magnum' as the concluding novel. It was 'delicate work' to 'chuck off' so large a number of copies 'before the public smell it as the conclusion of the magnum', but he would try it on the calculation of 'seeing the said Siege in the spring', for which purpose he would postpone any announcement of the closure of 'the magnum' as long as he possibly could. 'You may consider £2000 at your command' for the three volumes of *The Siege of Malta*,[6] which Scott, in another letter from on board the *Barham*, claimed was written—as far as the first volume was concerned—'with great confidence and ease'. It was better, in his opinion, than *Count Robert of Paris* and *Castle Dangerous*. He expected to bring back to Britain 'a thousand pounds' worth of valuable literary material' provided he had the full benefit of his trip, so that he did not envisage returning 'till the year is somewhat advanced'. In contrast to his princely reception at Malta he felt that 'here we are less kindly treated', for the Neapolitan authorities 'threaten us with imprisonment when we are dismissed from the frigate'. In that event 'I might go back to Malta' with Captain Pigot, who 'does not, I think, quite understand the freedom his flag is treated with'.[7]

Charles was officially informed, however, that 'they will not be more than seven days in the vessel', for which reason he began to think where they had best be accommodated after their detention. He thought it better that Scott should take apartments in a hotel for a few days, and then they could find out exactly what would suit him. 'Walter's leave is out on 31st January, but has written for six weeks more.' His own stay at Naples was quite uncertain, as the limited extension granted him by the Foreign Office would expire at the beginning of February. In the meantime he continued to go alongside the *Barham* despite a high sea, which on one occasion gave him 'a complete ducking'. Walter handed him Scott's letters for Cadell before he passed to Anne a letter that he had received from Sophia containing 'very bad accounts of poor Johnny Lockhart'.[8]

In ignorance that Johnnie had, in fact, died of his long illness a day or two after their departure from Malta, they became anxious for further news of him from Sophia, to whom Anne, in her reply, complained that owing to 'Walter's great hurry to get us away from Malta' they had missed their letters. 'Walter was sick yesterday which rather pleased me, and tomorrow will be the *same*, as he has been dining in the gun-room. I was glad to hear papa tell him that he must alter his way of life at Naples.' As to Charles, she had found him looking remarkably well despite his rheumatism. It was hard to her feelings that they would probably be spending Christmas in the *Barham* as 'our prison-house', from which nevertheless they were released on Christmas Eve just before Vesuvius, which had hitherto only been smoking, 'burst forth in all its terrific grandeur, the burning lava running down its sides for about two miles in a complete stream, and every explosion sounded like the discharge of a heavy artillery'.[9] Scott, with his instinct for humour and superstition, remarked that 'my arrival has been a signal for the greatest eruption from Vesuvius which that mountain has favoured us with for many a day'. 'I can only say, as the Frenchman said of the comet supposed to foretell his own death, "Ah, messieurs, la comète me fait trop d'honneur".'[10]

After going into lodgings for a few days in the Hotel della Gran Bretagna in great joy at now really seeing Charles again, he agreed to dine on Christmas Day with Mr Hill, resolving that 'it should be my first and last engagement' of that kind in Naples, as he had become a little alarmed about himself after his last attack at Malta. Besides the weather had become bitterly cold, and he suffered from that and, much more, from irritation at the continued absence of money from Cadell.[11] 'For God's sake send me what cash you can,' he again begged him just after Cadell had, in point of fact, received and promptly answered his letter of 4th December from Malta with an estimate that 'the magnum' had made £17,000 in one year, and that, as the trustees of Scott's estate contemplated paying a third dividend to his creditors before many months were over, this would 'take £20,000 more of the sum against you'. In other words, Cadell revived the old idea that the balance of Scott's debt would soon be paid off. 'This is moving pretty smartly to my view', so that, 'to use the present fashionable phrase, we will be able to burke [= kill] the whole affair'. He agreed with Scott that in view of James Ballantyne's long printing experience it would pay them to retain him for *The Siege of Malta* instead of engaging young Andrew

Shortreed. Nevertheless 'I shall send a copy of each sheet to Mr Lockhart before it goes to press' for an opinion.[12] It was a pleasure 'to see you writing in such spirits', on which he was also congratulated by Skene in a reply by the same conveyance and containing the information that Skene had not only received the paper for the Royal Society of Edinburgh about Graham Island—'the hide and seek island', as he called it—but had read it to a very full meeting as a communication from 'their absent president'.

Skene had no doubt that 'La Valette cannot have failed to delight you', and that 'Vertot must have made your pen, like Major Weir's stick, take post without its master's leave' in allusion to Scott's cane, which Anne had wittily named 'Major Weir', because 'it is so often out of the way that it is suspected, like the staff of that famous wizard, to be capable of locomotion'.[13] Having read the whole of Vertot during his own visit to Malta, Skene still recollected 'the delight which that interesting history and the presence of the scenes on which the events were acted, reciprocally gave to each other'. As the cholera had not yet come to Edinburgh, he gave Scott no information about it, unlike Lady Louisa Stuart, who wrote by the same packet to Malta in reply to 'your dispatches', which 'came in good time to cheer and comfort Sophia' over the loss of Johnnie Lockhart. Although the old year was ending sadly on account of 'the poor boy', his death was rather 'a release than a deprivation'. Meanwhile it was good for Scott at the moment to be living in a past age with the Knights, for 'everything anti-chivalrous seems to be the order of our present day' after the riots and the passing of the Reform Bill by the House of Commons by a large majority before the Christmas recess. Although the cholera had certainly spread in the north, it was still confined to the most dirty quarters, where the apprehension it had caused had resulted in 'a general scrubbing and cleaning and white-washing', so that 'Auld Reekie, I am told, will feel the benefit through all her closes and wynds'.[14]

In contrast to Lady Louisa's good wishes to Scott for 'the year now so near at hand' were his own forebodings that it was likely to find him 'in the condition of those who are sick and in prison, and entitled to visits and consolation on principles of Christianity'. If it had not been for Walter's money, 'we must try a begging box', since 'they seem to have abandoned me so particular[ly]'.[15] Anne shared his low spirits not only on his own account but also in consequence of her own ill-health combined with some loneliness at finding herself having to sit alone with him in the evenings, while 'Walter and Charles except *dinner* sometimes are never at home day or night'. It was 'gaiety to a degree' not only for them but also for Captain Pigot, who had accompanied them to San Carlo for the opera after the Christmas dinner, followed by an exciting climb up Vesuvius when the lava was running down its side.[16] Anne felt that at Malta it had been better for Scott, with Frere, Dr Liddell and Dr Davy visiting him every day in much warmer rooms than those of their hotel, although she trusted 'in time to get some quiet society for him' after he had himself heard that 'there are

many English here'. He had 'some knowledge of most of them' or was connected
with them through friends they had in common.[17] There was Lady Drummond,
for instance, to whom Charles had gone for dinner after the ascent of Vesuvius.
She was the widow of his friend, Sir William Drummond, the diplomat, who
as a classical scholar had also known John Morritt. Then there was Lord Hertford
—Croker's employer in England—who came to Naples regularly in the winter
with Lady Strahan and her two beautiful daughters. Scott looked forward to
renewing 'an old acquaintance mad[e] up in the days of George IV'.[18] He was
the prototype of Lord Monmouth in *Coningsby*.

Scott's own kinsman, John Scott of Gala, had mentioned two or three other
English residents to him in London when he had cautioned him against over-
exertion in visiting the old parts of Naples. Foremost among those parts in
interest to him was the historic site by the ancient castle associated with the
rebel, Masaniello, and the French adventurer, the Duke of Guise, both of whom
he had treated at length in an article written only two years previously for the
Foreign Quarterly Review.[19] So he went on an airing to see the site, particularly
the tower of the Church of the Carmelites, where Masaniello 'was shot at the
conclusion of his career'. There he also marked 'the striking and affecting'
epitaph of Prince Conradin, the son of a German Emperor, to complement the
tombs of the Knights of Malta as additional material for the journal of his tour.[20]
Conradin was one of the many foreign rulers of Naples, especially in the Middle
Ages, of which Scott had extensive knowledge combined with a passion for the
ruins of that period in contrast to his indifference to classical antiquities.

The passion soon found an outlet in a picturesque ruin of a palace in the same
street as that of his hotel and originally put up by the wife of one of the Spanish
Viceroys of Naples. The street was the celebrated Via Nuova, 'a new access of
extreme beauty which the Italians owe to Murat', a brother-in-law of Bonaparte
and a former King of Naples.[21] Scott had traced Murat's rise and fall in *The Life
of Bonaparte*[22] besides explaining how Naples had been drawn towards England
and Austria in her foreign policy by Sir John Acton, her former Prime Minister.
Although Acton, who was of English descent, had died a few years before
Murat, his widow was another prominent member of the English colony on
Scott's and Anne's list of prospective acquaintances. Anne for her part looked
upon the Via Nuova as 'the Hyde Park of Naples and the most splendid drive
in the world' against a background of Vesuvius on one side and the Bay of
Naples on the other. Scott could see Vesuvius from the window of their hotel,
now no longer erupting but smoking. He described it as 'controlling' the Bay
of Naples, itself 'a vast amphitheatre' for countless vessels of different forms and
countries, including the *Barham*, which sailed away for Malta after he had
promised Captain Pigot to present him with a set of *Waverley Novels* inscribed
by himself in gratitude for the passage to Malta and Naples. The present was in
keeping with the advice about naval etiquette that he had received from Captain
Hall in London. Despite his intention to return home overland through Ger-

many to meet Goethe at Weimar, the rumour ran among the *Barham*'s crew that they would be returning to Naples to fetch him back to England in the summer after a tour of duty in the Adriatic.[23]

Anne appears to have remained in correspondence with Captain Pigot, and was afterwards linked with him in marital gossip. It was a great comfort to her to hear of 'a good English doctor', who might attend Scott.[24] He was Edward Hogg, a former friend of Scott's great favourite, Lady Northampton, whom he had last mentioned in London when he had told one of his callers that he was looking forward to meeting her at Naples. Although he had temporarily forgotten on that occasion that she had died in Rome the year previously,[25] he now remembered not only her death but that of another dear friend, Lady Abercorn, the wife of his father's employer in legal business, so that he had mixed feelings for Naples on going on another airing in remembrance of 'friends much beloved who have met their death in or near this city'. His feelings again drew out his sense of mediaeval history combined with his gift for calling up quotations from memory, for he drew on Lockhart's *Spanish Ballads* for a parallel between himself and King Alphonso of Aragon, who had 'summed up the praises of this princely town with the losses he had sustained in making himself master of it'.[26] His memory, however, operated only fitfully in a manner corresponding to the 'cloudiness of words and arrangement' that had continued to mark all his writing, including *The Siege of Malta*.

It was with shock, in fact, that Charles had noticed this symptom *after*—but not *before*—his father's release from quarantine, for, although Sophia's letters had prepared him to find Scott 'feeble and speaking with difficulty, I was not aware that his mind had been so much affected'. He had no hesitation, therefore, in deciding that, contrary to the Foreign Office instructions that he should return to London within a month, he could not leave Scott alone with Anne in the event of Walter's leaving them within a fortnight to rejoin his regiment. Accordingly he wrote to request another extension of his stay at Naples, where Scott proposed to remain for three months on moving out of his hotel into more comfortable apartments on the ground floor of Palazzo Caramanico in Strada di Chiaia.[27] On transferring to Palazzo Caramanico, Scott became more cheerful, as he found some friends to sit with him in the evenings, including an old Scottish acquaintance, Mr Laing Meason, who engaged his interest in 'the villas of the middle ages'. He was a fellow-member of the Bannatyne Club. Scott also hired a coach by the week for daily excursions, and put himself under the care of the same doctor who was looking after Anne, as Dr Hogg had retired from regular practice since he had settled in Italy from Cheshire on a comfortable income. Nevertheless Hogg also sat with him or accompanied him on his airings, which took him to the more remarkable places in the neighbourhood of Naples, such as Pozzuoli and the beautiful Lake of Agnano, where he was particularly struck by the sight of the leaves still lingering on the trees at so advanced a period of winter. The scene quickly recalled to his mind a lake in

Scotland, which was evidently his chief source of gratification in visiting it.[28]

His Italian doctor was called Roscalli, and could tell him about the distinguished Neapolitan family after whom his *palazzo* was named, particularly about Prince Caramanico, who had been the favourite of Queen Caroline of Naples until Sir John Acton had ousted him in order to become Prime Minister. Roscalli was an agreeable person, much liked by Scott's friends, whom he joined from time to time in the evening, or else he called at lunch-time after Scott had done his reading and writing.[29] For he still toiled at *The Siege of Malta*, 'with fingers never weary', as he put it himself in a letter to Lockhart. He had finished 'about two volumes of good value', and meant to send them to Lockhart for an opinion 'by the first safe opportunity', depending on whether Walter would leave or remain with them on getting an extension of his leave of absence. He had a notion that his numerous letters could not have reached their destinations despite the supposedly more frequent posts in Italy than in Malta, and despite his scrupulous avoidance of all mention of politics, in keeping with his earlier warning to Cadell from off Gibraltar, that 'much politics will not make letters very safe'.[30]

In fact, he wrote to Lockhart that 'my interest in politics is greatly diminished' almost on the day that Lockhart was himself writing from London to give him news of the Reform Bill before its second reading in the House of Lords. 'There is, I fear, no doubt', he told Scott, 'that the King has at last consented to make 37 new peers' to ensure the Bill's passage. He considered the long letter that Scott had written him from Fort Manoel in Malta 'a high treat, and I look forward to something of and concerning the Knights which will cheer the world ere long'. He then turned, in a lighter, half-bantering mood, to Scott's old friend, James Hogg, the Ettrick Shepherd, who was in London from Edinburgh to bring out 'an edition of his works *à la Waverley*'. 'I fancy he will succeed in his *start*. He seems likely to be a great lion among the ten-pound interest' in allusion to the newly enfranchised voters of the lower orders, and in reflection of Lockhart's mixed attitude to Hogg on grounds of class and education. He had invited Hogg to dinner together with Scott's other old friend, Theodore Hook, the famous wit, whose jokes they had so often enjoyed at the same table. In fact, he repeated the latest of them, since it related to the proposed creation of new peers by William IV, who had allegedly been brought to consent to this measure—as Scott had himself first heard in London—by the offer of coronets to his illegitimate children, the Fitzclarences, by Mrs Jordan—'one of whom, Hook says, must be Lord Jericho, "as they have all got beyond Jordan" '.[31]

Although Lockhart did not refer to Johnnie's death, Sophia had already broken the news of it in a letter which reached Naples in the New Year after Scott and Anne had read an obituary notice in an English newspaper, so that 'we were forewarned for the sad intelligence'. 'The poor boy is gone, whom we have made so much of,' Scott wrote resignedly in his journal. In sympathy for Sophia and Lockhart he proposed through Anne that 'you should come here' whenever

Lockhart could leave London. They had plenty of room in their *palazzo*, and 'you would so delight in the place', where there was much to be seen and the drives were so beautiful. Despite the low temperature there was 'a delightful feeling in the air' corresponding to Scott's changed spirits thanks to 'the very good society' they had found for him. Sir William Gell, the classical topographer and a key figure in the English colony of Naples, was driving out with him every day after he had been introduced to him by Mr Laing Meason. Scott had lately called with him on Gell's neighbour, the venerable Archbishop of Tarentum, 'who almost rivals my fighting bishop of Malta'.[32] Scott was, in fact, now looking upon Gell as 'one of my chief cicerones', his other companion being Gell's friend, Mr Richard Keppel Craven, a son of Baron Craven and formerly, like Gell, in the entourage of Princess Caroline of Brunswick during her residence on the continent in separation from the Prince of Wales. Keppel Craven had written a travel-book on the south of Italy, which Scott had read with pleasure.[33] Gell, according to Anne, was witty, and Keppel Craven, besides being accomplished, 'is so well acquainted with everything here that he is a great advantage in a morning drive'.[34] Scott would have wished to supplement Keppel Craven's information by independent research with Gell's assistance, but he hesitated to draw Gell away from his own classical investigations. Besides, Gell was handicapped by poor health, for he was crippled with gout and rheumatism, so that he was more disabled than Scott, being dependent on a wheel-chair for indoor movement and on a very low carriage for their excursions.[35] None the less he soon became a sort of Boswell to Scott for anecdotes and carriage-talk, which afterwards formed the principal source for Naples in Lockhart's *Life of Scott*.

Anne usually spent her mornings with the English lady living in apartments above them. She was Mrs Ashley, 'a fashionable London beauty for two seasons', who was proving 'such a nice person' without showing the least sign of being a flirt, as Anne had heard her represented in England. Her mother-in-law, who lived in London, was one of the many Scottish ladies with whom Sophia was acquainted. She was accompanied by her brother, Henry Baillie, a member of parliament for Inverness-shire, who was also, like Captain Pigot, afterwards linked with Anne in talk of marriage. Indeed he was said to have proposed to her, and that she accepted him, but nothing came of it. She herself was to protest to her father's friend, Susan Ferrier, the novelist, that 'the generous public has been so good as to give me two husbands, which is *contrary to law*'.[36] There is no mention of Baillie, however, in her extant letters to Sophia from Naples. He was very friendly with Dr Hogg, and was spending most of the evenings with Scott before returning to London with yet another letter to Cadell signed 'yours in necessity', but otherwise reassuring. Even Anne was 'in the way of mending', and this time had no complaint to make of Walter to Sophia, for he 'has been quieter'. '*His stomach attack has done him much good.* He stays at home more and is kinder.' On the other hand, she could not stand the 'horrid' wife of Mr Laing Meason. 'She has an Italian prince attached to her.' It was difficult to keep clear of her, 'as she comes at all hours'. Anne, unlike Scott, had not yet met Lord Hertford, who, according to Charles, 'is looking very well'. Scott recorded with pleasure that 'he has got a breed from Maida', Scott's favourite deerhound, 'of which I gave him a puppy'. Anne gathered that he gave a ball every winter for Lady Strahan, while 'Lady Acton gives private theatricals, but they are all stupid'. She regretted that she was not yet strong enough to go to the splendid birthday celebrations of King Ferdinand II.[37]

Scott went to the royal palace with Walter and Charles in his uniform of a brigadier-general of the Royal Archers of Scotland, 'and looked as well as sixty could make it out when sworded and feathered *comme il faut*'. 'I passed well enough', surviving even his fears of a fall on the slippery floor of the magnificent apartments. 'The King spoke to me about five minutes, of which I hardly understood five words. I answered him in a speech of the same length, and all I'll be bound equally unintelligible.'[38] For the reading knowledge of Italian that Scott had acquired in his youth for romances of chivalry had become so rusty that he had found during his call on the Archbishop of Tarentum, who had no English, that he could get on better with French, and even that, as proved by his attempt to speak it with the King, was only a little better than his Italian, although in the past he could speak French fluently. Nevertheless he bore witness in his journal to his pleasure at being introduced to 'many distinguished persons' and their ladies in fine dresses and jewellery, including 'a pretty Spanish ambassadress', who spoke English, as did the wives—both of them countesses—of the Austrian and Russian ambassadors. The Austrian countess, in particular, seemed to be 'very clever'. 'I will endeavour to see her again', as both he and Anne had already made her acquaintance through Gell, who was also on dining terms with Lord Hertford.[39]

After the ceremony he went to San Carlo for 'the opera to see that amusement in its birthplace, which is now so widely received over Europe'. It was a 'superb' building, so large as to be seldom quite full, but on this particular evening it was, as the opera formed part of the birthday celebrations, so that the same brilliant scene of the royal palace was re-enacted with the King himself in attendance. He was accompanied by Prince Charles, his brother, who was looked upon as likely to succeed Ferdinand before very long in view of the latter's 'great corpulence' and fits of epilepsy. Scott thought it a pity that the King's health was so prematurely undermined, for he was only twenty-two and seemed to be popular. As to the opera itself, Scott thought it 'bustled off without any remarkable music' or poetry, the only redeeming feature being 'the *coup d'œil*, which was magnificent'. He was 'dog sick of the whole of it', and left without waiting for the ballet.[40]

He was evidently much more in his element in the National Library, commonly called the Studio, where the scholars of Naples, according to Gell, 'crowded round him to catch a sight of so celebrated a person, and they shewed him every mark of attention in their power, by creating him honorary member

of their learned societies'. On rummaging among the ancient manuscripts, he
detected a folio of old English romances, including the tale of Sir Bevis of
Hampton, similar to the famous manuscript of *Havelock the Dane* that Sir
Frederick Madden had discovered in the British Museum before its publication
for the Roxburghe Club of London. He thought the folio suitable both for the
Roxburghe and the Bannatyne, but, on applying to have it copied for quick
dispatch to Cadell, he was told that 'it is an affair of state', for which the King's
permission was necessary. He therefore addressed a formal request to the
Minister of the Interior in ignorance at this stage of the Italian manner of
conducting business.⁴¹ While waiting for an answer, he at last received from
Malta—after 'a mo[n]strous time'—Cadell's letter of early December about the
preliminary good reports of the sales of *Count Robert of Paris* and *Castle
Dangerous*. 'This puts a period [= an end] to my anxiety,' he wrote in his journal,
and at once replied with a long letter seeking an assurance that Cadell had settled
the overdraft on Coutts, and proposing that, in return for *The Siege of Malta*,
Seventeenth-Century Letters and the journal of his tour, 'you should advance me
£200 a month regularly, which would be enough to live upon'.⁴²

He had now regulated his expenses, which were 'far from being excessive'.
In addition to his carriage and horses, he had engaged two servants, 'one a
valet de place, another a cook', who also saw to all their provisions, including
'excellent wine', as much as they needed, 'but few care to drink it'; in fact, 'if
you see Dr Abercrombie, tell him with my love that I have given up the wine at
last' in compliance with the *régime* prescribed by Dr Roscalli, of which he gave
Cadell some details: 'bread and butter and a bunch of grapes, never butcher
meat' at breakfast, followed by a drive 'for amusement or instruction with some
friend' until it was time for early dinner at home, after which other friends of
both sexes called for a chat, but they always 'break up at eight or nine and think
themselves well used with a dish of coffee'. In this way they were seeing 'some
of the most distinguished persons both for rank and interest in this celebrated
city', including the Austrian countess and her husband, the ambassador, who
had apparently been encouraging Scott to visit Vienna on the return journey in
view of his explaining to Cadell that 'I would attempt to come home by way of
Vienna and perhaps some of the northern courts, where I have had invitations'.

They were also seeing a good deal of Lady Adam, the Greek wife of Sir
Frederick, the Governor of the Ionian Isles, who was in London on official
business. She was waiting for him to return—not without impatience, according to Anne, for her good looks were attracting unpleasant attentions from the
Neapolitans. Naples, in fact, seemed a place of scandal to Anne, although
neither she nor her father was contemplating an early return to Scotland, so that
Scott explained to Cadell that 'if my health agrees with the climate, it would be
foolish to leave it for half a year or thereabouts'. Therefore he wished to give
Naples 'a fair trial', since 'it is now just beginning' to turn milder after the
stormy weather that they had been having since their arrival from Malta. His

'old facility of composition has been as much at my command as ever it was', and 'my hand is generally speaking much improved', enabling him to add 'a great many pages' to *The Siege of Malta*, which was written 'clear out'.[43] In other words, it was a 'clean' manuscript, complete with separate sheets for corrections, that he was preparing for dispatch to Cadell in proof of the great pains that he had been taking to make up for Laidlaw's absence as amanuensis.

Cadell, for his part, had received Scott's first urgent letter from on board the *Barham* at Naples, 'and I lose not a post of assuring you, as my letters from Malta will testify, that I have not been a negligent correspondent, no more than you yourself'. As he surmised that his other letters addressed to Malta 'will not reach you so soon as this', he not only recapitulated for Scott all the excellent news of the sales of 'the magnum' and *Count Robert of Paris* and *Castle Dangerous*—'deil ane remains' ['hardly one remains']—but he confirmed that the trustees of Scott's estate would soon be paying a third dividend to his creditors, which 'will bring down the principal to £40,000!!!' He did not say, however, that Scott's debt had been paid off—there was after all a balance of £40,000 still to be paid, excluding interest on it—he simply held out a prospect, as he had repeatedly done in the past, that it would not be very long before the debt would be paid off, so much so that he added, 'my hat will soon cry victory as sure as anything' in view of a long-standing bet with Scott that he would buy himself a new hat when the debt would be paid off.[44]

Scott was in a mood of euphoria at feeling that 'the mist attending this whoreson apoplexy', as Shakespeare had forcefully, if somewhat coarsely, put it through Falstaff, 'is wearying off'; and he went again to the Studio to finish *Seventeenth-Century Letters* and to inquire about an answer from the Minister of the Interior to his application to copy the ancient folio. He was told that no answer had come, and that his request might be 'granted in two or three days to a man that may leave Naples tomorrow'. Even the offer of 'a loan of whatever books I need' involved another long delay. 'I think really the Italian men of letters do not know the use of time made by those of other places, but I must have patience.' Eventually the King granted the favour he had requested, and Gell let him have his amanuensis to copy the romances at a rate so cheap by English standards that 'I am ashamed at the lowness of the remuneration', for which he made generous amends by asking Sgr Sticchini, the copyist, to break-fast and dinner. He was delighted to find that the Studio was rich in old Neapolitan and Sicilian ballads corresponding to his own *Minstrelsy of the Scottish Border*, and he set about forming a collection of them.[45]

Dr Hogg kindly supervised the copying of the romances by Sticchini and at the same time praised Scott's skill and experience to Gell in reading old scripts. Scott himself began to study the dialect of Naples for the ballads, assisted by 'the gentleman with the classical name', as he called Gell's neighbour, Sgr de Licteriis, the royal librarian.[46] Walter and Anne engaged two Italian masters for the language after Walter had received an answer in the affirmative to his

5
Sir William Gell (1777–
1836), classical topo-
grapher: Scott's principal
cicerone in Naples.

From a drawing by
R. Unwin

6
Paestum and the
Classical Temples, which
Scott visited from Naples
in the spring of 1832.

From a drawing by
W. Brockedon, engraved by R. Brandard, in Brockedon's *Italy, classical, historical and picturesque*

7. Benedictine church and monastery at La Cava, as seen by Scott on his memorable excursion from Naples in the spring of 1832.

Drawn by J. D. Harding, engraved by T. Jeavons. From *The tourist in Italy*, by Thomas Roscoe, 1833

request for an extension of his leave of absence. He could now remain in Naples till March, when Scott was much disposed to go to the Ionian Isles on the invitation of Sir Frederick Adam, who had come to Naples from London, and had offered to send his steamboat to Naples whenever Scott could visit him at Corfu. He would thus have more material for the journal of his tour, as *The Siege of Malta* was 'near done'. He had added a long tale to *Seventeenth-Century Letters*, which he sent to Cadell with a request that a proof should be sent to Lockhart 'if within reach, and to myself if possible'. In deference to Lady Louisa Stuart's wishes the *Letters* was 'to come out incognito'. He was still dependent on Walter for money, and had written so many letters on this subject that 'I am quite tired of it', although he could not believe that this 'total interruption of correspondence' arose from Cadell's neglect.[47]

Cadell was distressed to hear that 'you are at a loss about money', and assured him that he had settled the overdraft on Coutts, and that he was sending him a large supply of money through Coutts's agent at Naples. 'Rely on it that all your drafts will be duly honoured—do not give yourself one instant's bother on this score. I would be a sorry chap not to do all this and more.' There was nothing new for him to report about Edinburgh except that the cholera was 'now very near us', and they were all preparing for it in contrast to the preparations at Naples for the traditional Carnival, which, according to Charles, 'is to be very long this year'. The Austrian ambassador was giving a fancy dress ball of characters drawn from Scott's novels. 'One beautiful Italian woman has been in tears for the last week because her family are too Catholick to allow her to take the character of Rebecca, the Jewess', in *Ivanhoe*.[48] Charles himself, according to Anne, did not care for the 'style of society', but he loved the country, as did his master, Mr Hill, who was fond of him but 'is very odd and unsociable'. They had never seen him except on Christmas Day at the dinner he had given in Scott's honour. Without 'the beastly society' Naples would be 'a perfect paradise' to Charles, who was not relishing at all, on account of his rheumatism and Tory politics, the prospect of 'a fog and the Reform Bill' in London in the absence of an answer from the Foreign Office to his request for a further extension. 'He tells us', Anne wrote to Sophia in her usual satiric manner, 'he has the charge of *twelve nations*, and upon my word, though I disbelieve the nations, yet he seems to have all the business.' As to Walter, she continued to get on very well with him, for 'having so very pretty a person as Mrs Ashley all day in the house keeps him in *good humour*'.[49]

Mrs Ashley, moreover, was of use to Scott in preventing him from being too cross with Anne over her house-keeping until his concern about money was completely turned into triumph and self-congratulation when at length he received 'an epistle from Cadell full of good tidings'. It was the letter with the forecast that 'he will soon cry *victoria* on the bet about his hat' in anticipation of the eventual liquidation of Scott's debt. It was proof that 'as yet my spell holds fast', and 'I might write myself [clear]', especially as he had 'two or three things', including *The Siege of Malta*, 'in which I may advance with spirit' in view of their alleged superiority to *Count Robert of Paris* and *Castle Dangerous*, which he had never imagined to deserve going into a second edition. It was the public, in his view, 'that are mad for passing these two volumes', as he made no scruple to explain to Gell, to whom he stated, however, that 'all his debts were paid' in misunderstanding of Cadell's letter and in repetition of what he had already said at Portsmouth to Captain Hall and Mrs Schetky. 'And now', he added, 'I shall have my house and my estate round it free, and I may keep my dogs as big and as many as I choose, without fear of reproach.' For he had already told Gell of his favourite dogs at Abbotsford, 'so large that I am always afraid they look too handsome and too feudal for my diminished income'.[50] There was a scene in *The Siege of Malta*,[51] in fact, between his hero and his favourite horse that might well have arisen from his own personal attachment to his deer-hounds. It represented the Spanish 'Knight of Malta', who, like himself, was elderly, leaving his home for the siege, and turning to his horse as his 'old companion of former labours', who instantly paws the ground in affectionate recognition.

Gell doubted Scott's wisdom in proposing to go to the Ionian Isles on the ground that his health was not quite up to it, but he could certainly give him information about Corfu and the neighbouring isles, which he had visited, years before, on a diplomatic mission for the British government besides publishing a book on the geography and antiquities of Ithaca.[52] In contrast to his doubts Anne was enthusiastic about the trip, and was anxious to hear from Sophia and Lockhart that they would join them, as Scott had proposed, at Naples whence they could go not only to Corfu but also to Greece. 'There is a good many men-of-war always at Corfu,' she wrote to Sophia, perhaps in the knowledge that Captain Pigot was in the Adriatic in the *Barham* with other warships, 'and Admiral Sir Henry Hotham says he will be only too happy to let us have one to go to Athens.' Her father continued 'wonderfully well', as he reported himself to Sophia: 'I have not had any return of the imperfection in my speech, but hope the remains of it will soon disappear. At present they give me promise of doing so. My wonted good luck promises that this year will put an end to all old troubles and pay off my debts.'[53]

Charles confirmed that 'my father's health has improved, and I think will continue improving, but still I cannot leave him at present', although it was likely that 'my leave will be prolonged'. Anne had gone to her first carnival ball at the Austrian ambassador's. It had been 'most splendid', with the King himself and Prince Charles in attendance. 'Prince Charles is rather handsome and very civil to the English, flirting with all the young ladies.' Her next ball —with Walter to escort her—was at Lord Hertford's, although she thought her hostess, Lady Strahan, 'vulgar beyond description, and tells such lies, but she is handsome and very good-natured'.[54] Lady Strahan was the future Madame Colonna in *Coningsby*.

Scott had bought a considerable number of books for his library at Abbotsford, and had them all bound in vellum in the belief that he could now afford to be self-indulgent in money before returning home to live again in the old style of the laird of Abbotsford. 'I have returned to my old hopes,' he wrote in his journal, 'and think of giving Milne an offer for his estate—£10,000.'[55] Nicol Milne was his neighbour, whose estate he had long dreamed that he would one day buy.[56] 'Everything in which we have any interest seems to thrive,' he wrote to Cadell on receiving copies of all the letters that had gone to Malta with news of 'the magnum' and *Count Robert of Paris* and *Castle Dangerous*. Estimating that he would not be needing more than a credit of £1000 on Coutts for the whole of his residence in Italy, he requested Cadell to provide for that amount through Coutts's agent at Naples. In approval of Cadell's plan to postpone any announcement about the closure of 'the magnum' until he had received *The Siege of Malta* in the spring, he explained that he wished 'to finish the magnum with a romantic poem in one volume called Rhodes, for which I have got a capital tale' of chivalry from Gell. It was based on the legend of the slaying of a dragon by a Knight of Rhodes, which had been the stronghold of the Knights before their removal to Malta. There was a version of it, in fact, in Vertot, although Scott appears to have had his interest in it roused by Gell, who had seen the skeleton of this reputed dragon on the roof of one of the gates of Rhodes. Being an excellent draughtsman, Gell had made 'some famous drawings' of the dragon and of other parts of Rhodes, which he had passed to Scott.[57]

In gratitude to Cadell as 'the horse I have rid the ford upon', he wished to present 'a first-rate harpsichord' to his musical daughters through Sophia, whom he requested to give an order for it to her old Edinburgh teacher, Mr Pole, who 'during the distress of my affairs behaved in the kindest manner possible', so that it would be extremely gratifying if the order were also to be of service to Pole. Lockhart, moreover, 'will be so kind as to subscribe to Hogg whatever he thinks right' for the projected edition of Hogg's collected works. Having been the first to discover Hogg's poetical gift, particularly for ballads and songs, some of which had gone into the *Minstrelsy of the Scottish Border*, he was pleased to hear that 'he is in a way of thriving'. Far from following Lockhart's earlier lead in personal satire with bantering comment on Hogg's uncouth appearance and manners, he prayed, in view of Hogg's notorious losses in farming, that 'God keep farms and other absurd temptations likely to beset him out of the way'. If Sophia were to hear of any club or public scheme having the Duke of Wellington at its head, Scott would willingly subscribe to it. 'I will always keep my own politics, but I am past the time to be active in them.' To their 'no small confusion' Skene's sister—'that most selfish and double-faced of all Aberdeenshire people', as he had described her, years before, to Sophia—had arrived at Naples with an American traveller, Miss Douglas. 'I wish I may survive the joint attack, but to say the truth Miss Skene is far the more tolerable of the two.'[58]

Charles—rather maliciously—wished them both to be 'the first victims of the cholera should it visit us', while Gell, who shared Scott's delight in Susan Ferrier's novels, asked him if Miss Skene was not the prototype of Miss Pratt, the well-known character in *Inheritance*. 'Well, I believe it may be so,' he replied, 'with a little ill-nature added.'[59] Anne had found the Duke of Wellington's nieces, who had also come to Naples, 'very agreeable', while Scott had made the acquaintance through Keppel Craven of a French diplomat, Le Duc de Ferronay, who had two very pretty daughters with 'a great deal of talent both musical and dramatic', although Anne expressed some reservations about them to Sophia after she had seen them act with Keppel Craven and his son in a rehearsal for a play at Lady Acton's. She could not understand how Sophia and Lockhart seemed not to be alarmed about the cholera.[60]

Scott was shocked to hear about its progress near Edinburgh, and hoped 'my poor people are all well and neither want medicine nor attendance' from Laidlaw, of whom he also inquired about his dogs, library and plantations. Although Naples had the most beautiful scenery he had ever seen, 'I would often give it all for a sight of Tweedside'. One of Sir Frederick Adam's assistants, a Captain MacPhail, had been telling him about the plantations of fruit and timber trees, which 'I shall see with rejoicing eyes'. Laidlaw, as his former co-collector of ballads, with Hogg, for the *Minstrelsy of the Scottish Border*, would be interested to hear of the old English romances that Sgr Sticchini was copying for him in a beautiful hand and very exactly, although Sticchini did not understand a word of the language. 'I have been stuffing my head' with enough literature to keep Laidlaw fully occupied as his amanuensis for lucrative publication after his return to Scotland.[61] If only he had Laidlaw with him as amanuensis, he would soon finish *The Siege of Malta*, and, more important, even though it did not occur to him then, Laidlaw would have helped him to remove some at least of its 'cloudiness of words and arrangement'. For Laidlaw would surely have noticed Scott's aberrations at once on dictation. Laidlaw was 'a kind clerk', Scott had himself told Lockhart at Abbotsford, 'I see by his looks when I am pleasing him, and that pleases me'.[62] Anxious in this instance to repeat to Laidlaw the praises of *The Siege of Malta* that he had already made to Cadell and others, he informed him that 'its interest turns on the changed manners of the European nations', who at the end of the sixteenth century 'began to renounce the doctrines of chivalry', exactly as he had already explained in the first volume containing the 'original story' about the Spanish 'Knight of Malta'. He wished Laidlaw would obtain for him from Cadell the standard history of the Knights—of later date than Vertot—which had been reviewed by Brougham in *The Edinburgh Review*. Its author was a French Knight called Boisgelin, and any vessel to Naples would bring it safe.[63] He needed it for the projected poem about Rhodes.

He was really beginning to enjoy the Neapolitan climate, 'which is of late turned delightful', so that Anne's earlier fear that Pompeii with its damp excavated apartments might be very bad for him no longer operated. They therefore went there in a large party, which was met by Gell, who was an authority on Pompeii. On arriving at the Street of the Tombs, Gell observed that Scott was already almost tired before he had advanced a hundred yards; so he persuaded him to accept his wheel-chair, and was enabled to pass through the city without more fatigue. Gell had meanwhile supplied himself with another wheel-chair, and was able to call Scott's attention to the more remarkable objects. 'To these observations, however, he seemed generally insensible, viewing the whole and not the parts, with the eye not of an antiquary but of a poet, and exclaiming frequently "The City of the Dead" without any other remark.'[64]

Gell and Keppel Craven had already heard him declare at the ruins of Pozzuoli that 'we might tell him anything and he would believe it, for many of his friends, and particularly Mr Morritt, had frequently tried to drive classical antiquities, as they were called, into his head, but they had always found "his skull too thick" '. For this reason and for the other relating to his health Gell hoped to dissuade him from going to Greece from Corfu,[65] but Scott was bent on going to Athens, and, even more, to Rhodes in 'ease and safety' in a frigate that Sir Frederick Adam had ordered for April from Constantinople in lieu of his steamboat. The frigate was to be H.M.S. *Brook*, not the *Barham*. Charles also thought that this trip might well be managed, as there was 'not much land-journey', but he was firmly opposed to Scott's idea of returning home in late summer via Vienna and Germany. This 'is out of the question and must not be attempted', he wrote to Lockhart, from whom he wished to know if he and Sophia had any chance of coming to Naples to replace Walter as companion to Scott in view of the impending termination of Walter's leave and his consequential departure for England. It was absolutely necessary, in Charles's view, for someone to be with Scott 'to arrange his money matters, as he cannot even draw a simple bill without explanation, and you know Anne is not overwise in these matters'. In the event of Lockhart's being obliged to remain in London, Charles would stay with Scott, 'and must take my chance at the Foreign Office, from which I have as yet received no answer'. He regretted that Anne 'has taken a great dislike to me and Walter, which is increased by her seeing my determination not to quarrel with her both for my sake and my father's'.[66]

Scott also informed Cadell of Walter's impending departure after Cadell had passed to the editor of *The Caledonian Mercury*[67] the news that Scott intended 'to make a considerable stay in Italy, and to return by the Tyrol through Germany'. *The Siege of Malta*, he added to Cadell, 'advances', and he would soon be sending 'the first volume' by Walter. He looked forward to hearing that Cadell had received *Seventeenth-Century Letters*, which, as his friend, Allan Cunningham, would have phrased it, were 'a humbug on the public' in view of their purporting to be authentic whereas in fact they were fictitious. For that reason, after Lockhart had seen the proofs, Cadell 'must get them out the best way you can, unless I stand convicted'. But, contrary to his earlier feeling that, on balance, they should retain James Ballantyne for the printing of *The Siege of Malta* rather than engage Andrew Shortreed for it, he now came out firmly against Ballantyne for *Seventeenth-Century Letters* on the ground that 'that scoundrel pirate Galignani picks the works out of his [Ballantyne's] printing-house' for publication as reprints on the continent at a handsome profit without paying royalties.[68]

Galignani was the famous English library established at Paris—where it still exists in Rue de Rivoli—by an Italian *émigré* in London, whose two sons, who now carried on the business, had offered Scott a small royalty on *The Life of Bonaparte* as a reprint on his last visit to Paris after Lady Stuart had informed him that they had pirated his *Lives of the Novelists*.[69] Now he had come to see for himself that Galignani had been pirating even his novels, including *Count Robert of Paris* itself, on, or even before, its appearance from Ballantyne's press, for he had just sent Lockhart a list of errata from a copy of the pirated edition. Therefore he wished to give *Seventeenth-Century Letters* to Shortreed. He 'hoped much' from 'this little work', and thought that the long tale he had lately added to it—'a romantic Italian adventure'—would not be found bad, although less 'capital' than Lady Stuart's contribution.[70]

Cadell was thinking of going to London for a business meeting with Lockhart, who felt that, although nothing could be more agreeable than Scott's proposal that he and Sophia should travel to Naples, 'I must adhere to my post' in face of the 'fierce season ahead of us' over the Reform Bill. Besides, the circulation of *The Quarterly Review* had again risen considerably, and he wished to keep up the momentum. 'We do, however, indulge the hope that ere summer closes, we may find it possible to make a run and invade your *palazzo*.' They had received 'more cheering news' of the *palazzo*'s inmates from Henry Baillie on his arrival in London from Naples. Lockhart did not doubt that *The Siege of Malta* would be welcomed whenever it would appear. 'Being here I shall of course be at your service to do anything in the way of revising the press which you and Cadell may wish.' As to the cholera, 'today we have the news of its appearance in Edinburgh, where admirable preparation has been made'. Although the book trade had not yet emerged out of the low state in which Scott had himself found it in London, 'your series, and a similar one of Byron's life and works are thriving capitally'.[71] The Byron series was the publication by Murray in imitation of 'the magnum', of which Scott had also heard in London.

Lockhart's information was confirmed by Cadell: '20,000 volumes trotted off last month—cholera and all'. Murray 'cannot touch us, do as he may' with Byron. The cholera itself was 'not yet here as an epidemic', and the post from Naples remained open, enabling Laidlaw to follow up Scott's request for Boisgelin, although, like Charles, he expressed disquiet at Scott's mental confusion over money: 'he mentions their living very cheap, yet he says they pay £150 a month for their palace'. If *The Siege of Malta* was, as Scott had been claiming, equal to *Ivanhoe*, 'it would not only be a literary curiosity but next to a miracle'. Laidlaw, in fact, was 'but half satisfied' with Scott's latest communication, and was disappointed that 'he never mentions his family at all', which is certainly not borne out by the letters that have survived, although a number of them, as Laidlaw himself informed Scott, did not reach him or else reached him after he made that remark to Cadell.[72] In any case Cadell did not share his misgivings and represented Scott to readers of *The Caledonian Mercury*[73] as 'in the highest health and spirits' and as intending 'to proceed shortly to the Grecian Isles' as far as Athens in Sir Frederick Adam's company. Cadell had received *Seventeenth-Century Letters*, and 'I shall forthwith put them into the hands of Shortreed and send the proofs to Mr Lockhart', who would forward them to Scott, 'if he can judge of your motions with sufficient certainty'. Cadell was waiting 'to welcome *The Siege of Malta*' on its delivery by Walter, 'who I suppose must soon look homewards'.[74]

Walter's intention was to return home by Rome and Milan at the end of the carnival, which, according to Charles, was 'unusually brilliant'. Even Scott referred to the balls as without number and to sugar-plum pelting as in high fashion. 'This town is certainly one of the gayest in the world', although 'somewhat too frivolous for my time of life and infirmities'. In consequence 'I rather prefer Malta'.[75] The chief amusement at the court was 'a perpetual round of dancing, good enough for young folk, but night after night scarce tolerable for old persons who patronize them with the same assiduity as the others'. This information and much else was in Scott's replies to the letters that reached him from Skene, Lady Stuart and others on the eve of Walter's departure. He not only answered them by Walter but also sent a packet of instructions to Cadell and Laidlaw, including an order for a pair of coach-horses and two clever ponies, 'as I do not think I will ever walk much again, so I must see how I am to be carried'. His exercise, 'as Parson Adams says, must be of the vehicular kind', but he was content to submit to it, so that, if Skene wished 'to revive old frolics', it would have to be a race in a pony-cart. Even the old high carriage, in which he had commuted between Abbotsford and Edinburgh, would have to be exchanged for a low one, precisely like that used by Gell for their airings. He was confident that no one was a better judge for finding the carriage and horses that he wanted than Laidlaw, who could also be relied on to look after the vellum-bound books in Italian that he was shipping to London for Abbotsford.[76] The chests containing them carried 'two volumes of the history of the Knights of Malta by Vertot, being the IV and the V which Mr Lockhart may need when revising the manuscript' of *The Siege of Malta*.[77]

'After much hesitation', however, he had settled against sending *The Siege of Malta* by Walter out of fear that 'it may miscarry' and because he wished it to be more advanced before parting with it. In fact, he had 'burned one half of it' after he had written 'the greater half of the three volumes', and was writing it over again. 'I will find a good opportunity of sending the precious stuff by a safe hand from this place, where the rule of the post is about ten days.'[78] In other words, he had a King's messenger in mind as the best mode of conveyance. 'In a month or six weeks I will be all ready again to go to press' in keeping with his undertaking to let Cadell have the manuscript in the spring—it was then the beginning of March—after which a final announcement could be made about the closure of 'the magnum'. It was unnecessary to send it sooner, 'as I will not write fast' in view of his infirm hand and of his attempt to achieve a legible manuscript, even though, according to Gell, he was sending Sgr de Licteriis, the librarian, occasional queries about books in the Studio 'in so indistinct a hand' that the poor Neapolitan could not read them.[79]

He was anxious to hear how Cadell proposed to bring *Seventeenth-Century Letters* out, and had lately been a little disturbed at hearing that Croker 'has on hand a selection out of the original letters of Lord Hertford's collection', which might clash with his own and Lady Stuart's publication. But, on second thoughts, 'perhaps they may rather help each other, as otherwise we must take our chance'. His only wish was that Lockhart might make the little work longer with a contribution 'in his own powerful person'.[80] In any case, since Shortreed was going to print it in lieu of James Ballantyne, Cadell must make sure that Shortreed looked to his printing-house, for 'that old pirate Galignani is making as much as anyone but yourself or the author by the magnum', and 'I will find a means of vengeance' on Ballantyne, if he continued to let his 'workmen steal proof-sheets and send them to Galignani'. Evidently his old quarrel with Ballantyne after the latter's wounding remarks about *Count Robert of Paris* as well as over the Reform Bill still rankled. As to the projected poem about Rhodes, which Cadell had so far not noticed, 'I will write it certainly' in the form of 'a vision', which had become fashionable since the turn of the century with the 'rediscovery' of Chaucer and the literature of the Middle Ages. 'If I find it did not come trippingly off, I can always burn it.' The drawings of Rhodes that Gell had given him could be turned into 'excellent vignettes' by a knowing engraver to complement the illustrations by Turner that were to appear after 'the magnum' in the new edition of his poetical works. At Corfu and Rhodes he would be helped by the weather, which at this time of the year was splendid, and Sir Frederick and Lady Adam were pressing him to go with them. Moreover, Cadell's advances had reached him just before Walter's departure, so that he was no longer dependent on loans for the house-expenses, which were now all settled. In fact, he had a balance 'which is much more than I shall need for a long time'. Walter would give Cadell 'all personal news' if he travelled to Scotland on a visit to his wife's estate at Lochore in Fife after his return to England. In that event Cadell would be informed of it from London by Henry Baillie before the latter rejoined Mrs Ashley in Naples.[81]

In the meantime Anne was recovering from a cold caught in the last week of the carnival, while Charles was 'not sorry that we have now entered upon the more quiet and rational season of Lent'. The Foreign Office had after all been 'very civil' to him, 'and have extended my leave of absence till May'. Whether he would be able to leave Italy in April would depend on his father's movements and on whether Lockhart could be persuaded to relieve him by coming out to Italy much sooner than he had last indicated. Although Charles had originally countenanced Scott's going to Corfu and Greece by sea in a steam-boat or frigate from Naples, he was now opposed to the whole idea, as Scott proposed to take ship from Ancona, the papal port on the Adriatic, for which he would have to travel overland to Rome and thence across the Apennines. It 'will never answer', Charles wrote to Cadell, to whom he repeated that 'as for his going home' from Greece by the route over the Alps into Austria and Germany, 'that is out of the question'. 'My father', he explained, 'is certainly stronger and will be much the better if he remains quietly here', as he had himself originally given Cadell to understand that he intended to do. 'Moving about always seems to make him nervous and unwell', as his last move from Malta to Naples had witnessed. So Charles asked Cadell 'to try and persuade him to stay here'. Moreover there was trouble near Ancona, for the people in Romagna were 'in open revolt' as part of the national movement for the unification of Italy, contrary to the settlement imposed by the victorious allies after Waterloo. 'The present state of affairs does not render the Estates of the Church a very desirable residence,' Charles explained to Lockhart. Unfortunately Anne 'seems to have set her mind upon going' to Rome with Scott in the spring, and in that event 'I must of course go with him' in the teeth of the deadline set by the Foreign Office. For he dared not even contemplate asking for yet another extension. 'I shall write no more but let them take *their will of me.*'[82]

He was tactfully supported, even if without much success for the time being, by Gell in the latter's airings with Scott, who was sometimes displeased to hear how distant Rhodes lay from Corfu, although he accepted an offer from Gell of a set of notes about Rhodes—additional to the drawings he had given him —which Gell believed would provide him with all the information he needed for the projected poem.[83] In the meantime, pending information about transport to Greece from Sir Frederick Adam, who sailed, with Lady Adam, for Corfu in advance of a move by Scott in the spring, Gell arranged an excursion to the celebrated temples of Paestum, which Scott had long been wanting to see when the weather became settled enough to warrant a drive to a place quite distant from Naples—some seventy miles—over country affected in parts by malaria and without ready facilities for board and lodging.[84] Even Charles had lately written to a friend that, 'although I have been there several times', the ruins of the Greek temples, one of which had been excavated only a year or two previously, 'are so magnificent that I cannot resist the temptation of paying them another visit'.[85] Fortunately for Scott he could have found no better guide for the ruins than Gell, who was the resident correspond of the Dilettanti Society of London for the antiquities of Italy, including Paestum. In fact, Scott had already advised him to send Lockhart a note about his work for *The Quarterly*

Review, which Lockhart for his part had promptly acknowledged in a letter on the way to Scott with the additional information that Cadell was expected in London from Edinburgh in a week or so when Walter might have returned from Naples.[86]

It was again fortunate for Scott that Gell happened to be very friendly with a hospitable English lady, Miss Whyte, who lived in a villa at La Cava on the route to Paestum. He had been wanting for some time to make her acquaintance after having heard of her brave, even if vain, attempt to assist two English travellers who had recently been murdered by Calabrian bandits. For he was now very close to bandit country, the mountains of Calabria being traditionally associated in English literature with crime of the 'Gothic horror' type, notably in the novels of Ann Radcliffe, about whom he had written a memorable essay in *Lives of the Novelists*. Indeed he had just sent Lockhart by Walter 'an Italian story of eruption and assassination' in proof of his interest in the subject. So it was settled that Miss Whyte should receive and lodge him and his party on the way to Paestum.[87] Gell took him in his carriage, while Anne and her maid, Celia Street, went in another carriage with Mrs Laing Meason and Dr Hogg. They went by Pompeii and Herculaneum in full view of the chain of mountains stretching from Vesuvius, which had destroyed both those cities. It drew out Scott's long-standing interest in the geology of mountains, exactly as the mountains of Andalusia had done on his way to Malta. The interest derived from his acquaintance with the border country of Scotland and, even more, with the Highlands. At Pompeii it was necessary to halt to refresh themselves and their horses in a tavern, where Scott—unhampered now, as he believed, by any need for economy—gave Gell a display of the liberality associated with him as laird of Abbotsford. Gell had certainly heard of his liberality but had so far not seen it. He did so now, for—to quote his own words—'after we had finished, not only the servants were fed with the provisions Sir Walter had brought, but the whole remainder were distributed among the poor who had been driven into the tavern by the rain'.[88]

Below Pompeii the fertile country bordering on the mountains stretched before them drew out his interest in plantations before he reminded himself that all the region around Naples was famous for Lacrima Christi: 'not a bad wine, though the stranger requires to be used to it'. The country itself had formerly belonged to the rich Republic of Amalphi,[89] a number of whose merchants had founded the Order of St John. He had read about this in Vertot, and he also knew—for he had stated it in the first volume of *The Siege of Malta*,[90] which he was about to dispatch to Cadell—that the Barbary pirates, including Dragut, had harassed the coast of Amalfi and indeed well beyond, as far as Genoa. In fact, his eye was quick to focus—as it had done on board the *Barham* in sight of the coasts of Spain and Malta—on a tower erected upon an eminence by the defenders of Amalfi as 'an exploratory gazebo, from which they could watch the motions of the Saracens, who were wont to annoy them with plundering excursions'. He called it 'the Knight's Tower' as long as it remained in sight,[91] and it was curiously reminiscent of 'the observatory' that he had created in *The Siege of Malta*[92] for his own Spanish Knight in a picturesque setting of mountains, wood and flowers. Gell was surprised to see 'how quickly he caught at any romantic circumstance, and I found in a very short time he had converted the Torre di Chiunso into a feudal residence and already peopled it with a Christian host'.[93]

It lay in a pass between the mountains in which La Cava was situated, and the drive over the height was 'so uncommonly pleasant as made me long to ride it', as in the past, 'on pony-back, at which no man on earth would ever have defeated me'. That, however, was impossible. At La Cava itself they received the warmest hospitality from Miss Whyte 'consistent with a sadly cold dwelling place'. 'They may say what they like of the fine climate of Naples—unquestionably they cannot say too much in its favour. But yet, when a day or two of cold weather does come, the inhabitants are without the means of parrying the temporary inclemency, which even a Scotsman would scorn to submit to. However, warm or cold, to bed we went, and rising next morning by seven we left La Cava' for Paestum on a cold drizzling day through wooded country, stocked with wild animals.[94] It drew out his old interest in field-sports, which was unmistakably reflected in *The Siege of Malta* in his frequent use of imagery connected with the chase and reminiscent of Shakespeare's similar practice. His love of field-sports, moreover, was shared by Charles, who had lately come to this place—which was called Persano—and had afterwards given him information about the hunting and shooting practices of the Italians, compared with their Scottish counterparts, for insertion in his travel journal and in his next letter to Laidlaw.[95]

The road from Persano led to 'the beautiful seaport town' of Salerno, famous for its medical school in the Middle Ages, but they made no stop and continued, within sight of the sea, 'to traverse the great plain of the same name, which is chiefly pastured by that queer-looking brute, the buffalo, concerning which they have a notion that it returns its value sooner, and with less expense of feeding, than any other animal'. At length they came to two rivers, one of which Charles had already referred to as 'the classic Silanus' in his account of the shooting expedition. On crossing it, they came to another plain 'displaying a similar rough and savage cultivation'. Scott's interest in primitive people—deriving from his love of ballads and from his excursions to the more remote parts of the Highlands and Lowlands of Scotland—was immediately stimulated by the external appearance of the shepherds, as wild as the savage herds under their guardianship. Their farm-houses were in very poor order. It was here, in fact, that the two travellers, whom Miss Whyte had vainly tried to help, had been murdered by banditti, and it seemed strange to Scott that 'in this wild spot, rendered unpleasing by the sad remembrance of so inhuman an accident, and the cottages which serve for refuge for so wretched and wild a people, exist the celebrated ruins of Paestum'.[96]

The ruins themselves, enclosed by 'a city wall in wonderful preservation', were so magnificent that his ingrained indifference to classical antiquities was temporarily suspended in admiration of the size and, even more, of 'the accuracy and beauty of proportion' of the temples, which had been the work of an ancient Greek colony, 'the Sybarites, a luxurious people', who had nevertheless been capable of a style of architecture 'so simple, chaste and inconceivably grand'. For this reason he evinced uncommon interest in a theory that Gell had elaborated about 'the origin of civilization' in the light of these and other ruins. He wished to promote it through Lockhart in *The Quarterly Review*, so that he afterwards followed up Gell's earlier note with a suggestion to Lockhart that 'it may interest you to see a short analysis of his work, which you may stick into the next journal'.[97] The subject itself had been treated in his lifetime from different standpoints by all the *literati* of Europe, including the Scottish philosophers of his own and earlier generations, notably Adam Ferguson, the father of his intimate friend and neighbour at Abbotsford, in *An Essay on the History of Civil Society* (1767). Ferguson had himself been influenced by the Neapolitan philosopher Gian Battista Vico, although there is no evidence that Scott heard of the latter from Gell or any of his circle. It is conceivable, however, that Dr Hogg, as an amateur Egyptologist, might have enlarged to Scott on 'the rise and fall of civilizations', on which he said that they reflected as 'we returned to our hospitable Miss Whyte in a drizzling evening, but unassassinated, and our hearts completely filled with the magnificence of what we had seen'.[98]

Miss Whyte for her part had arranged for him to visit, after proper rest and refreshment, the splendid Benedictine monastery of La Trinità della Cava, superbly situated in a very large ravine and approached through a beautiful forest of chestnuts spreading over picturesque mountain scenery. For this and other reasons the invitation from the abbot to the monastery was to prove the highlight of his excursion. He set off, with Gell, after breakfast on a fine day, and their carriage traversed the steep and precipitate roads over the ravine, which reminded him 'of the bed of the Roslin river' near Edinburgh. The views were not only beautiful but changing incessantly, and the advancing spring— to quote his own words, for he broke into poetry—'was spreading her green mantle over rock and tree, and making that beautiful which was lately a blighted and sterile thicket'. Gell heard him recite, 'with great emphasis and in a clear voice', the whole of *Jock of Hazeldean*, one of the most popular of his own Border ballads and originally written for Sophia.[99] The convent itself, lying 'most romantically' on the projection of an ample rock, was large but not handsome, 'the monks reserving their magnificence for their churches'. But it was surrounded—and this was of great appeal to Scott—'by a circuit of fortifications, which, when there was need, was manned by the vassals of the convent in the true style of the feudal system',[100] exactly as he had represented the Maltese vassals of the Knights offering to do at any time of crisis in *The Siege of Malta*.[101] La Cava, in short, answered to his ideal of the Middle Ages, particularly as the system itself was still 'in some degree the case at the present day', contrary to the state of affairs in Naples, where, as he was to write to Laidlaw, 'the feudal government is totally destroyed', and the taxes levied by the King had been raised 'to an exorbitant extent, so that money-jobbers, lawyers and attorneys are the only men who thrive'.[102] Certainly he was not alone among English travellers in complaining of excessive 'regal duties' in the various governments of Italy before unification.

At the convent he and Gell were received with the greatest politeness by the abbot, 'a gentlemanlike and respectable looking man', descended from a family related to St Thomas Aquinas, who had not belonged, however, to the Benedictine Order but to the Dominican, and had, in fact, been buried in one of the latter's churches in Naples. The Benedictines formed 'the most gentlemanlike order in the Roman church', so that the monks attending the abbot 'shewed their superior pretensions over other ecclesiastics to birth and breeding'. Gell and Miss Whyte had taken care to request that a Pontifical Mass should be sung in Scott's presence, after which, with the music of 'a grand organ, with fifty stops' still ringing in his ears, he was conducted, not without difficulty, through the long and slippery labyrinths of the vast building to the apartments containing the archives of the monastery. Here all the antiquary in him was rapturously drawn out by the ancient deeds placed before him not only of Christian sovereigns but also of Saracen rulers in this corner of Italy. So absorbing were the manuscripts that he was quite unconscious of a young Neapolitan painter, Vincenzo Morani, who chanced to be on the spot and made a sketch of him for Dr Hogg in what Gell afterwards described as 'his best manner and most natural position'. Gell, in fact, valued a copy of it presented to him by Hogg.[103] It was to be the last portrait of Scott, and complemented the more formal and better-known one by John Watson Gordon, that had been painted two years before, after his first stroke, and that Cadell had lately published in an engraving to illustrate *St Ronan's Well* as the latest volume of 'the magnum'.[104]

Never during the whole of Scott's residence in Naples did he regret more than 'on the present occasion the not having refreshed my Italian for the purpose of conversation'. Fortunately he had Gell, who spoke Italian fluently, to assist him. The monks pressed them to stay for dinner, but they were already engaged to return to Miss Whyte for the same purpose. On the way back, in the forest of chestnuts, he again recited, at Gell's request, *Jock of Hazeldean*, and when Gell praised 'his astonishing memory, he observed that he possessed at one time the art of repeating whole poems'. Gell had already asked him why he had given up poetry for novel-writing. 'Because Byron bet me,' he answered, pronouncing 'beat' short and with emphasis. Dr Hogg had in the meantime arranged for Morani to make copies of pictures of the Lombard Kings from a book of the monks that had enchanted him, while Miss Whyte had prepared 'a mighty dinner', which he ate with relish in the teeth of his late professions to Cadell about his diet, and in confirmation of Anne's remark, also to Cadell, that 'I have seen so many of his good resolutions broken through that I put little faith in them'.[105] After enduring another night in Miss Whyte's cold interior he set out with Anne, after breakfast, in his own carriage on the return journey to Naples. Before reaching Pompeii they passed through Nocera, which, like Amalfi, had been subject to incursions by the Saracens, so that he was told that 'the complexion and features' of some of the inhabitants were 'peculiarly of the African cast and tincture',[106] not unlike 'the sun-burned visages' of the Maltese peasants and fishermen that he had described in The Siege of Malta.[107] Although they had intended to have another look at Pompeii, the weather, which had again become drizzling, did not permit them, but near Portici he heard of 'two assassinations, still kept in remembrance', and wrote them up in his journal, particularly as one of the murders—a typical Neapolitan crime of passion—illustrated 'how congenial, at this moment, is the love of vengeance to an Italian bosom'. The stories complemented his large collection of printed trials—an interest in which only Dickens was to rival him—complete with the contemporary ballads about the criminals and their victims. The ballads included one by his friend, Theodore Hook, which he repeatedly quoted.[108]

It was now the second week of Lent, and the churches were full of wor-shippers, as he found for himself on going with Anne to 'the most august of the Dominican churches' to see the tomb of St Thomas Aquinas as well as that of the celebrated Marquis of Pescara, 'one of Charles V's most renowed generals'. His guide on this occasion was Sir Henry Lushington, the English consul, who had been recommended to him in London by John Scott of Gala. Anne for her part was accompanied by Lushington's sister and by an old friend, Marianne Talbot, one of the two daughters of Sir George Talbot, a leading member of the English colony of Naples. For Anne, according to Charles, 'has picked up some very decent friends and guardian angels' besides Mrs Ashley.[109] They included 'the two lovely Ricciardis', the daughters of an Italian dowager-countess, with whom she was seen by a young English traveller, newly arrived at Naples, who was to cross her and Scott's and Charles's path on and off as far as Venice. He was Owen Cole, and was travelling with an Anglo-Irish friend, Augustus Fitzroy, who was a cousin of Captain Pigot and apparently related to the Duke of Grafton.[110] When he was presented to Anne, it was at 'an assembly given by the Garniers at Naples, to which all the élite were invited', so that 'in the saloon of the Palazzo Garnier were more than a hundred guests of various nationalities, style and rank—counts, marchesas and bediamoned dowagers'. Lord Hertford was there, 'seated at whist, his well-developed leg graced with the garter and gallant motto, on his breast the star'. Lady Strahan was also there with her two daughters, and Cole anticipated Disraeli's raillery in Coningsby in remarking that Lord Hertford 'was guardian to the Miss Strahans; they were his 'wards'; their almost equally beautiful mother, who was in her autumnal bloom, was his 'reward''.[111] Scott was not there, to Cole's great disappointment, for his head was stuffed with the more notable characters and pointed pieces of dialogue in *The Waverley Novels*, which accounts for the striking allusions and parallels in his subsequent recollections.

On walking up to Anne, he told her how 'extremely desirous I was to be introduced to her illustrious father'. He thought her 'very pretty', admiring, in particular, as Susan Frere had done in Malta, her dark eyes and hair, and also her tall figure, although he was in error in representing her mother as having been of 'Irish extraction'. By the side of the Ricciardi girls she seemed to him 'the fairest of the three', although he too heard that 'by some she was reproached with peevishness', which in his admiration of her he seemed very willing to discount—as willingly, in fact, as, in his admiration of her father, he discounted the taunts of 'some Scotch people at Naples—Glasgow or Greenock bodies, who tried to undervalue their illustrious compatriot, speaking of the Laird of Abbotsford as one of those self-made men who would have done better to have kept their place'.[112] It is impossible to tell what Anne thought of him or of his friend—or indeed of all her newly made acquaintances—in the absence, from this point onwards, of her own letters to Sophia just at the time that, ironically, Scott was informing Lockhart that 'all our letters come now pretty exactly in about twenty days' from London.[113] Her silence henceforth is regrettable not merely on her own account—for it implies the withdrawal of a voice that had always been sharp, lively and spontaneous, even if at times a trifle incautious—but also because Scott, after the excursion to Paestum and the visit to the tomb of St Thomas Aquinas, abandoned his journal for nearly a month, perhaps to expedite the writing of *The Siege of Malta*.

He informed Lockhart that he was sending him by King's messenger the first volume and a half of *The Siege of Malta* as a first instalment on the assumption that Cadell was now in London and would thus be able to compare notes about it with Lockhart.[114] It incorporated the theme of 'the changed manners of the European nations', as represented by the Knights at the time of the Siege, about which he had written to Laidlaw in his last letter. He had now linked it with his own beloved Cervantes, who, 'far from undermining the principles of chivalry in *Don Quixote*', had only 'pointed out the extravagancies to which they may be carried out'. For he had remembered that Cervantes had 'served against the Moors' with the Spaniards as allies of the Knights, first, in the Siege of La Goletta and, then, in the battle of Lepanto a few years after the Siege of Malta. For these reasons he had inserted Cervantes in the novel in an original piece of dialogue between his hero and La Valette, both of whom pay tribute to his genius. Indeed his hero, the Spanish 'Knight of Malta', tells La Valette that 'I studied to find the author and bring him out with me to this Siege of Malta' only to find that, having lost an arm in the battle of Lepanto, he had been rendered unfit for further service.[115]

As to the theme of 'changed manners' Scott may well have seen in it a parallel with his own times under the shadow of the Reform Bill, which was about to be introduced in the House of Lords without the creation of new Whig peers. 'All the opinions of our fathers', he had made his hero say to La Valette in the same dialogue, 'are now held up to the ridicule of their descendants', exactly as Don Quixote had been in the romance of the Spanish author, whose object, however, had not been to represent his hero as a madman of chivalry. 'On the contrary, all in Don Quixote's temper, which springs from his own sentiments and his own heart, is brave, just, generous and disinterested', thereby pointing him out, despite 'all his weaknesses', as being 'the real model of an accomplished gentleman'.[116] Certainly Scott looked upon himself as 'a kind of Don Quixote in our age', on the evidence of what he had lately disclosed confidentially to Skene, as living 'in a matter-of-fact age', and as inclined on that account to sympathise all the more with 'those who are acted upon by the feelings of the more imaginative age which preceded us'.[117] The disclosure seemed to explain the double impulse behind *The Siege of Malta*, which represented gold as a factor in the 'changed manners' of the Knights, while celebrating at the same time 'the feelings' of those among them who acted in the best traditions of the earlier ages of chivalry. The Spanish 'Knight of Malta', therefore, bore 'the marks of the "hero born in other times"', while the dialogue in the novel relating to 'changed manners' contained allusions to Richard Coeur de Lion as the paragon of the earlier ages of chivalry.[118] Scott had already celebrated him in *The Talisman*.

'Having taken so much pains' with *The Siege of Malta*, he was reluctant to leave it unfinished, and would therefore proceed as fast as he could with the other half, pending a report on it by Lockhart. 'I must take my chance when I hear how you get on with the perusal', though he remained confident that it was at least as good as *Count Robert of Paris* and *Castle Dangerous*. He was impatient to hear a probable date named by Lockhart for his arrival in Italy to take the place of Walter, who 'I suppose is nearly home' with the material that he had sent by him for Cadell and Lockhart additional to *Seventeenth-Century Letters*, which 'I conclude have found their fate in the printing-house'. Pending Lockhart's departure for Italy, 'you must correct as boldly as you can the gross and obtrusive errors' in *The Siege of Malta*, of which he was soon to send both Lockhart and Cadell an example that occurred to him after the dispatch of the manuscript. Lockhart could be relied on to correct the errors, as he had done for the two earlier novels, although Scott, despite his late professions that his hand had improved, feared that it was still 'bad enough', unlike his speech, which he continued to hope would be 'quite well again' on the evidence, for instance, of his late recitations to Gell.[119]

Gell had already heard him say 'laughingly' that he had put a part of *The Siege of Malta* into the fire by mistake, but that he thought he had re-written it better than before. He now feared, however, that 'there will be some difficulty in arranging the copy' for Cadell and his printer, as he was sending it in two instalments, numbering each instalment separately by parcel. The first instalment consisted of three parcels. He thought it best to let the proofs wait till his return to Abbotsford, 'for it will scarce be possible to correct them with all Europe between them and the author'.[120]

The money from *The Siege of Malta* and from his other projects would pay off any remaining debts 'and buy me a pair of good carriage horses and two clever ponies', that he had commissioned Laidlaw to find for him. Although that commission still held, he was thinking of buying 'a handy britzka' for the return journey to Abbotsford. 'The carriage is London built, quite new, and has performed the journey' to Naples. Being low, it was 'convenient for my going in and out', and moreover the taxes on it were already paid, which was a saving. It was offered for £150, but would be sold more cheaply. 'This will save me a landau or coach when I return and bring me snug and perfect', as it carried two passengers inside, on occasion three, and two outside, 'which will suit us exactly': that is, Anne, Charles and himself would sit inside, and John Nicolson—who would drive it—and Mrs Street would sit outside. It was, therefore, 'of great consequence' that Laidlaw should attend to his commission, for 'I am now think-ing of my motions', which he begged Cadell to mention in public only in *general* terms, 'as all special information goes into the papers directly', to his great annoyance from the prying Italians, including Galignani's agents in Naples, 'who cast about to steal whatever they can lay hold upon'. In fact, once the rest of *The Siege of Malta* was completed and delivered, he did not wish it to be advertised, 'for there is a great chance of stealing stray copy and we should lose much by such roguery'.[121] He had lately seen an Italian trans-lation of *Old Mortality* on top of Galignani's pirated edition of *Count Robert of Paris*. He even had an Italian translation of *The Lady of the Lake* in his sitting-room.[122]

It was also shameful that several of his letters to Laidlaw should have been stolen in the post 'by people who are willing to satisfy their senseless curiosity at such an expense of feeling and good manners'. Even Lockhart had reported that 'many autographs have fallen into foul hands somehow'. He had therefore been obliged to repeat the commission to Laidlaw, suggesting at the same time that he 'make a drive through the walks for the said low carriage', and inquiring how the latest plantation—called Jane's Wood in honour of Walter's wife—was coming on in the advancing spring in proof of the increasing pull of Abbotsford upon him. 'I think of and dream of all at Abbotsford even more than when I was there in person.' He was gratified, in fact, to hear that 'my poor people' were not affected by the cholera, which was itself being contained in Edinburgh, according to his latest information from Cadell before the latter's departure for London. On the other hand, he sympathised sincerely with Cadell over the death of one of his daughters. 'I had a share of the same distress in poor Johnnie Hugh Lockhart.'[123]

As to his movements, he would first go to Rome on the termination of his lease of Palazzo Caramanico in mid-April, by which time he hoped to have heard from Sir Frederick Adam about a frigate from Corfu for 'the promised peep at Greece', followed, if possible, by a visit to Rhodes for the projected poem about the Knight and the Dragon. Although Cadell was still silent about it, he wished to hear if he approved of it. 'The tale is wild and pretty', and he would soon find out 'whether I have any pith left' for it. It was true that Greece 'is in great confusion' as an aftermath of the War of Independence, 'but I do not mean to expose myself to the least danger'. Failing a frigate from Sir Frederick Adam, 'I will strive to fight round Rimini and Venice' in the know-ledge that there was trouble in Romagna, 'and so to Britain by the Rhine and Holland' despite Charles's opposition and in preference to the route from Naples to Marseilles by steamer for France and England. The route by sea, admittedly, was shorter, more comfortable and free of 'regal duties', as he had himself first heard from Croker for the outbound voyage before the offer of a passage in the *Barham*. But 'this is a horrid dull route' compared with that over the Alps into Austria and Germany, where he would pass through Innsbruck for a sight of the celebrated tomb of the Emperor Maximilian, surrounded by an unparalleled assemblage of kings and rulers, all familiar to him from his reading in the Middle Ages. He had lately been shown an engraving of them by Anne's friend, Marianne Talbot, who was to testify—as did Gell—to the pleasure he anticipated at seeing them. They would complement the tombs of the Knights in Malta and the pictures of the Lombard Kings in the book of the monks of La Cava that Morani had copied for him, not to mention the tombs of the Stuarts that he would soon be seeing in Rome as their last residence.[124] Finally there would be the pleasure of the long-meditated meeting with Goethe at Weimar.

Even Charles was now resigned to the impending move from Naples. 'I think we have fairly settled about Rome, where we shall go in about three weeks,' he informed Sophia, who herself wrote to tell him that Lockhart would be joining them 'some time about June for a week or two' without her and their children. Lockhart had also agreed to Cadell's proposal that he should revise *The Life of Bonaparte* for publication in 'the magnum' on the completion of the novels and the poetry with Turner's illustrations. This, in fact, had been Cadell's purpose in going to London: to put Turner's drawings in the hands of the lead-ing engravers and to explain to Lockhart an old idea of Scott's 'of harnessing some clear-headed hand to revise' the whole of *The Life of Bonaparte*. He was delighted to inform Scott of Lockhart's acceptance, and that Turner's drawings 'are very beautiful'. But he made no mention of the outcome of *Seventeenth-Century Letters*, nor acknowledged the delivery of the first instalment of *The Siege of Malta* by King's messenger from Naples, although he did explain that he would be seeing Lockhart again about *The Life of Bonaparte* before returning to Edinburgh shortly, again without indicating whether he expected to see Walter at Lockhart's on his arrival from Naples. 'Business is very fair indeed' regarding *The Waverley Novels*.[125] As he was uncertain whether Scott was still at Naples or on the way to Greece, he addressed his letter to Charles. He had apparently missed, on account of his move to London, Charles's request that he try to persuade Scott not to go to Greece and, even more, not to return home via the Alps and Germany. He could not have been responsible, therefore, for the other communication on the way to Scott—this time from John Gibson, the secretary of the trust of his estate—to the effect that the life-insurance companies might object to his going to Greece, which was not covered by his policy.[126] Consequently Gibson advised Scott to wait, pending an answer from the companies. He had apparently come to know of the projected trip to Greece from the repeated notices of it in *The Caledonian Mercury*[127] and other news-papers.

Charles for his part was hopeful that in the intervening three weeks 'something will prevent the Greek expedition' either because of a change in the plans of Sir Frederick Adam at Corfu or in consequence of the political situation in the Balkans and the Adriatic, which had only lately involved even Captain Pigot in an incident with a Russian frigate. Scott gave it as his opinion that 'I never saw a man more like to take a hint of incivility' than Captain Pigot, even though he had mildly complained, during his quarantine in the *Barham* in the Bay of Naples, that 'he does not, I think, quite understand the freedom his flag is treated with'. Indeed he now likened Pigot to an American naval officer whom he had lately met on a mission 'to settle accounts' with Naples, failing which he had threatened to bombard the capital. Nevertheless he had found 'this military transatlantic negotiator' quite civil and modest in conversation in comparison with his compatriot, Miss Douglas, who was still in Naples with Miss Skene. Miss Douglas was 'truly detestable'. They had asked her and Miss Skene to dinner, but she had taken 'great offence at my not having fixed a date to dine with her'. Even after he had 'got off with difficulty', she had chanced to meet him again at Lady Drummond's, and after dinner 'in a large company she came across the room to me in order to make long speeches to show how intimate we were'.[128]

There was no question, therefore, of inviting her or Miss Skene to join them in a large party of English residents under Gell's escort on a tour of Cumae near Naples, followed by dinner provided by Scott, in another gesture of liberality, at one of the inns of Pozzuoli. Although he had already seen Pozzuoli with Gell and Laing Meason, the weather had not then been so inviting as now, and in any case he had not yet seen the beautiful lake of Avernus near Cumae, which was itself of great classical interest as the site of the earliest Greek colony in Italy, older, in fact, than that of the Sybarites at Paestum. Moreover the road to Cumae commanded a view of Monte Nuovo, a volcanic mountain of the same formation as Vesuvius, and which had already struck his imagination with its history, for Gell had told him how it had risen, like Graham Island, in one night to its present elevation not without destroying a whole village. For many reasons, therefore, Gell 'considered it my duty in quality of cicerone to enforce the knowledge of the locality', particularly as 'several of these places he would hear mentioned in society', even if he discounted the numerous references to them in Virgil. Although he agreed to listen to Gell's explanations, and answered him that he had the spot perfectly in his mind, Gell found that 'the place had inspired him with other recollections of his own beloved country and of the Stuarts', for he relapsed into the poetic vein that had marked the drive to the monastery of La Cava, and, on proceeding along the road, he began to recite a Jacobite song by James Hogg under the influence of the fresh foliage of the oaks in spring, followed by his favourite ballad verses by Theodore Hook at the sight of a solitary lane leading to the citadel of Cumae.[129]

Much of this contrast between him and Gell was admirably caught by Owen Cole when he had the long-wished-for pleasure of being presented to Scott at a *conversazione* in Palazzo Caramanico a few days after he had made Anne's acquaintance. Again he was accompanied by Augustus Fitzroy, and they found Scott in an elbow-chair, wearing 'his Caledonian club dress'—blue coat with thistle buttons and tweed trousers—which, in Cole's eyes, 'became his bulky form, though it gave him more the baronial appearance' of a laird or of 'a gentleman farmer' than of an author. Beside him sat Gell in his wheel-chair, 'the polished courtier, the classical topographer and foreign *habitué*, with features modelled as from Parian marble'. So dissimilar did they look that Cole likened Gell to 'Eurystheus by the side of Hercules'. Every now and then an explosive laugh escaped from Scott at 'some *bon mot* of Gell's, whose cold blue eyes and curvilinear lip would imply sarcasm'. After praising Captain Pigot to Fitzroy, Scott began to recite his favourite 'Sea Song' by Allan Cunningham, keeping time with his paralysed hand. Cole was not slow to note Scott's broad Scottish accent, as Madden had also noted in London. To a Russian lady—not the minister's wife but another countess called Wallendoff—who spoke of *Count Robert of Paris*, Scott exclaimed that it was not worth reading before he pointed to the Italian translation of *The Lady of the Lake* on the table of his sitting-room, and asked her if she had read that.[130]

For all his admiration of Scott, Cole had to admit that 'his demeanour was sometimes the reverse of refined', as when, on over-hearing a young diplomat trying to make Anne promise to ride with him in Rome, he 'unhorsed' him by almost shouting, 'No, you shan't ride with her!' Anne had all this time been making herself agreeable to every guest in a gay company of various ranks and nationalities, all intent upon her father. 'There was little or nothing of the parental Doric in her accent.' By contrast Charles had sat alone in a corner of the room, perhaps in one of his moods against 'the beastly society'. Cole had nicknamed him 'the Diogenes', and had mistaken him for 'the family physician in attendance' until he perceived his error when Anne opened her album and displayed a water-colour, which she said was by Lord Castlereagh, at which Charles—perhaps knowing that, like her father, she was sensitive to peers and peeresses—stepped forward and drawled in Cole's hearing :'Only a daub—

just because a lord painted it, you think it right to praise it—quite a mistake!'
The remark did not really bear out his earlier protestations to Sophia that he
had striven to keep the family peace by remaining silent even under provocation
from Anne's temper. To divert the attack, she sent him for eau-de-cologne,
complaining of headache. It seemed to Cole that 'there was a something granitic
in the father's roughness, which degenerated into what rather resembled slang
in the son'. Yet he had already perceived a kindly heart behind Scott's rough
exterior, and 'a gentleness in his smile, though from the moribd state of his
lips less of such than formerly'. It pained him to see him arise from his seat after
what he described, perhaps a little hyperbolically, as 'a trial of strength' with his
infirmities, hobble across the floor to take leave of his guests in that benevolent
manner that had struck Mrs Davy at Malta, and afterwards prop himself for
some time on his stick between the two rooms of his apartment before finally
retiring, at his usual early hour, to bed.[131]

Cole does not appear to have been aware that Charles was a victim of
rheumatism, and 'although I have escaped my usual rheumatic attack this spring',
his foot was still swollen, and he was expecting it to get worse in London at the
Foreign Office, as he explained himself to Sophia in reply to the news that
Lockhart intended to join them in June. For at last he could now comply with
the deadline set by the Foreign Office for his return, 'and I must certainly go
back to my duty, for the Foreign Office have been very kind and forbearing'.
Accordingly, unless Lockhart changed his mind, 'or my father take it into his
head to go to Corfu, I shall, after seeing that they cannot make any blunder
about money etc., leave for England' at the end of April. He was anxious that
Sophia and Lockhart should—as Cadell had earnestly requested Scott—give
Coutts notice of a bill for £200 drawn on them for the britzka that Scott had
just bought for the journey to Rome and afterwards for home. Far from getting
it, as he had forecast, cheaper than the offered price of £150, he had had to pay
£200 for it, and, according to Charles, it 'is worth about half'. 'I offered my
services to get them one, but Anne's experience prevailed, and first trial the
forewheel refused to move, and altogether it is a most useless concern.' They
were getting on 'pretty smoothly', however, and 'papa, I think, is stronger,
but eats and drinks a great deal too much, which is very naturally not prevented
by the good advice he receives from Anne, who, by the way, if she took proper
care of herself, might be as well as anyone else'.[132] For she had lately had a recurrence of her stomach complaint, to which even Scott had referred in his last
letter to Laidlaw in further proof that Laidlaw had been in error in his allegation
to Cadell that Scott 'never mentions his family at all'. Like Charles, he had
seemed to suggest that Anne's complaint would not recur 'if she will take care'.
Indeed he echoed Charles in a later letter to Lockhart: 'Anne has got sound of
her stomach complaint, but will hardly take enough of care'.[133]

She was dining, with Scott, at Lord Hertford's at the very moment that
Charles was answering Sophia, but he expected to be able to enlarge on 'papa's

further plans, as I see a letter for him from Sir Frederick Adam'. It was to the effect that Sir Frederick hoped that H.M.S. *Rainbow* would be able to take Scott from Naples to Corfu and thence to Greece about the middle of April. She was commanded by the famous Arctic explorer, Sir John Franklin; and Lady Louisa Stuart knew of a lieutenant serving in her, and had recommended him to Scott in her Christmas letter to him. On the other hand, there was no certainty that Sir John Franklin would be able to come. Moreover, as Scott informed Cadell after the dinner at Lord Hertford's, he had received John Gibson's advice that he should not go to Greece until he had learned whether the insurance companies would sanction the journey. If they did not, 'why, they will not, and there is no help for it'. In that event 'I will hold my course northward, and look at Italy or return by Venice and the Tyrol'. 'I have not a complaint of any kind, and am as able to endure travel as ever I was in my life.'[134]

He regretted that, although he had received Cadell's last letter from London, 'you do not tell me what is doing about' *Seventeenth-Century Letters*, 'which is not like your exactness'. Neither did he know if Cadell had received the first instalment of *The Siege of Malta*, the proofs of which he would not be able to correct—'and there is a good deal to be corrected'—without Abel Boyer's *Annals*, 'which I must have if possible', although in fact Boyer's *Annals*, of which he had found a copy in the Studio of Naples, seemed to relate more to *Seventeenth-Century Letters* than to *The Siege of Malta*.[135] Boyer, however, had published another book containing an explanation of such terms of fortifications as Scott had used in large measure in *The Siege of Malta*.[136] He might therefore have had that book in mind in the absence of the fourth and fifth volumes of Vertot that he had shipped to England for Lockhart's revision of the manuscript. Without Boyer, he stressed to Cadell, 'I will have much difficulty in sending this book to press in England without my eye going over the proofs'. On the other hand, he thoroughly approved of Cadell's action in assigning the revision of *The Life of Bonaparte* to Lockhart, who could be relied on 'to keep the same line of politics'.[137]

Pending further news from Sir John Franklin and Gibson, 'I will go to Rome for a week till I learn how I am to be determined'.[138] It would be Holy Week in Rome, and he would 'view the ecclesiastical shows' there as a sequel not only to the High Mass that he had listened to in the monastery at La Cava but also to another original and imaginative scene that he had inserted in the first instalment of *The Siege of Malta*,[139] in which his hero and La Valette, after their dialogue about Cervantes, hear 'the anthem float round in solemn chorus' from St John's Cathedral—precisely as Scott had himself heard it on the spot in Valletta—'with the devotional feeling, which it is the peculiar property of so many of the hymns of the Catholic Church to impart'. Indeed he had lately written to Lockhart that in *The Siege of Malta* 'there is a place where there is a species of Christian hymn which I will fill up' after his return.[140]

The only disadvantage at present about the Easter ceremonies at Rome was that they were 'diminished in splendour' owing to 'the pope's poverty' in allusion to the financial embarrassments of the Church from Gregory XVI's lavish expenditure on architectural and engineering works combined with his magnificent patronage of learning.[141] Nevertheless Scott added to Cadell that the fine weather for travel had set in, and he would meet in Rome some of the friends of his old favourite, Lady Northampton. Gell was going too—in fact, before Scott—for he had the free use of a house in Rome with a pretty garden, of which he was very fond, particularly in spring for its trees, under which he could sit in his wheel-chair and meet friends without having to climb stairs. He would, therefore, continue to make himself useful to Scott as cicerone. Indeed it was a further inducement to Scott to go to Rome that Gell was going at the same time—and not only Gell but also Mrs Ashley and so many of the recent visitors to Naples, including Owen Cole and Augustus Fitzroy, in keeping with the traditional practice of travellers on the grand tour to flock to Rome for Easter. Mrs Ashley was expecting her brother, Henry Baillie, from London, so that Scott might perhaps have confirmation from him of Walter's arrival in England and perhaps also of the delivery of The Siege of Malta for Cadell by the King's messenger. Even if Walter himself did not write, there was always Sophia, whom Charles had already advised to address letters for him to the care of Mr Freeborn, the British vice-consul at Rome.[142]

As to the britzka that Scott had just bought for the journey, he held it 'a capital thing' and would 'save us a monstrous deal of trouble'. Although 'I have put myself to some expense for it', it would have the added advantage— once he got to Abbotsford in it—of replacing, as he had already explained to Laidlaw, the old family 'chariot, which my lameness will no longer permit me to use with comfort'. In that respect 'I could not expect the shadow to go backward on the dial, and if I get no better, I must be contented with not getting worse' in much the same sensible manner as that in which he had enjoined himself at Portsmouth 'to make myself as easy as I can, without suffering myself to be vexed about what I cannot help'.[143] Estimating that altogether he had spent about 20,000 dollars in Neapolitan currency, he admitted that 'this is a large sum, yet not excessive' in view of the literary material that he had dispatched to Cadell, or had accumulated in his travel-journal, which he took up again in anticipation of entering his tour of Rome in it. He also wished to enter the nucleus of a tale of a Calabrian bandit called El Bizarro, which he had heard from a resident English apothecary. Although he could not vouch for its truth, it had come from 'a respectable authority', and was another horrible story of revenge and murder. He meant to write it up at length as El Bizarro at leisure in Rome or on the homeward journey. There were reports that half a dozen of these bandits were active between Naples and Rome, 'and many carriages stopped'. So many stories about them were afloat that one could make 'a popular work' of them, as his old friend, Washington Irving, had done in Tales of a Traveller.[144]

Since Scott was in the dark as to 'what has come to hand or been lost', he dared not expose the second instalment of *The Siege of Malta* to the hazards of the ordinary post; so he entrusted it to 'a son of Lord Cowper, who only leaves a month after this [it was then mid-April], but it is the earliest and safest opportunity I can hear of'.[145] In consequence it would not reach Cadell, as they had originally calculated, in the spring but in the summer, too late for inclusion in 'the magnum', the closure of which could no longer be deferred beyond *Count Robert of Paris* and *Castle Dangerous*. The second instalment, like the first, consisted of three parcels, again numbered separately, and making altogether—in Scott's own words to Cadell—'six parts'.

The second instalment 'contains all I at present think of adding to the Siege of Malta', which he considered 'long enough' to fill the projected three volumes, so much so that he did not now consider it necessary 'to take up and finish my original story' about the Spanish 'Knight of Malta' in the first instalment, although 'I could easily do it'.[146] What he meant, therefore, was that it was *finished* as it stood, and that he had abandoned the 'original story' for a straightforward narrative of the Great Siege, heavily derived, in the last two parts, from Vertot. In other words, *The Siege of Malta* had been turned into a chronicle, perhaps under pressure to bring it to an end before the deadline agreed with Cadell, and in the belief that the numerous scenes of his own invention in the early and middle parts, including the more memorable battle-scenes, would be adequate compensation for the phasing out of the 'original story'. 'The spirit of chivalry blazing in its ashes', he had already written to Lockhart about one of these 'excellent' battle-scenes, 'gave many a bright and striking flash.'[147] It was in that sense that he had equated *The Siege of Malta* to Laidlaw and Cadell with *Ivanhoe*, particularly as he had fully exploited those 'modes of resistance' connected with mediaeval sieges similar to that of Torquilstone in the earlier novel. Certainly the wide range and variety of original scenes before the chronicle bore out the claim he had been making to his correspondents and to Gell, that he had been writing with much more ease and fluency.

Without referring again to the earlier 'difficulty in arranging the copy' for Cadell, he advised him that, if Lord Cowper's son delivered the second instalment after Lockhart's departure for Italy, 'I would trust no one else with this copy; it will be much better to wait for myself', particularly as there was now a distinct possibility of his being able to deal with the proofs himself at home rather than in Italy, and sooner than he had been envisaging only lately. For 'it is said that Sir Frederick Adam goes out to Madras to make a little money'. In other words, news had reached him of the impending appointment of Sir Frederick Adam as Governor of Madras. Consequently 'there is a great chance of our not going to Greece, so my vision of Rhodes goes to the devil, which is a great pity'. At all events he would draw on Cadell through Coutts at Rome for £500, 'which will I trust bring me home again'. He was 'beginning to tire of being so far from the shop'.[148]

In this state of uncertainty as to whether Sir John Franklin would come in the *Rainbow* or not during their week in Rome, he assembled, with Charles and Anne, in Palazzo Caramanico on the termination of their lease to bid goodbye to several friends. The party included Countess Wallendoff, the Russian lady, whom Scott had encouraged to read *The Lady of the Lake* rather than *Count Robert of Paris*. On this occasion she was persistent in asking him to write some lines for her album. He had never been very fond of doing so. 'The invasion of albums has become rather tiresome,' he had written to Cadell from Portsmouth; and even at Abbotsford, before his departure for the Mediterranean, he had consented to write a few lines for Dora Wordsworth largely for her father's sake, and in the event had made 'an ill favoured botch' of them. So this time he resisted Countess Wallendoff's importunities on the pretext that his writing days were over. But he changed his mind when some other friends assembled with him on the eve of his departure, and he seemed less tired and more cheerful. For he sat down at his writing-table, and wrote for a few minutes, after which he handed three stanzas to Anne, saying, 'Here, Anne, are some verses for your Russian friend'. 'Why, she left this morning,' Anne exclaimed, 'and I don't know her address—even if I did, they are much too good to be wasted on that tiresome Russian, who probably won't understand them.' Turning to her father, she added, 'Why did you trouble about that old bore?' 'My dear,' he replied, 'as I am good for nothing else now, I think it as well to be good-natured.'[149]

The verses were the last he ever wrote, and in them he returned to the image of 'the shadow on the dial', that he had lately used in the letter to Lockhart as a symbol for the acceptance of his fate as an apoplectic. The image was evidently dear to him, as he had used a variant of it, much earlier, in the *envoi* to *Castle Dangerous*, in which he had equated his infirmities with 'the shadows and storms' of old age.[150] The verses themselves combined a mood of fortitude and resignation with a sense of pathos at 'life's decline', touched with nostalgia for 'loved visions' and 'forgotten dreams' of 'an earlier day'. Although not free of his 'cloudiness of words and arrangement', nor faultless in rhythm, they were not quite the 'ill favoured botch' in Dora Wordsworth's album. Anne, in fact, gave them to Henry Baillie before they left for Rome on 16th April three weeks after Goethe's death at Weimar.

Although Scott was to be understood in Rome as saying that 'he had been in correspondence with Goethe before his death',[151] there is no record of it in his letters and journal, which do not even suggest that he had heard of Goethe's death when he left for Rome. The correspondence to which he was to refer probably related to the letters that had passed between them much earlier, well before his journey to Malta and Naples. It is true that Lockhart was to represent him in *The Life of Scott* as not only in possession of the news of Goethe's death before he left for Rome but as actually *deciding* to move from Naples on hearing of Goethe's death: 'His impatience redoubled: all his fine dreams of recovery seemed to vanish at once—"Alas for Goethe!" he exclaimed: "but he at least died at home—Let us to Abbotsford." '[152] There is not one word, however, in Scott's or Charles's letters to bear Lockhart out. On the contrary, they flatly refute his allegation of Goethe's death having a decisive, if not catastrophic, influence on Scott's morale *at Naples*. Even Gell—a key witness—did not provide any evidence in support of Lockhart's statement. In fact, he did not mention Goethe at all. On the other hand, Goethe had certainly heard or read in the newspapers of Scott's residence in Naples and of his intention to visit him at Weimar, for a few days before his death he had written to a German friend in Naples asking him to assure Scott, 'should [he] still be in your vicinity', that he would not fail 'to feel in every respect at home under our roof, and meet with the respect and attention which are due to him not only as the author of a host of important works but as a right thinker and a man of exalted mind'.[153]

Although Scott was soon to hear in Rome of Goethe's death, it was a mercy for his feelings and his pride that he was never to see the letter that Cadell had just dispatched to Naples from Edinburgh.[154] In it he informed Scott that he had remained in London specially till Walter's return, and that he had had 'many communings' with Lockhart about the literary plans that Scott had enumerated in writing by Walter. They had come to the conclusion that *Seventeenth-Century Letters* was 'too short to make a volume of any size, and there is a want of a leading interest' in it. The long tale—'a romantic Italian adventure'—that he had added to it 'is not in tone with the others', and although Lady Stuart's contribution was clever, 'Mr Lockhart's acute views of literature and my bookselling qualities cannot well doctor this little episode'. The projected poem about Rhodes could not come at the end of the novels, for 'whatever closes a series of prose works should be prose'. As to *The Siege of Malta*, Cadell confirmed that its delayed delivery, which was now inevitable, would exclude it from 'the magnum', and 'I cannot at present see anything but an announcement of volumes 48, *Count Robert of Paris*, being the last'. *Count Robert of Paris* itself and *Castle Dangerous*, he had learned in London, had been selling less well than he had been giving Scott to understand in his letters, although he himself and Whittaker had sold off all their copies. 'Still the miscellaneous booksellers have a good many—and growl a bit.' Fortunately 'the magnum goes on admirably'. 'I have not one ground of complaint to allege against it.' For that reason he again sought to set Scott's mind at rest about money. 'Do not give yourself one moment's uneasiness about money—money you must have.' But Cadell had not yet received a complete account of all the money that Scott had drawn on him through Coutts, supplemented by the debts that had accumulated in the form of open accounts from other sources. Neither had he yet attempted to look at the first instalment of *The Siege of Malta*, that he had brought with him from London, to find out if what Scott was writing could be published or not.

References for Chapter 4

1. *Journal* 690; Skene 202; MS 1553, f. 246.
2. MS 1553, ff. 246–47; Skene 202; *Journal* 690.
3. *Caledonian Mercury*, Feb. 2, 1832.
4. MS 1752, p. 437.
5. MS 917, ff. 19v–22.
6. MS 5317, f. 120.
7. MS 1752, p. 440; *Journal* 692.
8. MS 917, ff. 17–22; MS 1553, f. 244.
9. MS 1553, ff. 246–47; MS 917, f. 22v; *Caledonian Mercury*, Feb. 2, 1832 (Letter from sailor in H.M.S. Barham called Woodrow).
10. *Journal* 691.
11. Ibid; MS 1553, f. 248; MS 1554, f. 3; MS Acc. 5131, f. 269.
12. MS 1752, p. 440; MS 5317, ff. 122–23.
13. MS 5317, ff. 212–13; *Journal* 270.
14. MS 5317, ff. 212–14.
15. *Journal* 692.
16. MS 1553, f. 248; MS 1554, ff. 3, 49; MS 1614, Dec. 25, 1831.
17. MS 1553, f. 248; MS 917, f. 22v; *Journal* 691.
18. MS 1614, Dec. 25, 1831; MS 917, f. 28; MS 1554, f. 4; *Journal* 695.
19. 'Le Duc de Guise à Naples' in *Foreign Quarterly Review*, 1829, pp. 355–403; *Journal* 548–56.
20. *Journal* 691. Cf. Scott's review, pp. 363–72, 401.
21. Gell 10; *Journal* 692.
22. *Miscellaneous Prose Works of Sir W. Scott*, Edinburgh, 1841, II, Ch. 52, p. 466; Ch. 60, p. 578; Ch. 74, p. 663; Ch. 85, pp. 734–36.
23. MS 1554, f. 9; *Journal* 693; MS 3009, f. 31; *Caledonian Mercury*, Feb. 2, 1832.
24. Cf. *Memoir and Correspondence of Susan Ferrier*, ed. J. A. Doyle, 1929, p. 256; MS 1554, f. 9.
25. *Memoirs of Sir W. Knighton*, ed. Lady Knighton, 1838, ii, 232–33; *Journal* 596; *Letters* XI, 359.
26. *Journal* 691–92.
27. MS 917, f. 22v.
28. MS 1554, f. 3; *Journal* 692; Gell 2, 5; MS 1752, pp. 449, 452; Madden iii, 488.

29. MS Acc. 5131, ff. 269–71; MS 1752, p. 451.
30. MS 1752, pp. 448–49.
31. MS 5317, ff. 91–92. Cf. *Journal* 235–36.
32. MS 1554, f. 3; *Journal* 694–95; Gell xvii, **1–2, 7.**
33. *Journal* 694; Gell xvii, 2; MS 1554, f. 3; Gell 2.
34. MS 1554, ff. 8–9.
35. *Journal* 697, Gell 2, 4; Lockhart x, 147.
36. MS 1554, ff. 3–4, 10; *The Times*, Aug. 19, 1932, p. 13, col. 5; Gell 6; *Memoir and Correspondence of Susan Ferrier*, ed. J. A. Doyle, p. 256; *Journal of Sir W. Scott*, ed. W. E. K. Anderson, 1972, 700 n[1].
37. MS 1752, p. 449; MS 1554, ff. 4, 10; MS 917, f. 28; *Journal* 695.
38. *Journal* 695; Gell 5.
39. *Journal* 694–95; Gell 7; MS 1554, f. 9; Madden ii, 79.
40. *Journal* 695–96; MS 1554, f. 9; MS Acc. 5131, f. 270.
41. *Journal* 696; Gell 14–15; MS 1752, pp. 455, 470.
42. *Journal* 695; MS 1752, pp. 450–52.
43. MS 1554, ff. 4, 10; MS 1752, pp. 451–454; *Journal* 695.
44. MS 5317, ff. 124–27.
45. *Journal* 696–97; Gell 15; MS 1752, pp. 455, 470; Lockhart x, 148.
46. Gell 15–16; *Journal* 697–99.
47. MS 917, f. 27; MS 5131, f. 270; MS 1554, f. 8; MS 1752, pp. 455–57, 495.
48. MS 5317, f. 128; MS 917, ff. 28–30.
49. MS 1554, f. 11; MS 917, ff. 27–30.
50. *Journal* 698; Gell 10–11.
51. f. 58.
52. E. Clay, 'Notes of Sir W. Gell to Sir W. Scott' in *Journal of the Warburg and Courtauld Institutes*, vol. 33, 1970, 336–43.
53. MS 1554, f. 8; MS Acc. 5131, f. 27c; MS 1752, pp. 454, 458.
54. MS 917, ff. 29v–30; MS 1554, ff. 9–11.
55. Gell 16; MS 1752, pp. 458–59, 470, 517; *Journal* 699.
56. *Letters* XI, 196.

57. MS 1752, pp. 469–70, 520; Gell 13–14; E. Clay, 'Notes of Sir W. Gell to Sir W. Scott' in *Journal of the Warburg and Courtauld Institutes*, vol. 33, 1970, 336–43; *History of the Knights Hospitallers of St John*, tr. from the French of L'Abbé de Vertot, Edinburgh, 1757, ii, 115–17.
58. MS 1752, pp. 458–60, 472. Cf. *Journal* 65, 274, 424; *Letters* VI, 247.
59. MS 917, f. 36; Gell 5–6.
60. MS 1554, ff. 9–12; *Journal* 699–700.
61. MS 855, p. 40; MS 1752, pp. 486, 503.
62. Lockhart x, 67.
63. MS 855, p. 40.
64. MS 1752, pp. 472, 486, 489; MS Acc. 5131, f. 270; *Journal* 699–700; Gell 8.
65. Gell 8; E. Clay, 'Notes of Sir W. Gell to Sir W. Scott' in *Journal of the Warburg and Courtauld Institutes*, vol. 33, 1970, 336.
66. MS 1752, pp. 470, 472, 476, 485; MS 917, f. 31.
67. Feb. 9, 1832.
68. MS 1752, pp. 473–76.
69. *Journal* 224, 233; *Lady Louisa Stuart*, ed. J. A. Home, 1899, p. 234.
70. MS 1752, pp. 473–76.
71. MS 5317, ff. 93–98ᵛ.
72. Ibid, ff. 132–34; Acc. 5188, March 18, 1832; MS 1752, p. 522.
73. Feb. 20, 1832.
74. MS 5317, f. 314.
75. MS 917, f. 34; Lockhart x, 171.
76. MS 1752, pp. 473, 485; MS 855, p. 40; Skene 203; Lockhart x, 172.
77. MS 1752, pp. 517–18.
78. Ibid, pp. 491, 495, 497; MS Acc. 5131, f. 284.
79. MS Acc. 5131, f. 284; Gell 19.
80. MS 1752, pp. 490, 497, 511.
81. Ibid, pp. 496–98, 500, 512, 515, 520; Skene 205.
82. MS 1752, pp. 503, 508; MS 917, ff. 32–37.
83. Gell 14; MS 1752, pp. 512–13; E. Clay, 'Notes of Sir W. Gell to Sir W. Scott' in *Journal of the Warburg and Courtauld Institutes*, vol. 33, 1970, pp. 336–37.
84. Gell 16; *Journal* 700; MS 1752, p. 506.
85. MS 917, f. 35.
86. MS 1752, pp. 506, 536; *Journal* 701; MS 5317, f. 99.
87. Gell 16; *Journal* 703–4; MS 1752, p. 490; cf. MS 917, f. 35.
88. *Journal* 700–1; Gell 16–17.
89. *Journal* 701.
90. ff. 23, 93.
91. *Journal* 701; Gell 17, 20.
92. ff. 4–6.
93. Gell 17.
94. *Journal* 702; Gell 18; MS 1752, p. 506; Skene 203.
95. MS 917, f. 35; MS 1752, p. 523.
96. *Journal* 702–4; MS 917, f. 35. Cf. *Journal* 584 for Scott's earlier interest in 'rural society' connected with his search for old ballads.
97. *Journal* 704, 706; MS 1752, pp. 505–7.
98. *Journal* 704.
99. Ibid 705, 569; Gell 18–19; MS 1752, p. 507.
100. *Journal* 705.
101. ff. 83–85.
102. *Journal* 705; MS 1752, p. 524.
103. *Journal* 705; Gell 18–19; MS 1752, p. 507.
104. Cf. *Caledonian Mercury*, Feb. 4, 1832.
105. *Journal* 705–6; Gell 19–20; MS 1752, p. 507; MS Acc. 5131, f. 269.
106. *Journal* 706; Gell 20.
107. f. 84.
108. *Journal* 706–7; cf. ibid 174 n².
109. Ibid 707; MS 917, ff. 21, 26.
110. Cole was in error in believing that Scott and his party, including Walter, had been in Rome during the Carnival (Cole 261).
111. Cole 258–59, 261.
112. Ibid 258, 261–62, 265.
113. MS 1752, p. 509.
114. Ibid, pp. 505–7, 509–12.
115. *Siege of Malta*, ff. 75–77.
116. Ibid.
117. Skene 202–3. Cf. *Journal* 88.
118. *Siege of Malta*, ff. 18–19, 73; 1932 typescript of *Siege of Malta* (Berg 64B4878) p. 10, l. 5.
119. MS 1752, pp. 509–14, 516, 533.
120. Gell 12–13; MS 1752, pp. 511, 515.
121. *Journal* 698–99; MS 1752, pp. 501–2, 513, 516, 519–21, 524, 526; Skene 203.

122. Gell 20; Cole 259. See Mary E. Ambrose, 'The First Italian Translations of Scott' in *Modern Language Review*, Jan. 1972, pp. 74–82, for *Lady of the Lake* in Italian.
123. MS 1752, pp. 502, 522, 524, 526–27; MS 5317, f. 136.
124. MS 1752, pp. 512, 520, 529; Gell 23–24, 49 n[58].
125. MS 917, f. 37; MS 860, f. 40; MS 5317, f. 138.
126. MS 1752, p. 530.
127. Feb. 20, March 22, 31, 1832.
128. MS 917, ff. 36–37; MS 1752, pp. 509–10.
129. Gell 21–23.
130. Cole 258–59.
131. Ibid 259–61.
132. MS 917, ff. 38–39; MS 1752, p. 529; MS 5317, f. 138.
133. MS 1752, pp. 527, 536.
134. MS 917, ff. 38–39; MS 1752, pp. 530–531; MS 5317, f. 215.
135. MS 1752, p. 530; *Journal* 696.
136. A. Boyer, *The Draughts of the most remarkable Fortified Towns of Europe ... to which is prefixed an Introduction to Military Architecture or Fortification*, 1701.
137. MS 1752, pp. 529–30.
138. Ibid 531; *Journal* 710.
139. ff. 39–40.
140. MS 1752, p. 514.
141. *Journal* 710.
142. MS 1752, pp. 520, 533, 536; Gell 24–25; Madden ii, 40–41; MS 917, f. 39.
143. MS 1752, pp. 531, 533, 536; *Journal* 671.
144. *Journal* 708–10.
145. MS 1752, pp. 533, 535; *Journal* 708.
146. MS 1752, p. 533.
147. Ibid, p. 490.
148. Ibid, pp. 533–34.
149. *The Times*, Aug. 1932, p. 13, col. 5.
150. MS 1752, p. 536; Lockhart x, 119.
151. Lockhart x, 195.
152. Ibid x, 175.
153. *Caledonian Mercury*, May 31, 1832.
154. Acc. 5181, April 13, 1832.

5

Rome and Northern Journey

Both Charles and Anne were unwell, and, according to Scott, 'in very bad temper' at the start of the journey to Rome in the britzka 'on the famed Appian Way'. Anne had her usual stomach pains, and appears to have needed more assistance than Charles, who was able to direct John Nicolson, their driver, from his experience of the road and from his knowledge of Italian and of the country. Scott described his own temper as 'not excellent', in keeping with his usual nervousness on moving about. They started from the famous reviewing-ground called Paese dei Marsi through 'a rich and fertile country' to Santa Agata, where they breakfasted at a wretched inn before they made Aversa, which Scott mentioned in his journal as 'remarkable for a house for insane persons on the human[e] plan of not agitating their passions'.[1] At Capua, while Charles was away from the britzka for a moment to attend to Anne, a soldier rode against the pole of the carriage and broke it off. In about half an hour it was cobbled, and all proceeded smoothly for about two miles till Nicolson declared, as Charles had foreseen, that 'the forewheel was parting company with the carriage'. Fortunately they were able to pull up, and Charles sent a postilion back to Santa Agata for men to drag them up. After they had sat for an hour in the dark—an easy prey to robbers—the wheel was put sufficiently to rights to enable them to return to Santa Agata, 'where we made a miserable lodging and a wretched dinner' at the only place between Naples and Nola where they could sleep. The people of the inn, however, were very civil, and no bandits were abroad, 'being kept in awe by the King of Westphalians, who was on his road to Naples'. He was Jerome Bonaparte, a younger brother of Napoleon and former King of Westphalia before his retirement to Rome.[2]

After about four hours' work on the wheel in early morning it was effectively repaired, and they started with some apprehension of the notorious Pontine Marshes, which they had to cross for a good part of the way to Rome. 'This is not the time when their exhalations are most dangerous, though [they] seem to be safe at no time.' Despite the shore the road had the appearance of winding among hills until it came into its more proper line 'at a celebrated sea marsh called Camerina', which Scott mistook for Camarina in Sicily, familiar to him from Virgil, who was the Latin poet after Horace that he quoted most often to correspondents in England with a public-school education.[3] They reached Camerina through a wild pass bordered by a rocky precipice with shrubs, flowers and plants on one side in contrast to the sea on the other. It commanded a fine view of the town and castle of Gaeta, where his favourite

Stuart, Prince Charles, had first distinguished himself in a siege before he had landed in Scotland for the campaign that Scott had described memorably in *Waverley* and, more systematically, in *Tales of a Grandfather*.[4] Gaeta was a stronghold that had changed hands continually in the war with Bonaparte. Its castle was 'of great strength', as was the position of Terracina, 'where Murat used to quarter a body of troops and cannonade the English gunboats, which were not slow in returning the compliment'.[5] The English had then garrisoned Calabria and Sicily under Sir John Stuart, the hero of the battle of Maida, of which Scott had given an account in *The Life of Bonaparte*[6] besides naming his favourite deerhound after the battle.

He found Terracina itself partly fitted up as a barrack and partly as an inn, where they supped and slept tolerably comfortably, to Charles's relief, for the stretch of the road ahead of them was less exposed to robbers. In fact, in spite of warnings to the contrary, they all fell asleep as far as Velletri, a drive of six and a half hours without villages and with very few houses. At Velletri they dined 'in an ancient villa and chateau'. Scott would have wished much to have explored it, but Charles wanted to make up for lost time and also to ensure that they would not reach Rome in darkness. Besides, 'the long pilgrimage on this beastly road' had tired Scott, and the bad air and damp of the Pontine Marshes had caused him a very sharp headache. Contrary to the confidence that he had lately expressed to Cadell, that 'I am able to endure travel as ever in my life', he began to fear that 'my time for such researches' in old mansions and castles 'is now gone'.[7] Fortunately it was in daylight that they approached the beautiful Alban hills, 'especially a forest or avenue of grand oaks, which leads pretty directly into the vicinity of Rome'. Inevitably he associated Albano with the Pretender, whose family had taken the titles of York and Albany, so that when one of his hosts later asked him in Rome if he had not found the road terribly rough between Velletri and Albano, 'That I did indeed,' he replied, 'and what was worse, the unfortunate Prince had not left even an old pair of red velvet breeches as a memorial of him when we got there.'[8]

They entered Rome on the evening of 17th April by the Porta San Giovanni, which caught his eye for a statue of 'one of the old pontiffs' surmounting it, in keeping with his interest in the Rome of the Renaissance and of the Middle Ages rather than of the emperors. Even the Forum, a short distance beyond the gateway, drew no notice in his journal. Although both Charles and Anne had asked Gell and Mrs Ashley respectively 'to bespeak a lodging for us', they omitted 'to give direction how to correspond with their friends concerning the execution of their commission', so that 'there we were, as we had reason to think, possessed of two apartments, and not knowing the way to any of them'. In consequence they 'paraded the streets by moonlight to discover, if possible, some appearance of the learned Sir William Gell and the pretty Mistress Astley [Ashley]' until at length they found Gell's servant, Pietro Pighetti, who guided them to the lodgings that Gell had taken for them in Via della Mercede off Piazza San Silvestro, a district of Rome traditionally associated with English travellers. The lodgings formed part of a large block called Casa Bernini after the celebrated sculptor, who had lived and died there. In their apartments 'all was comfortable, a good fire included, which our fatigue and the chilliness of the night required'. They dispersed as soon as they had taken some food, wine and water, after which, refreshed with sleep, Scott wrote a summary of the journey in his journal with many misspellings and some missing words, but at least much longer than the mere mention of places and inns with which Charles contented himself in his own diary.[9] Scott then abandoned his journal for good without making up for it with letters to Lockhart and Cadell in view of his intention to remain in Rome only a week, pending information—presumably through Mr Freeborn, the British vice-consul—as to whether the Rainbow would be coming to take him to Corfu or not. They had heard nothing of her on their departure from Naples.[10]

In the absence of his journal Gell again proved the principal source for Scott in Rome, supplemented by a second cicerone, who was presented to him a few days after his arrival, and who, at Lockhart's request, afterwards submitted a short account for The Life of Scott.[11] He was Edward Cheney, a retired army captain, long resident in Italy as an art collector. He was a bachelor, in his early manhood, and his brother was with him at the time in Rome, both of them living in a style of 'fine gentlemanism', as it was later described by Richard Monckton Milnes, the future Lord Houghton and biographer of Keats. Monckton Milnes met them just after Scott's departure.[12] Their family had long lived, according to Lockhart, on terms of the strictest intimacy with Scott's old favourite, Lady Northampton, 'so that Sir Walter was ready to regard him [Captain Cheney] at first sight as a friend'.[13]

Before he was introduced to him, however, Scott made known to Gell that he was keenly bent on visiting the house where Benvenuto Cellini wrote in his autobiography that he had killed Duke Charles of Bourbon, the Constable of France, in the sack of Rome with a bullet fired from the Castle of St Angelo. Gell arranged for an Italian friend to take him to the place, of which, though he quickly forgot the position, he yet retained the history firmly fixed in his mind, and to which he very frequently recurred, always calling him "the Bourbon" '.[14] He continued to show much curiosity about him as one of the many figures associated with the history of Charles V, which he had come to know very well, largely from a work of the eighteenth-century Scottish historian, William Robertson, thereby explaining why he had mentioned Charles V not only at different places in the course of his journey but also in The Siege of Malta[15] as the patron of the hero of the novel and as the original donor of Malta to the Knights after the loss of Rhodes. Robertson's History of Charles V gave 'an admirable view of the state of the continent in the 16th century', so much so that Scott had recommended it to Charles as part of his general studies on entering the Foreign Service.[16]

Charles V's troops had been led by 'the Bourbon' in a war against the latter's own king and countrymen before the sack of Rome. So Scott also called him 'a traitor', although on hearing that a suit of armour belonging to him was preserved in the Vatican, he eagerly asked if 'the Bourbon' had worn it on the day that his troops had captured Rome.[17] That event had greatly struck his imagination, and he later told Cheney that 'he had always had an idea of weaving it into the story of a romance, and of introducing the traitor Constable as an actor'. Only Caesar Borgia rivalled him in interest as a potential character for a novel, since the history of the Cenci, which he had also once thought of applying to romance, was 'too atrocious and disgusting to be rendered available in the drawing-room of the present day'.[18] Indeed, although Shelley had written a tragedy called *I Cenci* during his residence in Rome a few years previously, it had been promptly rejected for the stage in London as offensive to public taste and delicacy. In consequence Shelley had published it in a very limited edition, in which Scott does not appear to have bothered to show any interest, for he looked upon Shelley as a discreditable revolutionary, on whom—as with Leigh Hunt, to whom *I Cenci* had been dedicated—'the world had set its mark'.[19]

Unfortunately it was impossible for Scott to ascend the rugged stairs of the Vatican Museum to see 'the Bourbon's' suit of armour, or indeed to negotiate its countless galleries and slippery floors to see the Stanzas of Raphael and *The Last Judgment* of Michelangelo.[20] In any case he had already declared to John Scott of Gala in London that he had little knowledge of Italian painting. He *did* go to the Vatican, however, or, more precisely, to the square of St Peter's for the traditional papal blessing at Easter on 22nd April. There he was again seen, and afterwards described, by Owen Cole, who was accompanied by Augustus Fitzroy. He was seated on the roof of one of the twin colonnades enclosing the square, and as Cole surveyed the countless 'heads ranged along the portico on the right as you face the Basilica, that of the bard-baronet was most conspicuous from below'. 'His visage, now altered by time or rather by suffering, showed to greater advantage at a distance' than when Cole had last seen it in close view inside Palazzo Caramanico at Naples: 'his countenance like the sun beamed forth, when, after a short period, Gregory XVI came forward to a window' in front of the square to give his blessing. 'Both were aged men, however dissimilar their physiognomy, resembling in this, that both inclined to corpulence.'[21]

Scott later told Cheney that he had been much struck with the benediction, and when Cheney asked him if he meant to be presented to the Pope, who, as a great patron of learning, had expressed an interest about him, 'he said he respected the Pope as the most ancient sovereign of Europe, and should have great pleasure in paying his respects to him did his state of health permit it'. In view of his love of pageantry he was advised not to leave Rome so soon but to wait to see the procession of Corpus Christi or to hear the Pope singing High Mass on St Peter's Day. 'He smiled, and said those things were more poetical in description than in reality, and that it was all the better for him not to have seen it before he wrote about it—that any attempt to make such scenes more exacting injured the effect without conveying a clearer image to the mind of the reader—as the Utopian scenes and manners of Mrs Radcliffe's novels captured the imagination more than the most laboured descriptions, or the greatest historical accuracy.'[22] Although the comment did not altogether tally with his recent enthusiastic response at Naples at *seeing* and *hearing* High Mass and organ music on the spot in the monastery at La Cava, it corresponded, on the other hand, to the imaginative scene he had inserted in *The Siege of Malta* about his hero and La Valette listening to 'the anthem float round in solemn chorus' from St John's Cathedral, which itself was not historically accurate, as the cathedral had then not existed. *The Siege of Malta*, in fact, exemplified all the liberties that Scott had commonly taken with places and dates in his historical novels.

His comment nevertheless was a significant contribution to the copious contemporary pronouncements by the English Romantic poets on 'imagination' as a creative faculty. The latest contributors had been Shelley in *Defence of Poetry* and Keats in his letters and poems before the latter had died in Rome only a few years previously after he had written *The Eve of St Agnes* under the influence, among other sources, of Scott's poetry, notably of *The Lay of the Last Minstrel*. He had died, in fact, in Piazza di Spagna, which was only a stone's throw from where Scott was staying. Scott cared as little for him as a man, however, as for Shelley not only because they were so removed by age, upbringing and social *milieu* but also because Keats, as another associate of Leigh Hunt, had been politically suspect, if not anathema, to him as well as to Lockhart. In fact, Lockhart had attacked Keats, as a member of Hunt's 'Cockney School', in *Blackwood's Magazine* before Croker had published the notorious article in *The Quarterly Review* which had been widely, even if wrongly, represented (by Byron among others) to have hastened Keats's death by tuberculosis.

Scott was much more in his element in the company of the German scholar, Christian (later Baron) Bunsen, to whom Gell presented him a few days after his arrival in Rome,[23] indeed before Cheney called on him at Casa Bernini. Bunsen was the Prussian Minister at Rome after a distinguished career as historian, philosopher and theologian. He lived with his English wife, *née* Frances Waddington, in Palazzo Caffarelli on the Capitol Hill, where, according to tradition, Charles V had lodged on a visit to Rome. As Mrs Bunsen had last seen Scott at Edinburgh in full health and vigour of manhood more than twenty years previously, she was naturally first shocked at his appearance, particularly as, like Mrs Davy in Malta, 'I was not prepared for his difficulty in speaking; but though his animation is gone, his conversation is much the same sort as formerly, therefore most interesting and original, and his expression of goodness and benevolence truly venerable in the midst of physical decay'.[24]

Although he was trying to keep his resolution of dining out as little as possible, he consented to dine with them at an early hour in a small company, the only other guests being Gell and Anne, who was accompanied by Miss Frances Mackenzie, a daughter of Lord Seaforth. Knowing of Scott's love of 'popular poetry', Bunsen had sought out 'the German ballads so enthusiastically sung during the "War of Liberation" in 1813', and after giving him an idea of the sense, made the two Bunsen boys sing them. Scott was pleased, and after praising 'that noble struggle', called the boys to him, and gave them a kindly pat on the head in much the same manner as that in which he had dismissed young John Ballantyne at Abbotsford on the eve of his departure for the Mediterranean. It was to Abbotsford, in fact, that he though the could best invite the Bunsens in return for their hospitality. So, before taking leave of them, he kindly urged them to visit him on their next journey to England; and inevitably he combined the invitation with a quotation from Shakespeare: 'I have had my losses; much is changed; but I have still "my two gowns, and all things handsome about me," as Dogberry says'.[25]

This was by no means the last that they saw of him, for both of them continued to call on him, usually on short morning visits, and on one occasion Bunsen found him alone, 'with his emaciated-looking son Charles, silent and unoccupied, in a corner', exactly as Owen Cole had first found Charles at Palazzo Caramanico in Naples. Scott had by then heard of Goethe's death, and he asked Bunsen questions about him and about Goethe's son, who had died in Rome only a year or two previously. Bunsen avoided giving the particulars of the manner of his death, which had been caused by habits of intoxication, and he merely said that 'the son of Goethe had nothing of his father but the name', and was startled by Scott's slowly turning his head towards Charles, and saying, 'Why, Charles, that is what people will be saying of you'.[26] It was as 'a wreck of a young man', in fact, that Mrs Bunsen viewed Charles, whom she had last seen as 'an engaging child at Edinburgh in 1810' without any sign of rheumatism and, even more, without the strain and tension of his attendance on Scott combined with anxiety about his own situation in relation to the Foreign Office. For it now looked as if he would not be able to leave Italy towards the end of April, as he had last informed Sophia from Naples that he would be doing, in order to resume his duties in London in May.

'We have been in great confusion', he wrote to Sophia on 24th April as their first communication from Rome, 'and have been waiting in hopes that the Great Unknown would give us some insight into his ulterior proceedings. . . . The greatest misery is the uncertainty of what we are to do.' They had received no further news of the *Rainbow*, 'and should she not arrive, I think you may count upon our leaving this [Rome] for Florence on our way home in about twelve days'. It was still his wish that they should take 'the shortest and easiest way' home by sea to Marseilles, but 'the cholera in France and my father's obstinacy will prevent our going' by that route. 'At present he talks of Germany, but I shall be thankful if ever he gets over the Alps.' In any event 'I shall write as soon as we have settled upon something' in the knowledge that, if they left for home in about twelve days, it would not be necessary for Lockhart to join them in Italy in June.[27]

It is curious that whereas Gell mentioned Anne several times in connection with Scott in Italy, and paid tribute to 'the constant and unwearied attention and anxiety with which she always watched and assisted her father',[28] he did not refer at all to Charles. Nor did Captain Cheney, who made Scott's acquaintance apparently at the time that Charles wrote to Sophia. He made the acquaintance through Gell, whom he asked, on the way to Scott's house, what were his favourite subjects of conversation, 'and I replied that he was the Master Spirit of the history of the Middle Ages, of feudal times, of spectres, magic, abbeys, castles, subterraneous passages, and praeternatural appearances, but that perhaps he was more animated on the history of the Stuart family than on any other topic, and when possible he always contrived to divert the conversation into that channel'.[29] It is understandable, therefore, that Gell should have recorded that Scott's acquaintance with Cheney—apart from their common friendship with Lady Northampton—'was productive of great pleasure to Sir Walter', for Cheney and his brother, in addition to having a town-house in Rome, were the proprietors at that moment of the Villa Muti at Frascati, which had been for many years the favourite residence of Prince Charles's brother, Henry Stuart, the Cardinal of York.[30]

It was at the Villa Muti, in fact, that Monckton Milnes was to meet the Cheneys and afterwards report to this father about their 'fine gentlemanism' without explaining whether it was through them or through his long-standing friends, the Bunsens, that he was to be presented to Scott, on the evidence of what Owen Cole was to write about him. Scott, according to Milnes as reported by Cole, 'was a mountain of a man, and a very rugged one too; he could not make him out—at one time he talked like a boor, without even the semblance of authorship of the commonest kind; again, he would for a moment or more be the Scotch Shakespeare'.[31] His impression of him, in other words, was not unlike that of Cole himself at his first meeting with Scott at Naples. Cole, however, was in error in representing Milnes as meeting Scott in Naples. He met him in Rome, as did several English travellers, who wrote home about him, so that extracts from their letters continued to be quoted in the British press.[32]

Even Lockhart informed Laidlaw that he had heard from a friend that Scott had been seen in Rome. 'I have *heaps* of letters from Sir Walter,' he added, all written from Naples, without indicating if he had received from Cadell the fourth and fifth volumes of Vertot that Scott had sent him to correct the manuscript of *The Siege of Malta*. He made very clear to Laidlaw, however, that it was with reluctance that he contemplated reading Scott's hand. 'The worst of it all is—I have received from the Major a whole sheaf of MS !'[33] The 'sheaf of MS' was not *The Siege of Malta* but the material that Scott had sent by Walter from Naples, which was short compared with *The Siege of Malta*. Cadell, for his part, had received his even more numerous share of letters from Naples, including the latest, in which Scott had informed him that he would be drawing on him at Rome through Coutts for £500, 'which I trust will bring me home again'.

Cheney confirmed the report of all the English travellers about the respect and attention that Scott received from the Italian authorities, and explained that the Romans were deterred from crowding to visit him 'only by their delicacy and their dread of intruding on an invalid'. His works were widely known among them, and by no means only by the upper classes, for the bookstalls were filled with translations of his cheap editions from Galignani's and numerous Italian printing-houses. Some of the most popular Italian plays and operas had been founded on his novels.[34] Moreover, the greatest Italian novelist, Alessandro Manzoni, was indebted to him in I Promessi Sposi, which he had himself read at Abbotsford only a year or two previously.[35] For all these reasons he was offered the use of villas, libraries and museums, which he politely declined, as he was content to live quietly in Casa Bernini, receiving calls from Gell, the Bunsens and Cheney, and, in the intervals, writing up El Bizarro as a short Calabrian tale. He showed it to a German gentleman called Mr Ganz, who had long resided in London, and who, according to Gell, became so great a favourite that Scott promised to make a present of El Bizarro to him when it was completed. He told Ganz that he had sent The Siege of Malta to Scotland, 'where it had only to be revised for the press'. 'He said that from his boyhood the Maltese knights had so interested him that after he had visited the island, the book, as it were, composed itself.'[36]

It is not clear whether Ganz was introduced to him by the Bunsens or by Cheney, who invited Gell to accompany Scott in the party that was formed on May Day to dine at the Villa Muti, where Gell had himself dined with the Cardinal of York some thirty years previously before his elevation to the purple.[37] Scott for his part had summed up the Cardinal, in his history of the Stuarts in Tales of a Grandfather, as 'a prince of a mild and benevolent character'.[38] The Cardinal's papers, containing a wealth of information about the Stuarts, had passed after his death to St James's Palace in London, where Scott had seen them and had proposed that Lockhart and himself should edit them. Accordingly they had been officially appointed to report about them, and only his illness had forced him to put off a visit to London that he had planned for them. If his present improved health continued, he could still take up the project after his return to Abbotsford, using, as he had suggested to Lockhart before his third attack of apoplexy, 'a cab to carry me between Regent's Park and St James's'.[39]

The sun was shining powerfully when he set off with Gell for the Villa Muti in a little droska, while Anne went in a larger coach—apparently not their britzka—with a group of ladies. Scott was in good spirits, and Gell had come to know well his utter lack of fear in a carriage, so that he had some difficulty in preventing Scott from falling in a very rough drive of twelve miles. Despite the heat and the glare the prospect of seeing the Cardinal's house sustained his spirits, and, on arriving in safety, Gell handed him to Cheney as his host, who showed him, in addition to the Cardinal's portrait, a painting of Prince Charles as well as an ivory head of Charles I, which had served as the top of the Cardinal's walking-stick. Above all, his interest was engrossed by a painting of the *fête* given on the Cardinal's promotion in the palace in Rome where the Stuarts had resided.[40] He fancied he could identify several of the followers of the exiled family in the painting, including the celebrated Highland chief, Donald Cameron of Lochiel, whom he had extolled, in the Jacobite campaign in *Tales of a Grand-father*,[41] in a manner curiously similar to that of the heroes of the Knights in *The Siege of Malta*: as a figure—to quote his own words—'not unworthy the best days of chivalry'.

Although he admired the beauty of the house, which commanded an extensive view of the Campagna of Rome, he remarked to Cheney that the prospect was 'a poor substitute for all the splendid palaces to which they [the Stuarts] were heirs in England and Scotland'. He derived, as both Cheney and Gell were to testify, great pleasure from this little excursion, and even Anne assured Cheney at dinner that 'she had not seen him so gay since he left England'. In fact, he ate and drank well in excess of his diet, and entertained the company with his anecdotes. His good spirits were kept up on the return journey, for which he contrived to place himself beside Gell in the little droska, contrary to Anne's arrangement that he should sit in her coach for safety in view of the food and wine that he had taken. In consequence he was even more fearless and careless of falling than he had been in the morning, so that Gell had to employ the better part of two hours in watching him, assisted by his servant, Pietro Pighetti. 'I was, however, well repaid for my trouble and anxiety, as he gaily recounted many histories of his favourite Stuarts, and told a thousand stories to beguile the way.'[42]

Unfortunately Gell was much less communicative about his response to the tombs of the Stuarts in St Peter's, which he was taken to see a day or two afterwards. Gell contented himself with dwelling on the formidable difficulty of getting Scott up the extremely slippery flight of steps to the marble floor at the entrance to the colossal nave of St Peter's, where fortunately the tombs of the Stuarts were in an aisle not far from one of the side-doors. Fortunately too they fell in with a Scottish traveller called Colonel Blair, with whose aid Scott accomplished his purpose after they had tied a glove round the point of his stick as a precaution against falling.[43] As to the tombs themselves, they had recently been embellished with a handsome monument by Canova, whose statues Scott, following the taste of his generation, had long regarded as the touchstone of beauty. 'I thought she might have rivalled one of Canova's finest statues,' he had, in fact, made one of the characters in *St Ronan's Well*[44] say of Clara Mowbray, the heroine.

Canova, however, was going out of fashion, unlike his fellow-craftsman in classical art, Thorwaldsen, who had long settled in Rome from Denmark.[45] 'I am told Mr Thorwaldsen is excellent in his art, second only to Canova,'

Scott had written many years before to the Duke of Buccleuch.[46] His own meeting with Thorwaldsen was recalled, several years later, to James Skene by Thorwaldsen himself, 'with tears in his eyes, saying that it was the most remarkable' interview he had ever enjoyed in his long life, during which he had been presented to most of the illustrious men of his time. They had included Byron, of whom he had executed a celebrated monument—now at Cambridge —to which Scott had subscribed handsomely.[47] Thorwaldsen, however, had been disappointed with Byron on meeting him in Rome and finding him eccentric and melancholy, whereas he responded at once to Scott's open and natural manners, even though their conversation appears to have been a replica of Scott's late meeting with the monks of La Cava and of his earlier presentation to King Ferdinand of Naples. For Thorwaldsen had no English, and Scott no Italian, and his German, like his French, had become very rusty, so that, although they met with the utmost cordiality, their conversation was 'singularly disconnected, for it was entirely composed of interjections and monosyllables'. Nevertheless 'the two new friends were so pleased that they seemed to understand each other perfectly; they shook hands heartily, clapped one another on the shoulder, and when they parted, each followed the other with his eyes as long as he could, and continued his demonstrative gestures'.[48]

Thorwaldsen himself was not reported by Skene to have referred to the bust of Scott that he modelled during the rest of his stay in Rome, but it was seen a few days later in Thorwaldsen's studio by a Scottish traveller called Cumming, who thought it 'not nearly so good' as the famous one by Chantrey.[49] Unfortunately it is not extant, but another bust, purporting to represent Scott, was made from a model and now lies in the Thorwaldsen Museum at Copenhagen.[50] It bears little resemblance to Scott, however, particularly in comparison with Morani's eminently natural drawing of him at Naples. Even the lost original is shrouded in some mystery in the absence of any reference to it—and indeed to Thorwaldsen himself—in Gell's and Cheney's reminiscences of Scott, which is perhaps not wholly surprising in Gell's case, as he does not appear to have shared the contemporary admiration for Thorwaldsen.[48a]

Cheney and his brother took Scott and Anne in their carriage to the Protestant burial-ground, as Anne was anxious to see the grave of her friend, Lady Charlotte Stopford, a sister of the Duke of Buccleuch. At the burial-ground, where the remains of Shelley and Keats lay beside each other by the noble pyramid of Cestius, Scott remained in the carriage with Cheney to avoid painful walking, while Anne went with Cheney's brother to look for Lady Stopford's grave. 'Infirmity', Scott explained to Cheney, 'had checked his curiosity.' Indeed 'much of what I saw at Naples, and which I should have enjoyed ten years ago, I have already forgotten'. Nevertheless he regretted to Cheney that he could not go to see where they had laid Lady Charlotte. 'She is the child of a Buccleuch; he, you know, is my chief, and all that comes from that house is dear to me.'[51] As Cheney was well read in Italian literature, Scott told him that he had formerly made it a practice to read through the *Orlando* of Boiardo and Ariosto once every year, and that it was the *novellas* of Cervantes that had first inspired him with the ambition of excelling in fiction. Cheney perceived that it was only at such moments, when warmed with his subject, that 'the light blue eyes shot from under the pent-house brow with the fire and spirit that recalled the author of Waverley'. On other occasions he was often abstracted.[52]

Cheney had the advantage—as did Gell—of being well acquainted with the descendants of some of the most ancient Roman families, several of whom were well read in Scott's novels in translation, including *St Ronan's Well* as the latest to appear in 'the magnum'. One of his most ardent admirers was the Duke of Corchiano. Cheney invited him and his duchess in a party to dine with Scott in his town-house. The duke as a man of much ability had played a part in the political changes of his country, and, as he spoke no English, he asked Cheney to tell Scott that 'in disappointment, in sorrow and in sickness his works had been my chief comfort'. A similar sentiment was expressed by the Marchesa Longhi, who, although young and beautiful, had had her share of sorrows. To these and other flattering compliments he replied with unfeigned humility, expressing himself pleased and obliged to the duke and the marchesa by the good opinion entertained of him, and delighted his admirers with the good humour and urbanity with which he received them. On the Duke of Corchiano's remonstrating against the fate of Clara Mowbray in *St Ronan's Well*, he replied that 'I am obliged to the gentleman for the interest he takes in her, but I could not save her, poor thing—it is against the rules—she had the bee in her bonnet'.[53]

The Marchesa Longhi's brother, who was also presented to him by Cheney, was a young man whom Gell had long admired for his talents. He was Don Michele Gaetani, through whose estate Scott had passed in the britzka on the way to Rome. He owned a large castle as heir to the Dukedom of Sermonetta, and his family, the Gaetanis, had figured among the most ancient and turbulent Roman dynasties in the Middle Ages, of which he had himself an extraordinary knowledge, so that, according to Gell, 'these historical qualities, added to the amenity of his manners, rendered him naturally a favourite with Sir Walter'. It was he, in fact, who, many years after Scott's death, was to unveil a tablet on the Casa Bernini commemorating Scott's stay there.[54] His ancestors, moreover, had been dispossessed of their rich fiefs by Caesar Borgia, one of whose swords was still in his possession. Scott examined with keen interest the long and broad blade, richly ornamented and inlaid with the arms of the Borgias, complete with Caesar's favourite motto—'Aut Caesar, aut nullus'.[55]

He had by now given up the *Rainbow*, and had definitely made up his mind to leave for home, so that Charles informed Cadell on 5th May that he had drawn two bills for £500 on him through Coutts, 'which I think will be sufficient to carry us home, if not cut off by the cholera on the road'. They would be leaving Rome in less than a week in their britzka, attended by John

Nicolson and Celia Street, for Florence, where they would be remaining at least two days. 'From that my father talks of returning by Innsbruck to Munich, Stuttgart and so to Frankfurt down the Rhine to Rotterdam. This route, however, may be changed, as there are all kinds of disagreeable reports such as a cordon at the frontier of Bavaria, and even the appearance of disease in Venice. I shall, however, try to steer clear of it.'[56] All their money arrangements were in the hands of the famous Roman banking house of Torlonia, the head of which had been created a duke by Bonaparte, and had been frequently mentioned by travellers for his two palaces, assemblies and lavish hospitality 'to all strangers who visit Rome, especially to the English'. He had died a few years previously after he had 'purchased the Prince of Wales's most valuable jewels', but his widow, the Duchess of Torlonia, was still alive, and was known to Gell. She invited Scott as guest of honour to a very splendid dinner in her palace in a large company, including Gell, Don Michele Gaetani, the Duke and Duchess of Corchiano, and Colonel Blair, who had helped him to see the tombs of the Stuarts in St Peter's.

The dinner was well after his normal retiring hour, and from the duchess's known hospitality it was feared that, in the heat of the conversation and servants on all sides pressing him to eat and drink as was the custom in Rome, he might be induced, as so often in the past, to eat more than was good for him. So Colonel Blair, who sat next to him, was asked to take care that this should not happen. Whenever Gell observed him, however, he always appeared to be eating, although even this did not satisfy the duchess, who, on discovering the nature of the office imposed on Blair, observed that 'it was an odd sort of friendship which consisted in starving one's neighbour to death when he had a good appetite and there was dinner enough'. On rising from the table, he spent the greater part of the evening listening to the amiable Duke of Corchiano, who told him that he had a vast collection of papers containing true accounts of all the murders, poisonings, intrigues and curious adventures of the great Roman families during many centuries, 'all of which were at his service, to copy and publish in his own way as historical romances, only disguising the names so as not to compromise the credit of the existing descendants of the families in question'. Scott was so captivated with all he heard that at one moment he thought of remaining for a time in Rome, and at another vowed that he would return there the following winter.[57]

Contrary to his late confession to Cheney that 'infirmity had checked his curiosity', he was eager to see the Castle of Bracciano, some twenty-five miles outside Rome, on hearing that it belonged to the eldest son of the Torlonia family, who bore the title of Duke of Bracciano. It had once belonged to the celebrated Orsini, about whom he cited a story in Gell's hearing. He was promptly given permission to go there with Gell in a party, and the steward had orders to furnish them with whatever they needed. They set off in burning sun, so much so that Mrs Bunsen, on hearing of it, feared that he might be made quite ill by the heat and the distance. As usual he went in Gell's carriage, while Anne, Gaetani and Cheney and another lady went in the britzka.[58] When they arrived at Bracciano—rather fatigued with the roughness of an ancient Roman road—he was pleased with the general appearance of the castle, which was finely situated on a rock commanding on one side the beautiful and wooded Lake of Bracciano. As neither their carriage nor Anne's could easily ascend to the court, he fatigued himself still more by walking up the steep and somewhat long ascent to the gateway, where he was struck with the sombre appearance of the Gothic towers, built with the black lava that had once formed the pavement of the Roman road, 'and which adds much to its frowning magnificence' in a manner that Ann Radcliffe would have relished. In the interior he could not but be pleased with the grand suite of state apartments, all still habitable and even retaining in some rooms the old furniture and rich silk hangings of the Orsini and their contemporary great family, the Odescalchi.

As these chambers overlooked the lake, he sat in a window for a long time during a calm and delightful evening to enjoy the prospect. A very large dog having come to fawn upon him, he told it he was glad to see it, for it was a proper accompaniment to such a castle, but that he had 'a larger dog at home, though maybe not quite so good-natured to strangers'. This notice of the dog seemed to gain the heart of the steward, and he accompanied him on a second tour through the grand suite of rooms, both highly pleased with each other's conversation, though it resembled that at Scott's late meeting with Thorwaldsen, for, as one attempted French and the other spoke Italian, little could be understood between them. At night they had tea in front of a large fire, and while he talked cheerfully, some of the party went out to walk by the battlements of the castle by moonlight. Inevitably a ghost was alleged to have been seen to complete the Gothic setting, and he said that a ghost was best made by painting it with white on tin, 'for in the dusk after it had produced its effect, it could be instantly made to vanish by turning the edge almost without thickness towards the spectator'.[59]

In the morning—true to his early rising habit—he was the first to be up and about after the steward, and together, with the dog, they made another tour over a part of the castle until he again seated himself in the deep recess of the window overlooking the lake, where he was found by Cheney, with whom he had a long and moving *tête-à-tête* before breakfast, reminiscent in some ways of the serious conversation that he had had with Wordsworth on the eve of his departure from Abbotsford for the Mediterranean. For even on this occasion the *tête-à-tête* took place on the eve of his departure from Rome. At first he speculated on the lives of the turbulent lords of the ancient castle, which he contrasted with the calm before him, while listening with interest to such details of history as Cheney could give him. Then they strayed into more modern times, and Cheney never saw him more animated and agreeable, so much so that 'he was exactly what I could imagine him to have been in his best moments'.

'Indeed I have several times heard him complain that his disease sometimes confused and bewildered his senses, while at others he was left with little remains of his illness, except a consciousness of his state of infirmity.'[60] It accounted for the late puzzling alternations of lucid and clouded passages in his letters and journal, and for the contrast, in quality of writing, between the opening and middle sections of *The Siege of Malta*. He talked of his impending northern journey, and regretted that he would not now be meeting Goethe at Weimar. On Cheney's telling him that he had himself seen Goethe the year before, and that he had found him well, and, though very old, in full possession of all his faculties, 'Of all his faculties!' Scott replied, 'It is much better to die than to survive them, and better still to die than to live in the apprehension of it; but the worst of all would have been to have survived their partial loss, and yet to be conscious of his state.'[61] It was an indirect revelation of his most haunting fear, that 'I should linger on, "an idiot and a show"', in Dr Johnson's words about Swift in insane old age.

He then talked of Manzoni, for whom he expressed a great admiration, followed by warm regard, as always, for Byron. On Cheney's asking him if he had ever seriously thought of writing a tragedy, he answered, 'Often, but the difficulty deterred me—my turn was not dramatic', in implied acknowledgment of the ill-success of the several dramas that he had attempted after his early translation of Goethe's tragedy. Some of the mottoes, Cheney urged, prefixed to the chapters of his novels and subscribed 'old plays', were eminently in the taste of the old dramatists and seemed to augur success. 'Nothing so easy,' he replied, 'when you are full of an author, as to write a few lines in his taste and style; the difficulty is to keep it up; besides the greatest success would be but a spiritless imitation, or, at best, what the Italians call a *centone* from Shakespeare.'[62] The remark applied admirably, in general, to all the tragedies that the English Romantic poets had attempted, including Shelley in *I Cenci*.

'No author', Scott added, echoing a remark lately made in a letter to Skene from Naples, 'has ever had so much cause to be grateful to the public as I have. All I have written has been received with indulgence.'[63] It was also gratifying that he had met with such a flattering reception in Italy, particularly as he had not always treated the Catholic religion with respect, although, as Cheney pleased him by remarking, 'no religion had any cause to complain of him, as he had rendered them all interesting by turns'. 'Jews, Catholics and Puritans had all their saints and martyrs in his novels', in which at the same time he had 'exposed all hypocrites of all sects'. Cheney perceived his light blue eyes sparkling with moisture, as he added, 'I am drawing near the close of my career; I am fast shuffling off the stage. I have been perhaps the most voluminous author of the day; and it *is* a comfort to me to think that I have tried to unsettle no man's faith, to corrupt no man's principle, and that I have written nothing which on my death-bed I should wish blotted.' Cheney made no reply, and while they were yet silent, Don Michele Gaetani joined them, and they walked through the vast hall into the court of the castle, where Gell and Anne and the rest of the party were expecting them for breakfast.[64]

Gell had made a drawing for him of the staircase in the court of the castle, and he presented it to him as an addition to the drawings of Rhodes that he had given him at Naples. After breakfast he was anxious to return to Rome to begin his journey the following day, which was a Friday. Wishing him to prolong his stay, Cheney reminded him of his superstition, and told him he ought not to set out on the unlucky day. 'Superstition is very picturesque,' he answered, laughing, 'and I make it at times stand me in good stead; but I never allow it to interfere with interest or convenience.' As Cheney helped him down the steep court to Gell's carriage, he said, as he stepped with pain and difficulty, 'This is a sore change with me. Time was when I would hunt and shoot with the best of them, and thought it but a poor day's sport when I was not on foot from ten to twelve hours; but we must be patient.' Cheney then handed him into the carriage beside Gell, and, as he was not returning to Rome with the party, Scott took leave of him, pressing him, with eager hospitality, to visit him at Abbotsford.[65]

During the return to Rome his conversation, according to Gell, 'was more delightful, and more replete with anecdotes than I had ever known it'. He talked a great deal to young Gaetani, and invited him to Scotland, but his anxiety to obtain another interview with the Duke of Corchiano on the evening of his return, presumably about the collection of Roman papers that he had offered to put at his disposal, was not gratified, as the duke was in the country, and, on arriving at Casa Bernini, Scott was overwhelmed with crowds of visitors, all calling to say goodbye to him, among them 'an English savant', whose report to London, that 'the author of Waverley seems in good spirits, and his health much improved', was soon after reprinted in *The Caledonian Mercury*.[66]

Even Gell believed that 'he was at the moment in such apparent vigour and spirits that I left him scarcely anticipating his loss, though I dared not look forward to another meeting', unlike Scott himself, who, before taking leave of him and of his servant, Pighetti, whom he thanked for his attention in the kindest manner, pressed him to be his guest at Abbotsford after he had promised to get Cadell to send him a presentation-copy of *The Waverley Novels*, with his autograph, in return for all that he had done for him. As Gell was by no means well off, and could scarcely afford the journey to Scotland, Scott told him that 'if money be the difficulty, don't let that hinder you'. 'I've £300 at your service, and I have a perfect right to give it to you, and nobody can complain of me, for I made it myself.'[67]

Although the gesture was characteristically liberal, and touched Gell so much that he afterwards recalled it to the public in tribute to 'the kind-hearted baronet', it was made in ignorance of his true financial situation and under the delusion that his debts had all been paid. In point of fact, taking into account the £500 that he had just drawn on Cadell through Coutts on Torlonia's bank for the northern journey, he had run up a debt of £2370 on Coutts instead of the £1000 that he had estimated at Naples would suffice for the whole of his stay in Italy. Moreover, Cadell had paid another £2400 on his behalf on various other occasions and on open accounts, so that, as he was about to put it to Walter, 'your father owes of new debt £5000', of which his pension would cover less than a third. In consequence 'your father is coming home to misery—yes, positive misery' in view of the fact that, whereas in the past he had succeeded, through sheer hard work, in cancelling excess expenditure with articles in keepsakes, reviews and so forth, he could no longer do so now not only on the evidence of the rejected *Seventeenth-Century Letters* but of *The Siege of Malta*. 'It is proper to tell you this, as I judge from a portion of manuscript now in my hands, what he writes cannot be published.' In consequence it behoved Walter and Lockhart to give him 'a full, true and particular account' on arrival in England, especially as 'there is some sort of hallucination in his mind about his pecuniary matters which must be fully and clearly explained so that there can be "no mistake" '. 'If your father, when at Naples, took it into his head that all his debts would be paid off this year, he must have been labouring under some unhappy delusion.'[68]

In fairness to Scott, however, it had been Cadell who had himself positively encouraged him in that delusion in all the letters that he had sent him to Malta and Naples, even though with a good intention, and even though admittedly he had never told him specifically that the whole of his debt had been paid off. Fortunately he was not to live to hear either the truth about his financial affairs or the verdict on *The Siege of Malta*, which since then has remained unpublished. Lockhart, for his part, was never to reveal how much of it he had read under the pressure of *The Quarterly Review* and the Reform Bill except to state in *The Life of Scott* that 'the manuscript of these painful days is hardly to be deciphered by any effort', thereby implying that he might not have achieved more than a few of the opening pages. In *The Life of Scott* he was also to state that Scott had started *The Siege of Malta* in Naples in lieu of Malta, and 'in spite of all remonstrances', which was contrary to all the encouragement he had received from Lockhart himself, and even more from Cadell, including an offer of £2000 for the manuscript. Lockhart, moreover, was to give out to the world that *The Siege of Malta* was unfinished, again contrary to what Scott had himself written both to him and Cadell from Naples.[69] In consequence, more than a hundred years after Scott's death, a completely different version of *The Siege of Malta* was published by S. Fowler Wright, purporting to be 'founded on an unfinished romance by Sir Walter Scott', and alleging that the manuscript had no plot, in the teeth of all the episodes of Scott's creation, complete with original dialogue, and of the theme of 'changed manners' preceding the chronicle borrowed from Vertot. Even so distinguished a scholar as Sir Herbert Grierson contended that Scott had drawn on his memory for the chronicle, not direct from volumes four and five of Vertot,[70] which Scott had himself shipped to Cadell from Naples for Lockhart's revision of the manuscript. So little, in short, that is *accurate* is known about *The Siege of Malta* that an attempt will be made to describe the manuscript, survey its later history briefly, and reveal its contents in a separate chapter as a postscript to Scott's death after the northern journey.

The journey itself opened on 11th May 1832 when Scott travelled through 'famous country' on leaving Rome for Florence by the Perugia road in preference to the Siena road, both of which were traditionally open to travellers on the grand tour, and both excelled in beautiful scenery, particularly in spring. He was attended by John Nicolson, who drove the britzka, in which sat Anne, attended by Celia Street, and Charles, who was in overall charge of the journey, as he had been on the Appian Road from Naples. Again as on that route, Charles contented himself with the briefest recital of inns and place-names in his diary, which nevertheless remains the principal source of information about the journey in the absence of material from Scott, and even when supplemented by the delightful but unfortunately fragmentary recollections of Owen Cole and one or two travellers, who met them casually at different stopping-places on their route. Lockhart is very brief and not always accurate in *The Life of Scott*.

The first place they stopped at was Terni in Umbria after they had been detained at Narni for repairs to the britzka, which this time do not appear to have ruffled Charles's temper.[71] Terni was celebrated among travellers for its waterfalls, which Byron, among so many writers, had described in *Childe Harold*.[72] They saw the falls by moonlight without the need, according to Charles, to ascend on donkeys for them, as the spectacle could be seen perfectly well from a carriage. They slept late at an excellent inn after going without food for many hours. Scott started, but never finished or posted, a letter for Sophia in apparent good spirits but in a semi-incoherent style to tell her that 'so far all is well and like to be so'. He was curious to know if Lockhart would be setting out for Italy before they returned to England. 'I wish he had come a month ago and met us at Naples and Rome.' It was now settled that after Florence they would be returning by the Tyrol and the Rhine, including Frankfurt, where Charles had advised Sophia to direct letters to the care of Poste Restante, so that perhaps they might hear something of Lockhart's intentions. In view of 'the prospect I have of being home in about six weeks' Scott was looking forward to seeing her again in London, and asked her to inform Cadell of his expected arrival before he left the rest of the journey to Anne.[73] In the Visitors' Book of the inn he wrote 'Sir Walter Scott—for Scotland'.

After another stop at Perugia for sleep they travelled a whole day to Florence, which they did not reach till the small hours of 13th May, and stayed there two days, Scott presumably spending the first day in sleep and at rest after such a fatiguing journey.[74] Having read in Vertot that the noble families of Florence had contributed many Knights to the Order of St John, he sent for the librarian of the ducal palace on his own initiative or through the British legation to ask if the public libraries of the city contained 'any remarkable works on the history of the Knights of Malta'.[75] The librarian was Giuseppe Molini, but, like his counterpart in Naples, he does not appear to have left a record of his meeting with Scott. According to Lockhart, Scott was only with difficulty prevailed on to see the Church of Santa Croce, where, as Byron had explained in *Childe Harold*, Michelangelo, Galileo and Machiavelli had been buried.[76] In front of the church was the huge statue of Dante, of whom Scott had lately confessed to Cheney that he knew little, finding him 'too obscure and difficult' in contrast to his delight in Boiardo, Ariosto and Tasso.[77]

It is not clear *who* exactly was 'the friend' who was afterwards reported to have asked Scott in what direction he travelled. Scott answered him: 'Home: it is after all the best place to live in and certainly the best to die in'.[78] Accordingly he endured 'a very cold and dreary journey' to Bologna over the Apennines, which had a good deal of snow on them well beyond Cavigliaio, where they dined off the provisions that they had brought in the britzka with them. After refreshing themselves with sleep at a good inn at Bologna, but without spending any time in sight-seeing, they made for Venice via Ferrara, where they stopped briefly for dinner before a longer pause, late at night, at Monselice for sleep. The journey to Ferrara itself was through rather dull country, which became a perfect plain from Monselice to the port of Fusina on the Adriatic. Although the flatness facilitated their speed, the posting along the road was very bad. Their attention, however, was arrested by many handsome Palladian villas, familiar to travellers on the grand tour and celebrated by Ann Radcliffe in *Mysteries of Udolpho*.[79] At Fusina, which was a free port under Austrian control, they embarked for Venice without delay at the Customs barrier, thanks to a *lascia passare* granted by the authorities to Scott in proof of the facilities accorded him for easy travel between the various frontier divisions of Italy.[80]

It took them only an hour and a quarter to sail over the lagoon to Venice, where they lodged at a very good hotel, 'The Leone Bianco', in apartments facing the Grand Canal and not very far from the Rialto. Although every room was occupied, the manager and servants were very civil and attentive, so much so that they earned not only an encomium even in Charles's terse diary but also from Scott himself, for he afterwards recorded his gratitude in the Visitors' Book of his hotel at Vicenza: 'I resided three or four days and could not have been more kindly or attentively served in my own house'.[81] The attention appears to have been an index of the general 'adulation and respect' paid to him by the authorities on the evidence of an anonymous English traveller, who was staying in the same hotel at Venice, and who afterwards sent Lockhart a short account of Scott for possible inclusion in *The Life of Scott*, but which Lockhart did not publish. The traveller—a long-standing admirer, even, on his own admission, an idolater of Scott—had heard in Florence of Scott's having landed at Naples from Malta, and had regretted that his own journey to Venice would prevent him from meeting Scott in Florence. He was, therefore, surprised and at the same time grieved when, standing in the balcony of the hotel in full view of the Grand Canal, he saw a party land from a gondola at the steps below him. The last of the new arrivals was evidently suffering from pain and fatigue, and looked 'so much changed from what I had seen him in Edinburgh in 1823 that, at the distance, I did not recognize his features, and it was not till an hour or two afterwards that I found I was under the same roof as the author of Waverley'.

Although he was anxious to pay Scott a visit of respect, particularly as they had friends in common, he hesitated, for 'an unwillingness to intrude upon his evidently enfeebled state prevented me'. But he did record that Scott dined twice with the English consul, and that on his return on the second evening he was 'followed by gondolas of serenaders who accompanied him to the steps of his hotel'. It was at the splendid close of an Italian day; 'the gondola that carried the author of Waverley was gliding past the palaces where Titian and where Byron had resided, and it was a sight not easily to be forgotten'. Even Charles recorded in his diary that 'the row to the Lido down the Gran Canale is delightful'.[82] He and his father and Anne, in fact, had lost no time in steering, well before the dinner, for Byron's former abode, Palazzo Mocenigo, at a short distance from their hotel, where they had been detected by no other than their old 'shadow' fellow-traveller, Owen Cole, who had apartments opposite theirs in common with his friend, Augustus Fitzroy. Cole had seen Scott embark in a gondola for Byron's *palazzo*—'there was a delightful radiancy in his countenace' —followed by Anne, whose tall figure and pretty eyes had revived the same warm feelings that he had first experienced for her in Naples.[83]

At the arsenal, according to the same anonymous English traveller, the gates were opened to admit Scott's gondola, 'a mark of respect which is generally only paid to princes'. The same deference was shown him in the Academy of Fine Arts, which contained a magnificent collection of Titians, Veroneses and Tintorettos. Scott met there 'an English painter of some celebrity', and, as they passed through the gallery, he was sufficiently cheerful to relate one or two of his anecdotes. It was probably an exaggeration on Lockhart's part to state afterwards that he 'showed no curiosity about anything except the Bridge of Sighs and the adjoining dungeons'.[84]

He left Venice on 23rd May, followed by Cole and Fitzroy, whose gondola gained on his more heavily weighted boat as they made for the landing-place, where horses were being got ready and boxes searched and repacked at the customs. Cole found Scott seated on an upturned barrel, imbibing 'the intense radiance of a mid-day sun'. As he approached him, 'his open hand was extended towards me with a courteous "How do you do, sir?" ' 'He did not recollect me, but that did not in the least detract from the genial urbanity of his greeting.' On Cole's mentioning that he had heard at the bank at Venice that the bankers there were inclined to lament with Byron over the 'Dogeless city's vanished sway', Scott replied that 'it is the habit with bankers to depreciate the market so that they may buy their stock cheap and sell with advantage'. Contrary to Byron, he predicted a future for Venice, so that Cole, who had something of a poet's vision, conjured up, under the spell of his words, the old glories of 'the Sea Cybele', complete with the launching of the Bucentaur from the arsenal that Scott had lately visited. From Venice to Vicenza Cole's and Fitzroy's carriage followed Scott's britzka at a little distance, never losing sight of him except during a tremendous thunderstorm near Padua, where he stopped for dinner. Cole's imagination was again kindled by the storm in apprehension for Scott's safety—'what if he were washed off the saddle!'—only to have his fears quickly dispelled at Vicenza, where the two parties stopped at a good hotel for the night. 'To my extreme delight there came an impromptu invitation from the Scotts, who were seated at the tea-table, just where I should most desire to find them.'[85]

At the table one of Scott's guests was a lineal descendant of the Stuarts. 'Sir Walter was in excellent spirits; Miss Anne as fresh as a rose, just washed by the shower; Charles in his very best humour. Hitherto I had never seen the "Lion" at any of his meals; how great was my gratification at being permitted to help him for the loaf!' For Cole experienced 'something of the realization of the evening party at the Castle of Branksome' in *The Lay of the Last Minstrel*, as Scott began to talk on a variety of Scottish subjects: from the Buccleuchs to Abbotsford, and from Scottish music to the Western Isles. About the Buccleuchs he told Cole, among much else, how much he regretted that the Reform agitation in London had prevented him from attending the christening of the son and heir of his chief. About Abbotsford, to which he invited Cole and Fitzroy, he told them that 'he indulged himself in the national vanity of a piper'. To Fitzroy he spoke of his having been challenged to a duel by a French general in resentment at certain passages in *The Life of Bonaparte*, which Cole imagined was 'evidently a joke', although it was perfectly true, whereas there does not seem to be confirmation in his journal or letters—although this does not necessarily mean that he was inventing—of his having had a pressing invitation to New York from an American lady, to whose proposal he had been obliged to give a flat refusal. ' "And yet" ', he added, with infinite humour, ' "none can accuse me of want of chivalry, having in my time done so much for women." '[86]

Cole was entirely preoccupied by Scott, who, on hearing of his having visited the Western Isles the year before, including a famous cave in the Isle of Skye, stopped him to tell him of a route that he ought to have taken ostensibly to the cave but in reality to the beautiful Rhymer's Glen at Abbotsford. Then while he wandered in imagination among his native hills and hollows, Anne arose and beckoned to him, and, assisted by Charles, he struggled to his legs, bowed slightly to his guests, and broke off in the middle of a sentence as he stood for a while at the open door, exactly as Cole had last seen him in Naples, propped on his stick between the two rooms of his apartment.[87]

On getting into the britzka, he made for Verona through a very rich country with the intention of sleeping in the city of Romeo and Juliet, whereas, according to Charles, they stopped there only for dinner at a hotel close to the tombs of the Scaligers, the family of the famous critic. While he was seated in the open carriage in front of the hotel, waiting for horses and the revision of his passport, he was again seen by Cole. He seemed thoroughly to enjoy the sunshine, which was almost as warm as it had been in Venice. Cole's head was still full of Scott's talk the previous night at Vicenza—he had aptly come to refer to it as another version of 'Tales of my Landlord'. On going up to the side-door of the britzka, he was again greeted by Scott with open palm and a slow syllabic, 'How do you do, sir?', which, however gracious, did not quite imply actual identification. On Cole's informing him that he meant to explore the abode of the Capulets, followed by a search for Juliet's tomb in the Franciscan convent, he replied, in the knowledge that Juliet's tomb was completely ruinous, that he should not go and see it, 'but go instead to the Church of Santa Maria l'Antica, in front of which stands the stately monument of the Scaligers', and to prove it Scott began to quote from one of his works, at which Cole's imagination, in admiration of all the wonderful spoils hoarded up in Scott's memory, was again aflame, this time conceiving himself as a sort of 'Mr Lovel in the sanctum of Mr Oldbuck' in *The Antiquary*. 'I could almost hear the voice of the imaginary possessor of the library while exulting over his literary spoils.'[88] The parallel could not have been more apt, and crowned Cole's recollections of Scott, besides providing another parallel with Captain Hall at Portsmouth, for Hall had also, in the parting scene with Scott, identified him with the same character in *The Antiquary*.

This was the last that Cole saw of him, for he pressed rapidly through the Alps after short pauses for sleep and dinner at Ala and Trento along the course of the river Adige. He reached Bozen, the first German-speaking town, on 25th May, and Charles appreciated the civil treatment they received at the inn there and at Sterzing at the foot of the Brenner Pass in very grand scenery. Sterzing itself was 'an odd-looking place', although it was famous in history as the site where the Tyrolese hero, Andreas Hofer, had defeated the Bavarians as the allies of Bonaparte, and had driven them out of his country. Owing to the cold it was better for Scott's party to sleep at Sterzing than to go on to Brenner, but it was even colder on the drive to Innsbruck despite the beautiful scenery. At Innsbruck they found the inn 'bad in every respect', and left after only a day, Charles recording in his diary that the chapel of the palace containing the celebrated tomb of the Emperor Maximilian, surrounded by bronze statues of kings in armour, which Scott had so longed to see in Naples, was well worth a visit. He did not say if Scott had accompanied him to it, so that it remains an open question whether Lockhart was again in error, or, at any rate, was exaggerating in stating that Scott would not even look at 'the fondly anticipated chapel at Innsbruck'.[89] Charles, and possibly Scott, also saw Hofer's tomb in the city, about which Charles surmised that the rides along its avenues must be beautiful.

From Innsbruck it was a fourteen-hour drive to Tegernsee along a narrow road as far as the Lake of Achenthal in picturesque scenery, followed, after sleep at midnight, by another six-hour drive to Munich along uninteresting country. At Munich they found a good hotel, although the town itself was 'very dull' to Charles, and the people 'all very vulgar-looking'. The garden of the royal palace provided an agreeable drive and promenade. They left Munich, after only a day, on 30th May for Ulm, dining at Augsburg, where they were followed, soon after they left, by the same anonymous English traveller, who had stayed in their hotel at Venice. As he now happened to put up at the same hotel in Augsburg, he heard from the owner of the place that he considered Scott's presence as 'having conferred a lasting honour upon his house, and related most minutely how the author of Waverley had asked for a flask of his best Stein Wein and tasted it successively from a large glass, a small glass and green glass in order to enjoy and discriminate its flavour'.[90] To the end, therefore, he kept up his 'three glasses of wine' despite Dr Abercrombie's warnings. Indeed Cadell was later to hear that 'he drank a good deal of wine, sometimes a tumbler of hock'.[91] Yet it was not he but one of his servants—either John Nicolson or Celia Street—who was taken ill at Ulm, where they were detained for two days, after which they made a short journey to Göppingen, pending their servant's full recovery. Their next stop, for dinner, was at Stuttgart—'a very pretty town with a beautiful approach'—before they drove through Ludwigsburg to Heilbronn, where they arrived a few moments before the most dreadful thunderstorm that Charles had ever witnessed.

They were now on the banks of the Neckar as a tributary of the Rhine, and early on the morning of 5th June they set off for Heidelberg in beautiful scenery, and reached it after a whole morning's drive, followed by an even longer drive to Frankfurt, which they reached at midnight on the same day, and put up at the Hôtel de Russie, 'the best hotel in Germany', according to Charles, who gave no indication in his diary whether they found letters at Poste Restante from Sophia or Lockhart as to the latter's intentions regarding his trip to Italy.[92] It is likely, however, that circumstances were against it in view of the dramatic turn that political events had lately taken in England. For the Reform Bill, after its second reading in the House of Lords, had been defeated in committee when Scott had been in Florence, and, on the King's refusal to create the necessary number of new Whig peers, the government of Lord Grey had resigned, only to be recalled to office, with a promise from the King to create the new peers, on Wellington's failing to form a viable ministry. It was not likely that Lockhart would leave his post in such a fluid situation. In fact, he was still in London, but without knowledge of Scott's exact date of return in the absence of the letter to Sophia from near Florence telling her of 'the prospect I have of being home in about six weeks': indeed even in less than that time at his rapid rate of travelling, which had been upwards of seventeen hours a day before Frankfurt, although not without symptoms of an approaching seizure, against which he had been bled more than once by Nicolson.[93]

At Frankfurt he entered a bookshop and bought the newly published *Legends of Alhambra* by his friend, Washington Irving. One of the salesmen, seeing him with Anne and Charles in an English party, offered to sell him a lithograph of Abbotsford. He said, 'I know that already, sir', and hastened back to the hotel unrecognised. He was later found by a lady reading Irving, of whom he spoke with respect and kindness. From Frankfurt he drove to Mainz, whence he sent the last letter he ever wrote in reply to a note from the philosopher, Schopenhauer, who had written to say he wished to pay him a visit. Scott politely declined on the ground that 'I am far from well'.[94] On boarding the Rhine steamer at Mainz, he had his attention temporarily revived by the celebrated scenery of crags and castles. For he found himself looking upon a more extensive panorama than that on which he had fixed his eyes in Spain and Malta and Amalfi for their towers and bastions. It was the panorama, in fact, that he had long since described in *Anne of Geierstein* at second-hand from Goethe after Byron had sung its praises memorably in *Childe Harold*.[95] But after Cologne was left behind, his curiosity dwindled, and on 9th June near Nimeguen he had his fourth paralytic seizure, and fell into the arms of Lady Strachan, who was close by. 'My poor father taken ill,' Charles wrote, followed by 'miserable day at Nimeguen'. Nicolson again bled him, and restored some signs of animation, but, in Lockhart's well-known words, 'this was the crowning blow'. Nevertheless he insisted on continuing his journey, determined that he would die at home.[96]

On 11th June he was lifted from the britzka into a small English steamer, *The Queen of the Netherlands*, from which a man—dead of the cholera—had just been removed. She carried him to Rotterdam, where he was again transferred into *The Batavier* for London. He lay on a bed spread in the carriage, from which the horses had been detached. His large head was covered with a black velvet cap. There was a solemn silence for some minutes among the passengers when the carriage was placed on board. In the words of an English eye-witness, 'the gayest, the most thoughtless among us seemed struck with awe'. Although they imagined that, on a nearer view, they would recognise the face from the many portraits that had made the world familiar with the features, they saw but the faintest outline. Its general paleness contrasted with the dark plaster fixed over the temples, where leeches had lately drawn blood. He seemed totally unconscious, his eye-lids falling heavily, but at length he raised them and spoke to Nicolson, who was always at his side in contrast to Anne, who was herself ill with strain and grief. When he was lifted from his carriage and borne in a chair to his cabin, he was ill again, and a Russian physician on board administered a sedative. On waking, he asked for pen and ink, but his hand dropped powerless.[97]

In this condition of stupor he was carried—on arriving in London late on the evening of 13th June—to St James's Hotel in Jermyn Street, as Charles feared that Sophia, having received no notice of the exact date of his return, might be out of town or unprepared to receive him. On finding her and Lockhart at home, he hastened back with them to the hotel, where, according to Lockhart, Scott 'recognized us with many marks of tenderness' before he again sank into stupor or delirium, so that it was not considered prudent to move him to their home. Walter was soon on the spot from his regiment in Manchester. The same doctors who had attended him before his departure for Malta—Dr Ferguson, Sir Henry Halford and Dr Holland—were called in and continued to see him daily, but there was nothing that they could do other than to ward off a fifth seizure with further bleeding. Dr Ferguson was impressed with 'the symmetry of the colossal bust' on the pillow with Scott's neck and chest exposed. 'He never seemed to know where he was, but imagined himself to be still in the steam-boat.' Dr Holland would not hear of his seeing Cadell, who had travelled instantly from Edinburgh, but Scott talked disconnectedly to him through Lockhart about his affairs, money and his works. In addition to hearing of the wine drinking on the return journey, Cadell was told that 'he had taken the home fever most thoroughly'.[98]

The information was echoed in the newspapers: 'Sir Walter insisted on performing the latter part of his journey with a continued rapidity, capable of disordering the constitution of the strongest body. . . . The placidity, which formed one of his most distinguishing characteristics, had yielded to the long vexation of disease.'[99] Even Captain Pigot, in acknowledging with gratitude the presentation-copy of The Waverley Novels that Scott had promised him at Naples, wrote to Walter from as far as Ancona, where the Barham was stationed, that 'the hasty journey he took, with the manner in which he lived, was no doubt the cause of his so soon having another attack'.[100] They but confirmed, in other words, the prediction that Charles had made in Naples without their suggesting or implying in any way that Charles had himself voluntarily contributed to the rapidity of Scott's movements, even though, owing to the delay in Rome pending information about the Rainbow, he appeared to have come to share his father's anxiety for as quick a return as possible in order that he might comply with the Foreign Office instructions that he should be back in London in May. As it was, he overran his time by several days.

Scott's wishes, as he lay in semi-consciousness in Jermyn Street, all pointed to Abbotsford, and after three weeks he recovered sufficiently to obtain his doctors' consent to his removal.[101] For at first it had been feared that he might expire in London. Indeed a report had spread—and had already reached Mrs Bunsen in Rome—that he had expired on board the steamer. He had himself solemnly blessed his children as if expecting death.[102] Even The Spectator had lamented that 'he is not permitted to revisit his cherished scenes and "familiar faces" of his native land', and on that account had paid tribute to him as a man. 'Sir Walter

Scott has had *political* enemies, as every distinguished individual must have who has taken so marked a political part as he has done ... but a *personal* enemy he has never had. His unaffected simplicity, his benevolence of heart, his integrity of character (which the latter circumstances of his life showed to be heroic) have made him the object of universal affection as well as respect. ... He is now cut off, at only 60 years of age, a victim of exertions beyond human strength.'[103] Dr Holland was himself to testify to *The Spectator*'s last remark: 'His frame was fitted for a longer life than sixty-one, and I cannot doubt that it was shortened by the anxious and compulsory labours of his later years.'[104]

On 7th July he was transferred into a steamship for Leith, accompanied by his two daughters, Lockhart and Cadell. Sophia trembled from head to foot and wept bitterly. As 'the child of his affections' she had drawn public sympathy in the press for her 'assiduous attendance on her father'. Anne, as she had herself lately written to Captain Pigot, still suffered from weak nerves and stomach pains.[105] Scott stood the journey as well as could be expected, and after a two-day rest in Edinburgh at a hotel he was lifted into a carriage for Abbotsford, where Laidlaw was waiting for him at the porch in circumstances very different from the prediction that he had made to him before his departure from London for Malta, and in which he had confidently expected 'to hail your return as at any former time I ever saw you depart'. Laidlaw had prepared his bed in the dining-room, and lifted him in, but he sat bewildered for a few moments until he exlaimed, 'Ha! Willie Laidlaw! O man, how often have I thought of you!' His dogs had gathered round his chair, and began to fawn upon him and lick his hands, as he alternately sobbed and smiled upon them until he fell asleep.[106]

Soothed on finding himself in his own house, he seemed to improve and said that he would disappoint the doctors after all. On asking to be wheeled in the garden, the library and the hall, he kept saying, 'I have seen much, but nothing like my ain house—give me one turn more'. From the library he looked down upon the Tweed in all the richness of summer before he asked Lockhart to read to him in a tone as gentle as that of a child. 'From which book?' Lockhart asked. 'Need you ask?' he replied. 'There is but one.' Lockhart chose the fourteenth chapter of the Gospel of St John. In the coolness of the garden by the shady court-wall he again asked Lockhart to 'read some amusing thing—read me a bit of Crabbe'. Lockhart read one of his favourite passages from *The Borough*, to which he responded with warmth. On the first Sunday after his return he got as far as his favourite terrace-walk in sight of the plantations and the hills beyond, and he listened to Lockhart reading the Anglican service. 'Why do you omit the visitation for the sick?' he asked, and accordingly heard it too. His memory seemed to be returning, but it was a deceptive ray of hope, for on asking to be wheeled to his desk and finding that he could not even hold a pen, he sank back in tears and asked to be taken to bed, where he lingered in a miserable state of mind and body for over two months with little relief from laudanum until the end came on 21st September 1832. 'It was a beautiful day,' in Lockhart's memorable words, 'so warm that every window was wide open, and perfectly still, that the sound of all others most delicious to his ear, the gentle ripple of the Tweed over its pebbles, was distinctly audible as we knelt around the bed, and his eldest son kissed and closed his eyes.'[107]

References for Chapter 5

1. *Journal* 711–12.
2. Ibid 711; MS 1614; MS Acc. 5131, f. 300.
3. *Journal* 711–12. Cf. ibid 10, 48, 122, 138, etc., for Virgil quotations.
4. Chs. LXXV–LXXXVIII.
5. *Journal* 712.
6. *Miscellaneous Prose Works of Sir W. Scott*, Edinburgh, 1841, II, Ch. 37, p. 430.
7. *Journal* 712, MS Acc. 5131, f. 300; MS 1614.
8. *Journal* 712; Gell 26.
9. *Journal* 712–13; MS 1614; Gell 26, 51 n[71].
10. MS 1752, p. 531; MS Acc. 5131, f. 300.
11. Lockhart X, 176–98.
12. *Life, Letters and Friendships of R. Monckton Milnes* by T. Wemyss Reid, 1890, i, 125.
13. Lockhart X, 176.
14. Gell 25.
15. ff. 2–3, 13–14.
16. *Letters* X, 370.
17. Lockhart X, 191.
18. Ibid; Gell 30. Cf. Lockhart VI, 391–92.
19. *Journal* 8, 423.
20. Gell 29.
21. Cole 260–61.
22. Lockhart X, 193–94.
23. Gell 25.
24. *Memoirs of Baron Bunsen* by Baroness Bunsen, 1868, i, 125, 374.
25. Ibid 374–75; Gell 25.
26. *Memoirs of Baron Bunsen* by Baroness Bunsen, 1868, i, 375.
27 MS Acc. 5131, f. 300.
28. Gell 38.
29. Ibid 25–26.
30. Ibid 26–27.
31. *Life, Letters and Friendships of R. Monckton Milnes* by T. Wemyss Reid, 1890, i, 124, 127; Cole 259–60.
32. e.g., *Caledonian Mercury*, May 31, 1832.
33. MS 860, f. 40.
34. Lockhart X, 197–98; Mary E. Ambrose, 'The First Italian Translations of Scott' in *Modern Language Review*, Jan. 1972, pp. 74–82.
35. *Journal* 606.
36. Gell 30, 50 n[67]; *The Literary Gazette*, Oct. 27, 1832, p. 681.
37. Gell 27; Lockhart X, 184.
38. ed. of 1925, introd. F. W. Farrar, Ch. LXXXVII, p. 1186.
39. *Journal* 515, 582; *Letters* XI, 214–15, 276; XII, 8.
40. Gell 27; Lockhart X, 185.
41. ed. of 1925, introd. F. W. Farrar, Ch. LXXV, p. 999.
42. Gell 28; Lockhart X, 185–86.
43. Gell 28–29.
44. Ch. XXI, p. 370, Oxford ed. of 1912.
45. Cf. *Letters and Correspondence of J. H. Newman*, ed. A. Mozley, 1891, i, 379.
46. *Letters* V, 216–17.
47. Skene 207; Lockhart X, 433.
48. E. Plon, *Thorvaldsen: His Life and Works*, tr. by Mrs C. Hoey, 1874, p. 114; Skene 207–8.
48a. E. Clay, *Sir W. Gell in Italy*, 1976, p. 153.
49. W. F. Cumming, *Notes of a Wanderer*, 1839, p. 59.
50. *Thorvaldsens Portrætbuster*, introd. J. V. Jensen, Copenhagen, 1926, plate 67.

51. Lockhart x, 188–89.
52. Ibid 184, 187.
53. Ibid 189–91.
54. Gell 31, 51 n[17].
55. Lockhart x, 191–92.
56. MS 971, f. 40.
57. Madden ii, 194 n; Gell 29–30.
58. Gell 31; *Memoirs of Baron Bunsen* by Baroness Bunsen, 1868, i, 375.
59. Gell 34–35.
60. Ibid 35; Lockhart x, 194.
61. Lockhart x, 194–96.
62. Ibid 194–95.
63. Ibid 195; Skene 203.
64. Lockhart x, 197.
65. Gell 35; Lockhart x, 194.
66. May 31, 1832; Gell 35–36.
67. Gell 35–36; Madden ii, 91.
68. Acc. 5188, June 4, 11, 1832.
69. Lockhart x, 148; Shortened version of *Life of Scott* (Everyman 1969), p. 624. See Chs. III–IV of this book, pp. 51, 55, 70–71, 88.
70. Scott files, departmental records, Department of MSS, National Library of Scotland, July 5, 1944. See also H. Grierson, *Sir W. Scott, Bart.*, 1938, p. 12.
71. MS 1614; MS 138, f. 51.
72. Canto IV, Sts 69–71.
73. MS 1614; MS 138, f. 51; MS 917, f. 40; Lockhart x, 198.
74. MS 1614. Charles merely recorded that he himself only had time to see the Pitti Palace, particularly Canova's Venus. The rest of his and Scott's time in Florence, which was then the capital of the independent Grand Duchy of Tuscany, may have been spent at the British Legation or as guests of the talented Lord Burghersh, who, with the other leading English resident, Lord Normanby, invariably entertained visitors of rank from Britain. Lord Normanby lived in a house which had originally been fitted up for the Pretender. (See C. C. Greville, *Memoirs*, 1874, i, 299.) Scott might have been invited to see it. This point has gone unnoticed by Scott's biographers.
75. W. M. Parker, 'Scott in Florence and Venice' in *The Scotsman*, March 10, 1962, p. 7.
76. Lockhart x, 199; *Childe Harold*, Canto IV, Sts 69–71.
77. Lockhart x, 187.
78. W. M. Parker, 'Scott in Florence and Venice' in *The Scotsman*, March 10, 1962, p. 7.
79. MS 1614; Lockhart x, 199; *Mysteries of Udolpho*, Ch. xv.
80. MS 1614; Cf. *Caledonian Mercury*, May 31, 1832.
81. MS 1614; W. M. Parker, 'Scott in Florence and Venice' in *The Scotsman*, March 10, 1962, p. 7.
82. Ibid.
83. Cole 261; MS 1614.
84. MS 1614; W. M. Parker, 'Scott in Florence and Venice' in *The Scotsman*, March 10, 1962, p. 7.
85. MS 1614; Cole 262–64.
86. Cole 264–65; cf. *Journal* 343–44, 347, 350.
87. Cole 264–65.
88. MS 1614; Cole 266–67.
89. MS 1614; Lockhart x, 199.
90. MS 1614; W. M. Parker, 'Scott in Florence and Venice' in *The Scotsman*, March 10, 1962, p. 7.
91. MS 786, ff. 108–9.
92. MS 1614.
93. Lockhart x, 200–1; *Caledonian Mercury*, June 21, 1832.
94. MS 1614; W. M. Parker, 'Scott's Last Journey' in *The Scotsman*, April 16, 1932, p. 15; Lockhart x, 199–200; *Letters* XII, 47–48.
95. Canto III, Sts 46–61; Lockhart x, 200; W. M. Parker, 'Scott's Last Journey' in *The Scotsman*, April 16, 1932, p. 15.
96. Lockhart x, 200; MS 786, ff. 108–9; MS 1614.
97. MS 1614; Lockhart x, 200; MS 786, ff. 108–9; *Life of Mrs Sherwood*, ed. Sophia Kelly, 1854, pp. 559–61.
98. MS 1614; Lockhart x, 200–2; MS 786, ff. 108–9; Sir H. Holland, *Recollections of Past Life*, 1872, p. 83.
99. *Caledonian Mercury*, June 21, 1832.
100. MS 1554, f. 49.
101. Sir H. Holland, *Recollections of Past Life*, 1872, p. 83.

102. *Memoirs of Baron Bunsen* by Baroness Bunsen, 1868, i, 376; Lockhart x, 201.

103. Reprinted in *Caledonian Mercury*, June 28, 1832. See also July 5, 1832.

104. Sir H. Holland, *Recollections of Past Life*, 1872, p. 83.

105. Lockhart x, 205–6; *Caledonian Mercury*, June 21, 1832; MS 1554, f. 49.

106. Lockhart x, 206–8; *Caledonian Mercury*, July 12, 1832.

107. Lockhart x, 208–12, 218; Skene 208–210; J. Hogg, *Familiar Anecdotes*, ed. D. Mack, 1972, p. 135.

6

'The Siege of Malta'

Description and Later History of the Manuscript

The manuscript of *The Siege of Malta*, which is now in the New York Public Library, consists of one hundred and fifty quarto sheets, specially supplied to Scott by Cadell from Edinburgh before he left London for Portsmouth and Malta.[1] Besides, there are about fifty-four insets, used by Scott for corrections, additions and footnotes, which in his earlier novels it had been his practice to make on the *verso* of the relevant pages. The majority of them are very brief. Thanks to the insets, the manuscript, as he explained to Cadell from Naples,[2] is, in general, 'clean'.

The entire text consists of about 77,000 words, in large part closely written in a hand that more often than not is small, thin, and in general, very difficult to read. It is perhaps most difficult in the opening chapters, which appear to have been written before Scott's marked improvement in health at Naples.[3] They are unlikely, therefore, to have been the part that he said at Naples that he had burned and rewritten better than before.[4] Certainly they are the part that suffers most from his 'cloudiness of words and arrangement' in the form of missing letters or words, repetitions, and confused or obscure constructions. After this bad start his hand, and even more, his grammar and syntax gradually improve, becoming, as has already been indicated,[5] much clearer and very fluent in the middle parts of the manuscript until, in the later sections, his hand again tends to shrink into thin letters in very close, steady writing. The 'cloudiness', however, in some form and in varying degrees, never completely disappears from the manuscript.

In keeping with a long-standing practice in his letters—by no means peculiar to him in his age—there is very little punctuation in the entire manuscript, and when there is any—as in the passages containing formal speeches or dialogue—it is often erratic. Its absence is thrown into sharper relief by Scott's peculiar method of sentence-construction, characterized as it is by a heavy number of subordinate clauses, sometimes running to paragraph length, without a single comma or stop. On the other hand, paragraphing is regularly observed throughout the manuscript, which consists of thirteen chapters varying in length from a few pages in the opening chapter to nearly a whole 'copy' in the later chapters. 'Copy' was the technical term used by Scott to denote each of the 'six parts' or parcels in which the manuscript was dispatched from Naples to Lockhart and Cadell in two instalments of three parcels each.[6] The first instalment of nine chapters constituted the 'first volume and a half'[7] of the three volumes in which *The Siege of Malta* was to be published.

The chapters themselves 'overflow', in one or two instances, from one parcel into another: for example, chapter 10 was largely contained, when originally dispatched from Naples, in parcel No IV, but its concluding part was contained in parcel No V.[8] Although Scott left the chapters unnumbered after chapter 2, the remaining eleven chapters are unmistakably marked off from one another by large centred headings. Originally five of the chapters had verse-mottoes appended to them, as had been customary with Scott for all his novels, but the leaves or pages containing them were removed from the manuscript many years after Scott's death, so that the mottoes now survive only in a version of the manuscript that was made anonymously in 1878. As Scott displaced the order of the chapters, in dispatching the first instalment from Naples, by putting four of the nine chapters in the third parcel instead of in the second, he attempted to indicate their proper sequence with directions at the end and beginning of the three parcels.[9] He also attempted to indicate where he calculated that 'vol. 2nd' started by means of a heading at the beginning of the third parcel.[10]

His displacement of the chapters in the first instalment, however disastrous for the sequence of the narrative, unless put right with his directions, did not affect his own numbering of the manuscript, although it may explain why he hinted to Cadell, precisely in dispatching the first instalment to him, that 'there will be some difficulty in arranging the copy'.[11] He numbered the 'six parts' of the manuscript *by parcel*; in other words, he numbered each 'part' or parcel *separately*, as can be observed in the top left-hand corner of each page. Inevitably, there was misnumbering by a man recovering from apoplexy, and this took the form of 'jumping' or duplication of numbers in several parcels.[12] On the other hand, two whole 'parts' in the middle of the manuscript are regularly numbered, thereby reinforcing the impression conveyed by their generally better quality of writing that they mark the point at which Scott had felt that—to quote his own words at Naples[13]—'the mist attending this whoreson apoplexy is weary-ing off'.

His numbering in the manuscript is in ink, whereas Cadell's numbering, or that of his scribe in Edinburgh, on receipt of the manuscript from Naples, was made in pencil in the top right-hand corner of each page. Cadell numbered the whole manuscript right through without slipping up once, but without restoring the displaced chapters of the first instalment. In consequence, the manuscript, in its *extant* state of pagination, is grossly misnumbered from the point of view of the order of the chapters and of the sequence of the narrative. Moreover, a vital page,[14] at the opening of parcel No III, which originally contained one of Scott's directions for the order of the chapters, is now missing, for a reason to be explained presently, although, of course, it was not missing when Cadell or his scribe numbered the manuscript in the order indicated in the following table, which also gives the corresponding parcels and chapters:

Parcel No I   = MS pp.   1– 23 (Chapters 1–2)
Parcel No III = MS pp. 48– 87 (Chapters 3–7)

Parcel No II   = MS pp. 24– 47 (Chapters 8–9)
Parcel No IV = MS pp. 88–111a (Chapter 10 almost complete)
Parcel No V   = MS pp. 112–135 (Chapter 10 finished; 11; 12 begun)
Parcel No VI = MS pp. 136–150 (Chapter 12 finished; 13)

The present structural disorder of the manuscript cannot be corrected by *internal* means without first making a complete transcription of it and then trying to establish its proper sequence in a literary jig-saw puzzle of about 77,000 words. Fortunately an *external* remedy is provided not only by the 1878 version of the manuscript but also by a typescript of that version, which was made in 1932 by a Maltese journalist living in New York, who merely initialled himself 'C.S.F.'. His identity, however, can be established from a series of articles on *The Siege of Malta* that he sent from New York for publication, under his name of Charles S. Frendo, in the now defunct newspaper called *The Malta Chronicle*.[15] Both the 1878 version and 1932 typescript now lie in the New York Public Library.[16] They appear to be even less known than the manuscript itself, at any rate, on this side of the Atlantic, where they are unknown even to the greatest living authority on Scott, Dr James C. Corson.

Thanks to them, it is possible to recover the text not only of the missing mottoes and of the page containing the vital direction relating to the order of the chapters but also of several other pages that disappeared from the manuscript many years after Cadell returned it to the custody of Scott's heirs at Abbotsford, following, or even before, Lockhart's condemnation of it in *The Life of Scott*. In other words, its return to Abbotsford laid it open to souvenir-hunting. In consequence, seven pages are missing, another ten pages have parts of varying size cut out, while another nine pages have parts cut out but fitted back with tape, perhaps by the copyist of 1878, fortunately without damage to the text except in two small instances[17] of incomplete or somewhat inaccurate restoration. All the missing and mutilated pages, with one exception,[18] are from what Scott called the 'original story', that is, the part of the manuscript containing incidents and characters of his own creation in a background of history derived from Vertot. The early pages, as was to be expected, proved most vulnerable to the souvenir-hunters, or perhaps more correctly, to the souvenir-givers, over an indeterminate period of time, but *after* 1878, except for three missing fragments, which were cut out *before* that date, on the evidence of notes attached to the manuscript. The notes record two dates and the names of the three receivers of the autographs.

The first name, not only in chronology but also in rank, is that of the 'Emp. of B.',[19] who was undoubtedly the Emperor of Brazil. He was in Scotland on a private visit in August 1871, which coincided with the centenary of Scott's birth. He went specially to Abbotsford before going round the rooms of a great exhibition in Edinburgh, giving 'evidence of possessing the closest knowledge of Scott's characters',[20] exactly like the Duke of Corchiano in Rome.[21] At Abbotsford the emperor must have been presented with half a page of *The Siege of Malta*, specially selected for him not only from the middle part of the manuscript but also from a page where Scott's hand is remarkably clear and the spacing between the lines most helpful for reading. It was larger than that cut out for 'Mrs Meiklau',[22] whose identity seems more obscure than that of Francis Scott,[23] the third named recipient, who may have been the fourth son of Lord Polwarth, in whose career Scott had been interested when Francis had been a young man.[24]

Fortunately the last page of the manuscript (f. 150) survived this distribution of autographs, thereby making it possible to understand why Lockhart had given out to the world the misinformation that *The Siege of Malta* was unfinished.[25] The explanation for this lies in the last line on that page, which has an incomplete sentence that reads: 'Thus a line of princes'. The reason for this is that Scott, having considered the novel, in his own words to Cadell from Naples,[26] 'long enough' as it stood for the projected three volumes, and having narrated in detail the history of the Great Siege of 1565, concluded, following Vertot almost word for word, with a description of Valletta as a legacy of the Siege in the sense that it had been built immediately afterwards by the victorious La Valette. Having said so, Scott, on the last sheet but one of the manuscript, proceeded to describe 'the present town of Malta, or, as it [is] properly called, of La Valette', including its quarantine harbour, where 'the author of these sheets passed ten days' in the autumn of 1831. Then, having added another paragraph, on the last sheet of the manuscript, he broke off, as it was really 'long enough', so that he and Cadell would, after his return to Abbotsford, decide whether to drop this after-piece altogether, or, if space allowed it, add another paragraph or two about the 'line of princes', as he called the Grand Masters, who had bequeathed such a splendid architectural legacy to Malta after the Great Siege. *Where exactly* to end was a small point that would be easily settled between him and Cadell in the light of the printer's report about space. The after-piece about *modern* Valletta, as he had himself seen it, was not strictly relevant to the Great Siege, or, if it was at all, only marginally so. It could even go into the journal of his tour; so he did not even bother to finish the last sentence. In consequence, when Lockhart looked at it, he assumed that *The Siege of Malta* was unfinished.

Lockhart's reputation in the nineteenth century, in virtue of *The Life of Scott*, was such that for nearly a hundred years his verdict against publication of *The Siege of Malta* remained unquestioned, just as his misinformation about its alleged incompleteness has continued to be repeated to this day.[27] *The Siege of Malta*, therefore, remained 'a mystery novel', in the words of a contributor to *The Scotsman*,[28] who first, in 1928, publicly pressed against letting Lockhart's verdict stand for ever. While admitting that even Lockhart's biographer, Andrew Lang, had respected 'Lockhart's ban' as 'sacrosanct', the contributor stressed that Lang 'was acquainted with a person who perused it [the manuscript], and who dissented from Lockhart's estimate to the extent of saying that "The Siege of Malta" was "not destitute of fine passages" '. A re-reading of it, therefore, by 'a modern literary critic' of standing was 'more than overdue', and 'if the opinion be favourable, let the novel be published as a contribution to the genius of Scott on the occasion of the centenary of his death' in 1932.

The plea appears to have had some effect, for the manuscript, together with the 1878 version, the author of which might perhaps have been Lang's anonymous acquaintance, was sold in 1929 by Major-General Sir Walter Maxwell-Scott to the publishers, Sheed and Ward. They, in turn, approached Sir Herbert Grierson for an opinion. Grierson was then preparing for the press the centenary edition of *The Letters of Sir Walter Scott* in twelve volumes. Even discounting this arduous commitment, it would have taken him months, if not a couple of years, to decipher Scott's 'woefully altered' hand in the manuscript, as Lang[29] had himself put it. The manuscript, moreover, was not only in structural disorder on account of the displaced chapters but shorn of many pages. Therefore Grierson must have read the 1878 version without being aware not only of its countless misreadings but that the copyist had more or less REWRITTEN *The Siege of Malta* in an attempt to correct Scott's 'cloudiness of words and arrangement'. The copyist, in other words, had carried out an editorial operation immeasurably greater than that originally envisaged by Scott himself for Lockhart in writing from Naples[30] that 'you must correct as boldly as you can the gross and obtrusive errors', pending Scott's return to Abbotsford.

Thanks to the editing, Grierson, unlike Lockhart, did not read the opening pages in quite the 'clouded' form of the original. Lockhart, on that account, may well have decided at once against further reading. Nevertheless Grierson advised against publication, and many years afterwards admitted in a private letter[31] that 'there were historical explanatory pieces, which read quite intelligibly', but alleged that 'it was when Scott launched into a scene such as he could do so well (e.g., the siege of Torquilstone castle in *Ivanhoe*) that he grew quite confused, and one did not know whether one was on the ramparts defending or on the trenches attacking'. The manuscript and 1878 version, therefore, were returned by Sheed and Ward to Sir Walter Maxwell-Scott, who refunded the purchase money. Shortly afterwards he wrote to Grierson that 'they had discovered that great parts of it [*The Siege of Malta*] were Vertot almost verbally', without informing Grierson by whose help the discovery had been made. Grierson had himself never read Vertot, but he knew from Lockhart's *Life of Scott* that Vertot had been 'exceedingly dear' to Scott ever since the latter had been a boy,[32] and that—to quote Grierson's own words from the same private letter—'one of the books he [Scott] fought his way through when confined to bed by the breaking of a blood vessel' in Scott's boyhood had been Vertot's *Knights of Malta*. Accordingly Grierson now attributed 'the historical explanatory pieces which read quite intelligibly' to Vertot, and allayed his misgivings over plagiarism by inferring that 'he [Scott] was drawing unconsciously on his early memories' of Vertot without having had Vertot's *Knights of Malta* with him or used it in the Mediterranean.

Meanwhile news reached New York that *The Siege of Malta* was again up for sale, so that Gabriel Wells, a well-known antiquarian dealer, crossed the Atlantic for Abbotsford, and bought the manuscript, with the 1878 version, from Sir Walter Maxwell-Scott in 1930 for a considerable sum.[33] Its sale, price, and, even more, a report that it 'contains a superb description of the Siege, and will reveal the author at the height of his story-telling powers', kindled the patriotic ardour of the Maltese journalist, Charles S. Frendo, who was invited by Wells not only to see the manuscript but also to read it through, and make a complete transcript of it, or rather, of the 1878 version, supplemented by a few marginal notes of his own, mainly on the missing pages of the manuscript. Naturally he tried to get up as much information as he could about Scott's journey and sources from Lockhart's *Life*, the *Journal*, and from several accounts of the Great Siege, but not from Vertot, of whom he appears to have never heard, so that he formed a completely mistaken estimate of Scott's achievement in the novel, on the evidence of the series of enthusiastic articles that he sent off to Malta for publication in *The Malta Chronicle*.[34] Moreover, despite Scott's 'woefully altered' hand, he misinterpreted the 'clean' manuscript as a sign of no 'physical and mental strain on the part of the author'.

His misinformation was promptly echoed, in the centenary year, in *The Glasgow Herald*,[35] in a jubilant cry of 'no decrepitude here' [in *The Siege of Malta*]. Grierson had lately published the first three volumes of the centenary edition of *The Letters of Sir Walter Scott*, while John Buchan brought out a biography of Scott, in which, without having read a line of *The Siege of Malta*, he 'hoped that no literary resurrectionist will ever be guilty of the crime of giving them [*The Siege of Malta* and *El Bizarro*] to the world'.[36] Grierson, for his part, added eight volumes, in the course of four years, to the centenary edition, until, in 1937, he completed the monumental task with the twelfth volume, which was intended to cover Scott's last years, including the numerous letters from Malta and Naples about the genesis, composition, completion and transmission of *The Siege of Malta*. Grierson, however, excluded all but four of them from the twelfth volume,[37] on account of Scott's apoplectic hand and 'clouded' writing, so that to this day they lie unpublished in the National Library of Scotland among the so-called 'discarded letters'. Grierson swiftly followed up the centenary edition with a biography, *Sir Walter Scott, Bart.*, as a 'corrective' of Lockhart's *Life of Scott*, in keeping with the reversal of Lockhart's reputation for accuracy that had come about in the twentieth century. In his biography Grierson referred, in the very first chapter,[38] to *The Siege of Malta*, which, he recalled, on the evidence of one of the four letters in the twelfth volume,[39] had been cried up by Scott to Laidlaw from Naples as 'one of his best novels'.[40] Then Grierson, although he had still not read Vertot,[41] but relying on the information that he had received from Sir Walter Maxwell-Scott, alleged that 'all that is coherent in that work [*The Siege of Malta*] proves to be an almost verbatim reproduction' of Vertot. Having said this, Grierson, bearing Scott's reading in Vertot as a boy in mind, but overlooking the information in the 'discarded letters' about Vertot's *Knights of Malta* as *vade-mecum* and source-book for Scott in the Mediterranean,[42] argued, in defence of Scott against plagiarism, that 'as the creative, controlling element in his [Scott's] mind failed him, the wonderful memory was still active, and he wrote as though it were his own what he had read and absorbed as a boy of fourteen'.

Meanwhile the expected rapid publication of *The Siege of Malta* in some form as a result of its transfer to New York had proved abortive, while *The Glasgow Herald* had not followed up Charles S. Frendo's further articles in *The Malta Chronicle* purporting to summarize the contents of the novel. It was, in fact, to know 'what *The Siege of Malta* really was' that S. Fowler Wright, a minor English novelist, went to New York and traced Gabriel Wells, who was now the owner not only of the manuscript and 1878 version but also of a carbon copy of the typescript made in 1932 by Frendo. It was probably the typescript rather than the manuscript or 1878 version that Fowler Wright read, for the typescript, in neat double spacing, could be easily and quickly read, unlike the manuscript, although Fowler Wright himself, in the foreword that he afterwards wrote to the novel purporting to be 'founded on an unfinished romance by Sir Walter Scott', stated that Wells had allowed him to 'inspect it' [the manuscript]. This, however, might have meant no more than that he looked at the manuscript before reading the typescript. In any case, his description of 'the original manuscript' as consisting of 'about 75,000 words' would seem to correspond more to the length of the typescript, and to suggest that, in default of a proper collation, Fowler Wright, like Grierson, was unaware of the systematic omissions of words, phrases, clauses, sentences, and even paragraphs, that had been made by the 1878 copyist, thereby accounting for the rough, perhaps conservative, estimate of 77,000 words already given in the description of the manuscript.

Fowler Wright, in fact, used the alleged 'brevity' of the novel as one of his arguments for asserting 'with entire confidence that he [Scott] would not have published it [*The Siege of Malta*] in its present condition'—in the form, that is, in which he had sent it from Naples—although Fowler Wright, having checked in Grierson's centenary edition and Scott's *Journal*, did admit that 'there is at least one reference by which he [Scott] appeared to regard it as a finished work'.[43] Of course, Fowler Wright, if he had had access to the 'discarded letters', would have found more than one reference to confirm what he had read in Grierson's edition or the *Journal*, and to disprove at the same time the other statement in his foreword, that Scott sent the manuscript 'to Abbotsford by sea'. Handicapped through this lack of external evidence, and for other reasons, on internal evidence, Fowler Wright formed his untenable theory that Scott had merely written 'the historical skeleton on which he would construct a complete romance in the leisure of the succeeding summer' at Abbotsford after the winter at

Naples. The theory was untenable, for one reason, because it was contrary to all Scott's past practice and methods of composition.

Fowler Wright put it forward in 1942, by which time Grierson had found 'some statement which implied that the book [Vertot's *Knights of Malta*] had been with him [Scott] in his voyage, so that he may have re-consulted it'. Nevertheless Grierson, who was never to read Vertot, remained sure that 'he [Scott] was trusting to memory, and had no intention of deceiving when he gave the words of the original'.44 Grierson wrote this in 1944, when Gabriel Wells presented the manuscript of *The Siege of Malta*, with the 1878 version and 1932 typescript, to the New York Public Library as a joint gift from himself and Dr Berg. Enough has been said about the 1878 version and 1932 typescript to make it needless to add that the following description of the contents of *The Siege of Malta*, preceded by a list of the principal *dramatis personae*, is based on a new and independent transcription, although the 1932 typescript will be used to fill in the gaps created by the missing pages of the manuscript.

PRINCIPAL DRAMATIS PERSONAE IN 'THE SIEGE OF MALTA'
IN ORDER OF APPEARANCE

DHALISTAN	A Pursuivant employed by Knights of Malta
DON MANUEL DE VILHEYNA	A Spanish Knight Commander of the Order of St John
JUAN RAMEGAS	A Brother Servant-at-Arms of the Order of St John, attached to Vilheyna
FRANCISCO	Nephew of Vilheyna
ANGELICA	Niece of Vilheyna
MORAYMA	Moorish Governess of Angelica
BONIFACE	A Maltese Sailor employed by Vilheyna
JEAN DE LA VALETTE	Grand Master of the Order of St John, and Commander-in-Chief of Knights of Malta
GUARGOGIN DE LA VALETTE	Nephew of Grand Master
MUSTAPHA	Pacha of Egypt and Commander-in-Chief of Turkish army besieging Malta
PIALI	Commander-in-Chief of Turkish fleet besieging Malta
LUDOVICK DE GARCIA	A Spanish Knight of St John
ZULMA	Wife of Mustapha and aunt of Suleman, Sultan of Turkey
DRAGUT	Renowned Corsair and Viceroy of Algiers, in overall command, with Mustapha and Piali, of Siege of Malta
ULICHIALI	Greek Renegade and Corsair under Dragut
HASSAN BARBAROSSA	Son-in-law of Dragut
CANDELISSA	A Corsair in league with Hassan against Mustapha

Description of the Contents: Part One

The manuscript of *The Siege of Malta* opens with a description of the Mediterranean Sea at sunset near Gibraltar in a mountain setting of Southern Spain, as Scott had observed it from the deck of the *Barham* on the passage to Malta. The scene is represented as enchantingly beautiful and tranquil, but disturbed for centuries by the wars between the Christians on one side of the sea and the Moors on the other. The exact locality is a Spanish fishing village called Aldea Bella, where a party of fishermen observe a small band of armed men, newly arrived in a vessel, whom they suspect of being Moors. The leader of the band asks one of the fishermen unceremoniously the way to the residence of the commander of the place, a Knight called Don Manuel de Vilheyna, renowned as 'one of the most severe scourges' in the wars against the Moors. The fisherman politely indicates a need on his part for caution, 'lest you should yourself be in the disguise of the infidels'. He is answered by the leader of the band, who is a Pursuivant called Dhalistan, that 'I am come officially to communicate with your master' to the effect that he must go instantly to Malta, where all the Knights are assembling from all over Europe in response to a summons from the Grand Master. The Pursuivant then shows the fisherman the blazon of his office.

At this point of the narrative the manuscript has three-quarters of a sheet cut off, but it is clear from the 1932 typescript that Scott used the missing fragment to introduce his readers to Don Manuel de Vilheyna before actually bringing him on the scene in person. His office of 'a commander of the Order' is first described. It entitles him to 'a benefice' of lands and rents, from which he remits a moderate sum regularly to the treasurer of the Knights 'as a quit rent for the whole' of his property. 'But when war threatened the Order, the commander lost the advantage, and remitted to the treasury the whole profits of its office.' In that event 'a formal intimation was made', as the Pursuivant is now doing to Vilheyna. Vilheyna himself is 'highly esteemed' by his brother knights, who have assigned him 'an important commandery on the coast of Andalusia, the rather that it was chiefly enriched by the gifts of his ancestors, Knights of Malta like himself, whose piety or zeal had bequeathed the property to the Order'. Vilheyna is 'remarkable for his skill in maritime affairs', and his vicinity to the Moors is particularly felt by 'the celebrated Dragut', Viceroy of Algiers, although in later parts of the narrative and of the dialogue he is also referred to as Viceroy of Tunis. Algiers is a stronghold, which, as Scott had noted in his journal on the passage to Malta,[45] the Emperor Charles V made more than one attempt to conquer, but which he was unable to keep in permanent subjection.

In the ceaseless warfare against the Moors, Vilheyna's general advantage has been so constant that, 'especially as the scenes of battle lay within hearing most frequently of the imperial court, he obtained a high reputation both with the famous old emperor and with his successors'. Accordingly he has received as a present from them two fully equipped galleys for the protection of the coast of

Andalusia or for cruising against the Moors, 'in both of which he was indefatigable'. Moreover, 'the Monarch', by whom Scott appears to have meant either Charles V or the present Emperor, Philip II, has added to Vilheyna's power 'in a manner equally distinguished by no equivocal mark of favour'. A considerable tract of country adjacent to the commandery has been 'erected into a royal government', and Vilheyna has received 'the power and privileges attached to the office', which constitutes 'a great augmentation of authority'.

Like most grandees of Spain, he leads 'a retired though active life' with his family, which consists of a niece, Angelica, and a nephew, Francisco, who, having nearly attained 'the regular age of chivalry', has already gone to Malta for formal acceptance as a Knight and has received a gift of broad lands 'in favour of his uncle's merits'. Otherwise he has lived close to Vilheyna and, even more, to the pretty Angelica, whose happy childhood and chivalric games he has shared under the tuition of an accomplished Moorish slave called Morayma. His future, like his property, is bound up with the fortunes of the Knights, while Angelica is intended by her uncle for a nunnery, although Vilheyna, who enjoys their company, is in no hurry to part with them. Accordingly they have remained in the castle of Aldea Bella, which also contains another member of the Order of St John, not exactly a Knight in rank, but a Brother Servant-at-Arms, who bears the same relation to Vilheyna that a squire bears to a Knight. He is a Castilian called Juan Ramegas, a name that Scott appears to have adapted from Commander Romegas, a famous sea-captain of the Knights, prominent in Vertot before the account of the Great Siege but not in the Great Siege itself. Juan Ramegas has become entirely dependent on Vilheyna for preferment, and 'the pride of the man was somewhat touched'. Nevertheless he holds several valuable offices on his master's private estates. It is he who has trained Francisco in the martial skills of the Order, particularly for service at sea in the galleys.

The castle of Aldea Bella itself lies about a mile from the fishing village where the Pursuivant has landed, and as he proceeds towards it, guided by the fisherman, he is informed that Vilheyna is to be found at this hour of sunset not in the castle but in the observatory, where he will be very angry if he is disturbed unless on important business. 'Spare fear on my account, vassal,' answers the Pursuivant, 'my business is such as will excuse my intrusion, even were he in his chapel.' The Pursuivant's dress of Malta cotton and light weapons are then described, as one of the fishermen has a closer look at him, still suspecting him in secret of being a Moor. On sighting the observatory in the distance in a hilly Andalusian landscape clothed in the foliage of advancing summer, he gazes at it with curiosity as a specimen of the fortifications dictated by 'the hasty and sudden attack and defence, which was the system of Spain and Arabia'. A stiff path leads him to the cliff supporting Vilheyna's watch-tower, the technical details of which are described in Scott's familiar manner but not without some clouded writing. The fisherman then explains to the Pursuivant that Vilheyna will not tolerate any stranger remaining in sight of the observatory without his

presence being made known to him 'by voice or by horn'. At this, the Pursuivant
replies haughtily that, when Vilheyna receives the orders he has for him from
the Grand Master-in-Council, 'he must attend the patience of the officer regular[ly] entrusted by them'. Anxious to act by his master's standing instructions
and alienated by the Pursuivant's tone, the fisherman sounds the alarm upon a
bugle horn, which is immediately answered all along the coast by the *tocsin*,
'being the general alarm sounded whenever a party of Moors had landed'.

At the opening of chapter two, the first few lines of which are missing from
the manuscript, but can be supplied from the 1932 typescript, Vilheyna starts
'from a rift of abstracted musing at the rude summons of the horn'. He goes to
a window of the upper storey of the watch-tower, throws it open, and appears
on the balcony. He is a tall, grey, old man, muscular despite his age, and bears
'the marks of "the hero born in other times"'. The only mark distinguishing
his rank is the eight-pointed cross of Malta, 'inscribed on his cloak in scarlet
cloth upon black'. His features betray 'something of anger and surprise', so that
the Pursuivant at once perceives that 'he would greatly exceed his commission
by talking in a high tone to a person of such great importance in the Order as
Don Manuel, and one who had lived so many years in the exercise of uncon-
trolled authority'. Accordingly he shrinks back, leaving it to the fisherman to
announce him as an officer from Malta.

Vilheyna, in a deep solemn tone, invites him to explain briefly his errand,
which he, deferentially and in a tremulous voice, declares to be an announcement that 'an instant and furious invasion of Malta is threatened by the force of
the whole Turkish empire' with the purpose of driving the Knights out of 'the
convent', as their official residence then used to be known. Vilheyna at once
understands that 'you come to intimate the Grand Master's pleasure that I should
as usual repair in person to the Convent with such troops as I can supply by the
revenue of this commandery'. On the Pursuivant's attempting to address him
about the summons from the Grand Master, Vilheyna promptly cuts him short
by telling him that he need not lecture him about 'my duty on this occasion'.
Vilheyna is then used by Scott to introduce the theme of the novel: that of 'the
changed manners of the European nations' when they 'began to renounce the
doctrines of chivalry' at the end of the sixteenth century.[46] For Vilheyna, without specifically touching on the issue of chivalry for the time being, hints at 'the
changed manners' by formally telling the Pursuivant that, although he is aware
that 'the Order, like other powers of Europe, have entrusted of late the manage[ment] of the relations with private persons or foreign states to diplomatists
of your character, I do not approve entirely of this new fashion'. Nevertheless
every able-bodied man within his commandery shall sail for the defence of
Malta, and he will himself implore the King of Spain for 'a right royal succour'
for the Order as 'the most powerful barrier against the Moors, who are such
plagues to His Majesty's dominions in the Mediterranean sea'.

The Pursuivant presumes to remark to Vilheyna that he never doubted his

8. Suleman the Magnificent, Sultan of Turkey (1494–1566), who, in 1564, when he was seventy years old, ordered the invasion of Malta for the spring of the following year.

From a portrait by Melchior Lorch. (By courtesy of the Trustees of the British Museum)

9. Grand Master Jean Parisot de la Valette (1494–1568), the hero of the Knights in the Siege of Malta.

From an engraving by Paul Girardet

response to the summons, only to be again told that 'it is not, however, for a gownsman such as thou art to measure forth my duties to the Order'. Accordingly, 'taking care to depress his voice and manner', he explains that, besides the summons, he is also charged to make known to Vilheyna 'the arguments which weigh with the present Sultan' and his advisers at Constantinople as to the wisdom or otherwise of sending an expedition against the Order, 'which derives so little encouragement from their attempt upon Gozo and Malta' in an earlier, unsuccessful, siege of 1551. Vilheyna assures the Pursuivant that he will consider with proper care 'whatever comes from my venerable brother, the grand master', even though communicated by a herald such as Dhalistan, whose 'rank is something new in the Order' as an office formerly discharged by the Knights themselves. Enjoining silence upon the Pursuivant about the communication from the Grand Master until they will reach the castle of Aldea Bella, Vilheyna invites him to be his guest for the evening, when 'I can hear you discourse at leisure'. He then disappears from the battlements of the tower to make his way to the castle, followed by his squire, Juan Ramegas, 'a tall, dark, severe-looking man', wearing a large silver chain around his neck, and having 'something [of] the aspect of Don Manuel himself'.

The Pursuivant, accompanied by the party of Maltese sailors that he has brought with him, walks close to Ramegas, well behind Vilheyna, and answers the questions that Ramegas puts to him about the state of affairs at Malta with special reference to 'the various preparations for receiving the enemy'. Before passing into the castle, which crowns a rocky mountain and is 'garnished with round and square turrets' similar to those noticed by Scott at Gibraltar,[47] they observe a small hunting party coming back with an immense wild boar as the spoil of the day. The party is led by Vilheyna's nephew, Francisco, riding a jennet. He is remarkably well mounted and distinguished-looking, and bears as 'striking a resemblance' to his uncle 'as a young man can present to an old one'. Vilheyna slackens his pace, while Francisco spurs his horse to ride up to him, and, on falling into his train, he is asked by Vilheyna to account for his delayed response to the *tocsin*. Francisco respectfully puts the blame on the obstinate defence put up by the boar, and assures his uncle that 'I lost no time to satisfy the clamours of the alarm bell'. Pleased with this answer, Vilheyna tells him that Morayma, the Moorish housekeeper, will order the cooks to prepare the boar for supper, as 'a brigantine from Malta has arrived with a messenger, one of those heralds whom the Knights of Malta have now taken into their service, and whom we must treat in complaisance to their new importance'. The Pursuivant's 'ideas of good freedom' urge him to suggest that they might 'waive any alteration of entertainment on his own account', but Vilheyna again rebuts the compliment by remarking in a dry tone that his house will fall back in the world's esteem if it is found to give 'a moment's thought in order to provide entertainment for such as him over and above other inmates of his family'. Blushing at this rebuke, the Pursuivant prudently resolves not to attempt

any further acquaintance with 'this haughty [knight], who had in no sense received him with that consideration which the young man's vanity expected'.

The scene inside the castle is busy with preparations for Vilheyna's galleys,
lying a mile off in the fishing harbour of Aldea Bella, to put instantly to sea.
Workmen, sailors and slaves are engaged in transmitting stores, ammunition,
soldiers and arms. Vilheyna, taking leave of the Pursuivant for a short while,
entrusts him to Ramegas, who resumes his questions about the situation in
Malta, particularly about the 'various improvements made upon the fortifications' since the earlier attack of the Moors of 1551, which had failed to achieve
the results expected by the Sultan, who had hoped to repeat the success he had
had at Rhodes whence the Knights had been expelled to their new home of
Malta. Ramegas avails himself of this opportunity to explain to the Pursuivant
that Vilheyna is unquestionably desirous of hearing accurately from him 'what
happened on the late occasion' of 1551, provided it is put to him with 'sufficient
deference' in keeping with 'our relative situation in the Order'. The Pursuivant,
although remarking that heralds 'are honoured when they have take[n] their
degrees in a college of eminence', assures him that 'my mode of addressing my
masters', including Vilheyna, 'shall be dictated by their ideas of what is proper'.
'Take notice if I give you a hint', answers Ramegas, 'to arise after the supper is
withdrawn, and it will serve as a signal to you to remain for an audience with
the Commander, which would not have been so long delayed if at your first
introduction you had entirely suited the humour of Don Manuel.'

The supper bell summons a large party of fifty dependents and guests to a
plentiful meal, all seated according to strict precedence: Vilheyna, Francisco
and Angelica, 'the three chief dignitaries of the family', alone at high table.
The Pursuivant and his Maltese attendants share a table with Ramegas and
Morayma as 'the chief domestics of Don Manuel's household'. The other ranks
converse together with 'a certain degree of independence' allowed by the
occasion, which is dominated by 'the approaching descent of the Moors' upon
Malta, 'and the consequences which it threatened' for the Knights. After mixing
occasionally in the conversation, Vilheyna, in 'a tone which left no difficulty
to comprehend his inference', tells Ramegas as his squire, who has been 'often
consulted in the affairs of the Order', that he cannot dispense with him in his
impending audience with the Pursuivant. The rest, therefore, are ordered to
leave the hall, and 'take care to prepare the galleys for Malta to launch with the
break of day'. Having pledged the lord of the castle in a grace-cup, they withdraw without noise, including Morayma, who during the meal has paid special
attention to her pupil Angelica, in whom she has spied 'a degree of distress'
unnoticed for the time being by the rest of the company, including Vilheyna.

The Pursuivant waits for Vilheyna to invite him to speak about 'the recent
attack upon Malta and Gozo', which Don Manuel had missed seeing in person
as he had been serving at the time in the German guards of the Spanish
Emperor. 'I am informed', he tells the Pursuivant, however, 'that both islands

were completely plundered and the inhabitants sold for slaves.' The Pursuivant glances at Ramegas for a signal to begin, and through him Scott gives for the benefit of his English readers, but in much clouded writing, an account, partly original and partly derived from Vertot, of the religious wars between the Christians and the Moors, which had eventually so incensed the present Sultan's father that he had besieged and captured Rhodes from the Knights, who in return had been given Malta by Charles V to secure 'a defensible island righ[t] in the middle of his own dominions'. On the Pursuivant's presuming to call Charles V 'that wily prince', he is immediately interrupted by Vilheyna, who served under the Emperor in the siege of La Goletta, the port of Tunis. 'Hold thy peace,' he tells the Pursuivant, 'it is not for such as thee to estimate the motives of the noble emperor's liberality, which it is your duty as a servant of the Order to assign to as firm a foundation as you can see possible.' Chastened by this rebuke, the Pursuivant proceeds to relate how the Knights had harassed Turkish shipping from Malta, culminating in the seizure, 'about a year ago', of a richly laden vessel belonging to the chiefs of the seraglio, which had 'made a great deal of noise' at Constantinople. In consequence the Sultan, who was no other than Suleman the Magnificent, had decided on another and much larger siege of Malta than that of 1551, which had been commanded by, among others, 'a person well known to your Lordship', namely, Vilheyna's old enemy, Dragut.

Vilheyna now begins to find himself increasingly interested in the Pursuivant's account, and orders him to go on: 'you talk it well, it must be owned'. Appreciating the compliment, but still suiting his words to 'the proud Commander's opinion of their different situations', the Pursuivant recapitulates for him—and for Scott's readers unacquainted with Vertot—the arguments, for and against, the projected Siege of Malta, that had been advanced at a council of war called by Suleman to sound the opinions of his principal generals and admirals, including Dragut and a wily old Pacha called Mustapha, who had driven the Knights out of Rhodes. The recapitulation enables Scott to develop the theme of 'changed manners'. For the Pursuivant explains to Vilheyna that Suleman had asked Mustapha, as a kind of old sage, if it was true that 'a great change has taken place among the Franks', including the Knights, 'subverting the very principles on which their ancestors made [war]' in the old days of chivalry, which the Moors connect in Palestine with 'Melec-Ric', that is, Richard I of England. Mustapha, for his part, had admitted that 'unquestionably the great change of principles has taken place among our enemies', principally under the corrupting influence of gold, but at the same time had contended that 'in other respects they press forwards in knowledge and discovery', so much so that he had unsuccessfully tried to dissuade his master from embarking upon the Siege of Malta. Dragut, on the contrary, as the inveterate enemy of the Knights, had urged that it should go forward.

Mustapha, moreover, had clashed on the same issue with Suleman's admiral called Piali, thereby enabling Scott—again through the Pursuivant's account to

Vilheyna—to give the first hint of his intention to develop this rivalry between the two Turkish leaders as a central feature of his novel in contradistinction to its existence only in embryo in Vertot, who also does not touch at all on 'changed manners'. For the Pursuivant recalls to Vilheyna how 'a placid but undisturbed smile hung on the features of Mustapha' as he had drily rebutted Piali's arguments in dialogue, which the Pursuivant reproduces for Vilheyna, who finds it 'highly agreeable' to learn that all this information has been gathered by the Grand Master from Greek spies at Constantinople in the pay of the Order. The conclusion of the Pursuivant's account of 'the Turkish politics' is that Suleman had closed the council of war by appointing Mustapha and Piali in command of the army and navy respectively against Malta with orders 'to take no measures in the siege without the consent of Dragut', who had gone back to Algiers to raise troops from there and—on the evidence of later information—from Tunis.

Thus, unlike the account in Vertot, the same leaders have been appointed for the present siege as in 'the late attack' of 1551, which the Pursuivant, complying with Vilheyna's wishes, now proceeds to describe, not without some confusion on Scott's part, for he appears to have fused it with incidents of the later siege, but otherwise well designed to give the reader a preliminary idea of Malta's fortifications. For the Pursuivant recalls them to Vilheyna in explaining how Mustapha had prevailed on Dragut and Piali to withdraw from a prolonged attack upon them out of fear of a relief force from Sicily under the famous Admiral Doria in the pay of the Spanish Emperor. He also confirms Vilheyna's information that both Malta and Gozo 'were completely plundered and the inhabitants sold for slaves', although he incurs a slight censure from Vilheyna for allegedly taking 'too much liberty in passing your judgement on the honour of a noble Spanish cavalier', who had cowardly surrendered Gozo to Mustapha.

Except for this slight censure, however, Vilheyna is now better disposed towards the Pursuivant on the latter's making an end of his narrative, so that he tells him: 'Young man, although I am one of those who think that your duty could be better performed as usual by the young knights themselves, yet I must allow that . . . you have delivered your message with simplicity and modesty'. 'Let me endure your indignation as a calumniator,' replies the Pursuivant in defence of his communication, including the account of the traitorous Spanish governor of Gozo, 'if I have spoken a word which is not delivered to me for your information by the Grand Master himself, who is most desirous that you especially shall stand fully possessed of the views of the Turkish captains on this important occasion.' Accordingly Vilheyna again invites him to proceed, 'if you have anything further to state which appears to concern your mission', but the Pursuivant explains that, having given him the particulars of the sacking of Gozo by Mustapha—which elicits the typical Scott touch that the episode is now recorded in 'many poems and songs' as part of the folklore of Malta—48'it becomes [me] to be silent, for it would [be] indecent to mention the drunken revels of the corsair Dragut . . . or the threats which he utters against the province of

Spain, which you inhabit, providing he does not meet with you at the Siege of Malta'.

Part Two

At the opening of chapter three in part two of the manuscript, Scott takes over briefly as narrator from the Pursuivant in an attempt to fill in more details of the aftermath of the sacking of Gozo and of the high expectations of Suleman from the impending Siege of Malta.[49] He then returns to Vilheyna, who declares —as Scott's hand begins to become clearer and his writing more fluent and surer—[50] that 'in answer to our neighbour Dragut, who calls himself Viceroy of Tunis, I will take care he is reminded that there never was a Knight of the Order who either loved or feared him, and that the present Don Manuel wears still the same sword which cleft Dragut's helm in the siege of Goletta so many years since'. Then taking up again the theme of 'changed manners' in the context of the religious wars between the Christians and the Moors, and in a formal style of epic declamation, he swears to 'cram the lie down the false throat[s]' of 'the infidels, who pretend our chivalry is degenerated from that which astonished Europe during the time of our fathers'. However 'loathe to compare ourselves to our fathers, who were great warriors, we have been sworn, as they were, to advance the cross, were it with the dearest blood in our body'. 'We therefore stand as much entitled to hope a blessing from Providence as our fathers in theirs, and in such hope and not in the vain confidence of earthly glory, we buckle on our armour', exactly like the old, heroic warrior in Scott's favourite ballad, *Hardyknute*, thereby explaining why he appended three stanzas of that ballad to *The Siege of Malta* as opening motto. It also explains why he was said in Mrs Davy's Malta diary[51] to have cried the ballad up in Malta at the time that he was appending it to page one of the manuscript.

Vilheyna reaffirms, in answer to the Grand Master's summons to Malta, that 'the morning bell shall not break sooner than the two galleys, which by the Emperor's commission I have quartered in the seaport of Aldea Bella, shall set sail with every creature on board, over whom nature and fortune give me any command'. In keeping with the rules affecting every Knight in an emergency such as this, he renounces to the Order 'all personal claim' to his commandery and to 'whatever of treasure I have collected' in a spirit of joy 'that thes[e] old eyes shall see what I have been able to save in this hour of need'. Although his order is for the galleys to sail at once to transport troops, stores, ammunition and the like, 'I must yet absent myself from the island of Malta for two or three days till I throw myself at the Emperor's feet and implore him in this emergency to show himself the same friend to the Order of Malta, which his predecessors in the House of Austria have ever proved themselves, to their own immortal fame and to the inexpressible benefit of Christendom'. In a farewell gesture, therefore, to his retainers, who may have joined the Pursuivant and Ramegas in the hall while he has been speaking, he orders them to 'crown me an bumper as befitting men who exchange their paternal seats to go where their duty calls them'. The pledge is received with 'the deep and enthusiastic cry, with which the Spaniards are in the habit of expressing their sentiments'. The Pursuivant and his Maltese attendants take their leave of Vilheyna to prepare for their return to Malta to report in advance to the Grand Master 'the ready zeal' with which his summons has been received by Vilheyna, 'and the succours which he had advanced toward the convent'. Vilheyna accepts their offer to transport some of his reinforcements in the vessel in which they had come to Aldea Bella, and exchanges some compliments with the Pursuivant, while Ramegas, who will command the two galleys with Francisco, leaves the hall with all those due to sail on the morrow to prepare themselves.

On going to look for Francisco, Ramegas encounters Morayma and Angelica returning to the castle in the midst of the bustle for the galleys' departure, which draws an explanation from Scott as narrator of the reason for that 'degree of distress' in Angelica that Morayma has secretly spied at supper before Vilheyna's audience with the Pursuivant. The explanation leads to the best scene so far in part two of the manuscript, marked by a typical Scott mixture of tender and heroic dialogue. Although Vilheyna, it is explained, has never intended Angelica to make his castle her permanent residence, having destined her for a convent, she has come to respect him over the years, and to exercise a certain influence upon him despite 'the gravity and occasional sternness of his temper'. He, for his part, has been 'willing to grant her any gratification in his power' as his favourite, and she has employed this influence on behalf of such domestics and slaves as have incurred punishment, thereby occasionally subduing 'Don Manuel's harsher determination respecting them'. Nevertheless 'the idea of mourning for a separation from her ancient relative' has never occurred to her imagination. 'The[y] would follow their natural duties, and he in war, she in the duties of the convent, would find their separate and peculiar avocation.' But it is otherwise with her feelings for Francisco as 'the intimate companion of her studies and her amusements' under the indulgent eye of Morayma, who has 'lost her complaisance' with them only when their play has turned on the defeat of the Moors by the Christians, which Francisco 'loved to represent that people as sustaining from the Cid and other Spanish champions'.

Having been born during the siege of La Goletta by the Spaniards, Angelica is now an 'elegant, dark-haired, bright-eyed young lady', deeply attached to Francisco, 'although she had not anticipated the age when this feeling was to awaken in its strength'. Vilheyna has himself never thought it necessary to take measures 'for their ultimate separation'. He is 'better acquainted with the winds, tides and currents than with the caprices of the human heart, and had little apprehension that the intimacy of Francisco might have consequences which should render either one or the other or both averse to the pious profession of a nun of Saint Clare or the chivalrous occupation of a Knight of Malta'. It is, therefore, with 'watery eyes and a tremulous voice' that Angelica approaches

Ramegas on observing the preparations for the loading of the galleys to be on 'the largest scale' consistent with 'the habits of [the] Commander and the customs of his castle'. She is accompanied by Morayma, who is herself 'a tall and fine-looking woman, a certain way advanced in life', and identical in name with a character in a play by Dryden that Scott had edited. The play was *Don Sebastian*. 'Have the Moors landed?' Angelica asks Ramegas, 'and are they in such force?' 'Not here, Signora,' he answers, 'their visits have of late been warmly received, [so] that, unless the infidels are delighted with bones and broken heads, it is not likely that so warm [a] welcome as they have received would encourage them to come here again in a hurry.' Then, echoing the theme of 'changed manners', he adds that 'it seems they are presumptuous enough to think the young men of the Order of Malta are not brought up, as their fathers were, at the sword-belt of the man-at-arms, but at the apron-string of the ladies, and so is shown by their chivalry'. 'What do you think of [this]?' he asks Morayma, 'no one ought to be a better judge.'

'My opinion is only a woman's,' she answers in a mild tone, for 'in the squire Ramegas she was wont to scent a species of enemy on account of the aversion which the old soldier, who had so much interest with her master, entertained to her race, and which in private she returned', even though aware that, if her sentiments are discovered, she runs the risk of dismissal from the castle, to her very great reluctance. She is concerned, moreover, about the impact of Ramegas's news upon Angelica, 'and by way of ascertaining its effect' she says, 'Do you hear, Lady Angelica? Our playfellow is summoned to leave us and go to Madrid with his uncle?' 'Not so, young Lady Angelica. Sir Francisco sets sail this next morning in command of one of our two galleys.' 'But I trust under his uncle's eye,' says Angelica with a stupefied voice, 'as that of one who scarce knew the import of the intelligence she had received.' 'His uncle', answers Ramegas, 'goes to Seville alone to transact some business at the Court of the Emperor, where the presence of Francisco would be somewhat superfluous. No, no, young lady, Francisco must learn to keep company with men, and learn other amusement than to fancy plays.' 'Undoubtedly', says Morayma, 'you at least go with Don Manuel.' 'No, no, Senhora, you have again guessed amiss; both our galleys go to Malta to meet the infidel invasion with Senor Francisco and myself, under my command, as the abler soldier, and I hope to discharge my duty.' 'Certainly,' says Morayma, 'nor is there the least danger, but under your well-known courage Don Francisco will learn to approve his valour without rashly endangering his life.' 'Certainly, Senhora, it must be my business to teach him to defend his honour as far as is consistent with the safety of his life. Adieu, Senhora Morayma. I would leave you with regret were it not that I had to meet some of your complexion long before I see you at Aldea Bella again. Send Francisco to me, should he come hither; we must both be ready to sail with peep of day to-morrow, and cannot spare time for leave-taking.'

Having said so, Ramegas leaves the empty apartment of the castle, and

Morayma does not fail to 'observe this important person's departure with a most ceremonious reverence such as prudent matrons render to those whom they at the same time dislike and fear'. Soon the deep tones of his voice summoning Francisco are heard sounding along the vaulted ceiling of the ante-room. On finding herself alone with Angelica, Morayma 'ventured to catch a glimpse of her charge, who now comprehended enough of what was going [on] to believe that the preparation was in progress, which should, with respect to the objects, for which they mutually hitherto existed, become perpetually changed'. 'A burst of hysterical passion' follows in a scene treated by Scott in the familiar manner of 'sensibility' in the eighteenth-century novel, complete with rhetorical questions for advancing the narrative. 'The tears ran in fountains to her eyes, but without obtaining the usual relief of overflowing the natural vent in which they are deposited.' Even 'the laces of her corsette became too tight for her bosom', and 'her sufferance at the moment nearly amounted to suffocation', as 'the veins of her arms and forehead were swelled and blue'. The whole appearance is 'that of a girl feeling for the first time an extremity of distress, though she scarcely could understand the cause'. 'If there was any room for lamenting Francisco, would not he himself express sorrow or gravity at least? But no horse-boy in the castle rejoiced more than did her cousin at the hopes of exchanging the dull hunting parties of Aldea Bella for the prospect of a serious war with the Turks in defence of what he had been taught to consider as the dearest duty of his life.' Besides, in view of his uncle's influence, he is likely to be 'placed in an honourable power of discharge' in the war.

As he hastily passes through the dining-chamber of the castle, having partly put on the dress indicating his rank as a Knight of Malta, his eye falls on Angelica, and reminds him of 'a duty which he had till that moment forgotten'. Advancing to her in haste, he takes her kindly into his arms, 'pressed her to his bosom, and kissed her as an affectionate sister would have on a similar occasion parted from her brother when he departed for the wars'. Poor Angelica, however, 'was formed with the strong warmth of her country women, and the touch of her lover's lips brought to a species of syncope the state of agony, under which she suffered'. 'The long eye lashes no longer withheld the flood of tears, by which Nature desired to express her feelings, and while she hung about Francisco's neck, and pressed her lips to his, her burst of repeated sobs, and the copious flow of tears rendered her like a person entirely out of her mind [rather] than a maiden undergoing for the first time the influence of a sorrow, which she felt as the first and most engrossing, which she had sustained in the course of her short life.'

Although the bustle and hurry in the castle are so great as to threaten constant interruption to Morayma, especially for the keys and articles under her charge, she becomes anxious 'lest her pupil should be surprised in the shadows of abandonment to her passion', which might elicit a reproach from Vilheyna that such conduct is incompatible with the duties of 'a young hospitaller' and of a future nun, so that Morayma trembles to think of the consequences of Vil-

10. Grand Master Philippe Villiers de L'Isle Adam (1464–1534), defender of Rhodes and First Grand Master of the Order of St John in Malta.

From a painting by Gillot Saint-Evre, engraved by Charles Amédée Colin

11. René d'Aubert de Vertot (1655–1735), historian of the Order of St John: Scott's principal source for *The Siege of Malta*.

From a painting by J. Delÿen, engraved by Laurent Cars

heyna's getting to know of this passionate embrace of the two cousins.
She therefore interfered between the two lovers, and bestowing a
number of tender caresses upon Angelica, contrived in that manner,
with an affectation of great sympathy, to interpose between her and
Don Francisco, with whom she had enjoyed a sufficiently long scene
of parting, and to which she earnestly desired a stop should be put
for the sake of the children themselves, to whom it might give
serious pain. At first there was some difficulty in accomplishing
this separation. Resigning herself to the blandishments, with which
her governess overwhelmed her, and in some degree ashamed at the
ecstasy of passion, which she could not [but] judge likely to prejudice
[her] in the opinion of her cousin, she yet resisted the efforts which
her cousin made to return the tokens of affection, with which she
had overwhelmed [him]; yet it was not without submitting to a
farewell kiss and embrace that, withdrawing from the arms of the
young man, she transferred herself to Morayma as a supporter, and
left the chamber in her company for their common bedroom.

There she also suffers distress for the dangers, in which she supposes Francisco
involved. 'Morayma endeavoured to comfort her by the common arguments
that what was put in peril was far from being lost, and that, not to go beyond
her family for examples, Don Manuel had taken arms three times at least for the
relief of Malta, and had returned home with victory and increased reputation
each time. The poor girl listened to such comfort as Morayma had it in her
power to bestow upon her, but tears and sobs were the only answers which the
afflicted maiden was able to return, while she endeavoured to anticipate the
return of her cousin Francisco, until, exhausted by the feelings which chased
each other through her mind, her sorrow at last gave way to sleep.' In her sleep
she is caressed by Morayma, who hopes that she may find Angelica, on awaken-
ing, composed and strengthened in mind 'to encounter the affliction which it
might be heaven's pleasure to send with the dawning of the new day, contrary
to the custom in the castle of Don Manuel'. Eventually Morayma, after a
succession of heavy thoughts, herself falls asleep.

The morning is filled with a number of warlike sounds, 'the consequence of
the orders which had been given to fit the galleys out to sea'. The *tocsin* is rung
in many parishes besides Aldea Bella, carrying from spire to spire 'the news of
the Moors being in motion', and warning 'the troops of every kind and where-
ever quartered' to assemble 'in convenient places to prepare resistance where
inroad might be expected'. Angelica rises from her bed even before the sun has
illuminated the neighbouring mountains, and, accompanied by Morayma, gains
the top of the village by ascending a secret staircase. There they find themselves
'among the walls and turrets of Andalusia, when the eastern horizon was already
edged with light, permitting them a view of the Mediterranean and a sight of
vessels, which had for various purposes taken arms at the summons of Don

Manuel'. The vessels that most attract the attention of 'the sorrowful young lady' are her uncle's galleys, particularly that commanded by Francisco, which has just put to sea. All the craft are deeply laden with soldiers, timber, beams and stores for assisting the besieged in Malta. After clearing the little harbour, they hold course to the east, as Ramegas and Francisco are anxious to comply with Vilheyna's special order that his troops should be among the foremost in appearing before Malta as well furnished as possible.

Vilheyna himself is on the battlements, watching with Angelica, and observes 'the eagerness with which she advanced her fresh spy-glass' to mark the disappearing vessels. Having given his niece 'a civil good morning', he notices on her cheeks and eyes the traces of tears.

> As Morayma was not near enough to suggest any answer to this question, the little maiden answered by pronouncing her cousin's name as the cause of her discomposure. Far from being disposed to blame her, Don Manuel answered her with perfect good temper: "Your concern in favour of your cousin, Angelica, is far from being blameable; on the contrary, I commend you for it. He has been our companion for many years, and now leaves us to encounter many dangers. Let us hope Our Lady will protect him, and do not forget him in thy prayers; the purity and piety of a creature at thy years finds access to the heavens, and the Virgin herself stoops to hear thee. Remember then to pray for the safety of thy cousin, and be confident in thy access to Our Lady of Grace, and forget not thy old uncle also, though he may at times seem little meriting thy prayers. But it is little I ask, Angelica, and that little is only a close befitting the life I have led for so many years under the influence of the blessed Cross. Even Our Lady may be reminded of the services of the House of Vilheyna and Aldea Bella, and all I ask for myself is one good blow at my old enemy Dragut; and even should the infidel savage get the better, he will not win more glory than a life of many victories can well afford to [see] deducted from its close."

Angelica exerts herself to maintain her composure in the tumult of 'the varied and mournful recollections' evoked by her uncle's speech to her. There is 'a stern, deep melancholy in Don Manuel's voice, which she had not observed on other occasions'. This 'vein of pathetic feeling' was not natural to 'his blunt and rugged temper'. He also recalls to her 'the nature of her own destiny, which she regarded for the first moment as a farewell to all the pleasures, duties and enjoyments of worldly existence, which were the share of more fortunate females'. Happily there is no time to indulge in 'the stream of thought, which would naturally have arisen on these recollections, and Morayma saw with pleasure that her charge saw the propriety of repressing them'. Morayma, therefore, indicates to Angelica that, instead of giving way to 'thoughts which could only be unavailing, she should see breakfast prepared for her uncle', who is about to set out for the Spanish Emperor's present residence at Seville. Vilheyna, however, who is in armour, himself orders his attendants to serve him with 'the chocolate which was now a general breakfast in such parts of Spain as were in the course of communication with the western world'. Morayma meanwhile ventures to express a hope that they may see him on his return from Seville for Cadiz, where he intends to embark for Malta. But he replies that another call at Aldea Bella would mean 'a longer delay than I dare venture to excuse' to himself at the moment, 'since I must go to Malta as a thief in the night'. From what he can discover, 'the infidels are already disembarked, and the service of every man whom we can command is peremptorily demanded'. As he leaves for his journey, at the end of chapter three, his brown horse, conscious of his approach, paws proudly on the paved court, and Vilheyna hastens 'to meet this old companion of former labours'.

At the opening of chapter four Scott shifts the scene rapidly from Spain to Malta, for he considers it unnecessary 'to mention the splendid manner in which our Commander of Don Manuel was received at the Court of the King of Spain', who makes 'the most magnificent promises of supports' to be sent in due course to Malta for the Knights. Accordingly Vilheyna sails from Cadiz in a Sicilian frigate, which, on approaching the coast of Malta, he exchanges for a very small, half-decked, light boat called a *speronaro*. In it, on the evening of the third day after his departure from Spain, he sights the northern coast of Malta, which Scott had himself approached in the *Barham* on the morning of 21st November 1831.[52] Vilheyna takes every possible precaution to avoid falling in with the Turkish cruisers, as it is widely known that the warships commanded by Admiral Piali and bearing the invading army under Mustapha, the Pacha of Egypt, have orders to rendezvous on the western side of Malta, 'so that about this time they were to be looked out for in almost every direction'. To escape what would have been 'a very mortifying capture', Vilheyna is rowed in the *speronaro* by six strong Maltese sailors, with long experience at sea, having served on board the largest of his galleys called the *Lynx*, which has already sailed for Malta under the command of Ramegas together with the other galley commanded by Francisco. Vilheyna's Maltese crew, thanks to their higher pay, have always been employed in the most dangerous service, 'like those who in modern times are called captains of the top'. Every precaution has been taken by them to conceal the real purpose of the *speronaro*, which, moreover, being flat and narrow, has the advantage of being able to go extremely near the shore and seek shelter, in case of attack or bad weather, in the rocky inlets. The Turkish galleys, in fact, often did not bother—contrary to their orders—to pursue the *speronari*, first, because their smallness rendered them petty as prizes, and, second, because of 'the great trouble of securing men who were so well acquainted with the shoaly and rocky coast'.

Despite all these precautions Vilheyna has a very narrow escape, which Scott relates with his familiar mastery of battle-scenes in graphic action, flavoured, as in *The Talisman*, with oriental touches, and interspersed, towards the end of the episode, with dialogue of epic courage in Scott's best manner. The action takes place in one of the many bays which render Malta 'so remarkably fitted for the marauding profession of the Knights'. Vilheyna's crew, emboldened by their supposed freedom from danger, enter the bay in the hope of running the *speronaro* upon the sands and getting safe to the shore by swimming, when they perceive to their horror that they are running straight in the teeth of a flotilla of stout Algerian galleys, displaying as their ensign a green turban above a drawn sabre in a sable field. The Maltese crew put about the *speronaro*, whispering to each other that "By Saint Mary, they were Draguntines", which is the name for 'the dexterous and dangerous corsairs' fitted out at Tunis and other ports where Dragut holds sway. 'The very recollection of his name stirred to action those mariners who had so often seen his sails sink before those of their master'; but just as the *speronaro* stands across the bay to gain the outward sea, her crew hear the close pursuit behind them, accompanied by 'the furious cry of the corsair calling upon her *ciurma*' or galley-slaves 'to urge their utmost exertions' in order that her sailors may dash from the bowsprit and yards upon the *speronaro* for booty, which they expect to be considerable from the prospect of its carrying a disguised Knight. The eager yell of the corsair's sailors combined with 'the extorted cry of the galley-slave, half expressing a sense of panic, half a feeling of sorrow, which followed every succeeding application of the terrible *tchabouk*' or lash, produces 'a motley chorus of noises', which, heard as it is by the *speronaro's* crew, 'who considered it as an inevitable [omen?] of death and endless captivity, was a shriek of an import the most frightful which could assail the human ear'.

Vilheyna's crew, however, show neither fear nor hesitation nor 'even a moment's doubt in the luck of the Commander, who had so often led them to victory'. They apply themselves to their oars 'with an agility surprising to their pursuers, although the latter had the advantage of being manned with seamen refreshed with rest and food, neither of which Don Manuel's crew had been latterly able to indulge in'. Holding on their course, therefore, and still keeping ahead of their pursuers, thanks in some measure to their knowledge of the navigation of the shoals of the rocky coast, they attempt to protract their flight by every means within their power in the hope of finding 'the shore occupied by some Christian post or protected by some Christian cruiser'. In time, however, they begin to perceive that 'the enemies' superiority of sail gained them an opportunity of firing on the chase with an effect which gradually increased'. 'As one thick cloud of smoke after another, preceded by a rapid flash, accounted for the almost momentary pause, which the rowers might make on their oars, to favour the marksman's aim, the ejaculation of some European intimated that the shot of the musketeer had been successful.'

At length a young man drops mortally wounded beside his comrade, an old seaman called Boniface, who is also his father, and 'hitherto one of the most active' of the crew. On hearing the groan of the young man as he is hit, he drops for one instant his oar, and falls forward, as if the same bullet has hit him too. 'Boniface,' says Vilheyna, 'I have seen thee laugh at a whole hail storm of shots such as this.' 'But those did not light in the heart of my son.' 'He has died by thy side, honest friend,' answers Vilheyna, 'Be comforted, Heaven is better than earth, and the mercies of God are to trust to rather than those of the infamous Dragut. Prove that you think so;' continues Vilheyna in a whispering tone, suggesting a desperate measure to avoid capture, 'when these infidels shall take this galley, fire our handful of powder, and God speed us all.' 'May God say Amen,' says Boniface, 'and my poor unfortunate's body shall go to the grave unmangled by the butchery of the infidel miscreants. Only one thing, my Lord, blame me not if I reserve this final sacrifice until the last moment, when it is the voice of the Deity himself who shall bid us strike.' 'Take thy time, but be faithful. Whenever that dog Dragut shall be the first to step over the side of the little boat, which still defies him, neither you nor I will survive to be termed his slaves. Be ready then,' says Don Manuel, 'and I will thank you in heaven.' Stretching his arm to embrace the dead body of his son, Boniface responds by holding in his hand 'a pistol which was pointed into the slender stock, to which the Commander's charge had relation'.

Boniface then changes his place to the first oar in the *speronaro*, and applying himself, renews the impulse which his son's mortal wound has for a short time interrupted, and 'the Christian bark once more sprang ahead of its pursuers with repeated cries of hope and despair'. At length she seeks refuge in a bay protected by one of the various batteries scattered on Malta's coast against sudden descents by Turkish corsairs to pillage and carry the inhabitants into captivity. The *speronaro* displays her colours to 'invite the succour of the Christian engineers, who immediately opened their fire upon the pursuers, and with a success by which one of them was sunk'. The captain of the largest and best armed of the corsairs, however, 'had urged the whole of his crew to the utmost exertion, knowing it was probable from the display of colours on board the *speronaro* that she was commanded by Don Manuel in person'. He, therefore, runs his vessel with her full weight against that of Vilheyna, taking his chance to escape on board the rest of the Algerian flotilla. But he does not reckon on the celebrated mortars of the Knights, which are capable of destroying any vessel within reach. As the corsair and the *speronaro* rush together, 'a voice from the shore called to discharge the mortars, preferring that both parties should perish together than that their Christian friends, with whose distinguished cognizance they were not [un]acquainted, should be made prisoners in their own sight'.

The bows of the corsair hardly touch the *speronaro* when Boniface discharges his pistol, 'and at the same time a concussion like that of a thunder cloud' ascends from the bay, 'and shot to the heavens the contents of the fatal mortar', which overwhelm both vessels with a perpendicular shower of missiles thrown up to the sky. 'The *speronaro*, from the desperate action of Boniface, made a sudden explosion', but immediately another galley, hitherto concealed by the rocks, 'entered upon the scene, apparently with the premeditated wish to share its dangers'. Her crew 'urge her with all the impulse that they could command to the pendent fragments of the vessels, which had met each other with so fatal [a] collision', but, though she loses several men by the shower of the contents of the mortar, 'yet she was far from suffering the ruin which might have been expected'. 'On the contrary, the exertions of her crew, particularly a young man, who appeared to be her commander, recovered from the wreck of the *speronaro* those of the crew who had not suffered, while the Moorish cruisers bore off and escaped from the Christian galley in different directions.' A boat, rowing swiftly, soon brings on board the galley a young soldier, who tells her commander, 'Noble my Lord, we have saved your uncle by holding our shields over his head, and defending him against the shower of stones.' Thus by a somewhat contrived coincidence so common in Scott's novels and in those of his period, the commander of the galley proves to be Francisco, who is reunited with Vilheyna, who justifies the faith of his crew in his luck by miraculously escaping —as does Boniface—with but minor injuries.

At this point of Scott's narrative, just before the end of chapter four, there is another sheet of manuscript nearly half cut off. The text of it is also missing from the 1932 typescript, but it is clear from the next sheet of the manuscript that, immediately after his reunion with Francisco, Vilheyna is warmly welcomed to Malta by the Grand Master, who may have been on a tour of inspection of the defences in the vicinity, for he is now actually on board Francisco's galley. He is, of course, the celebrated, or rather, the soon-to-be-celebrated Jean de La Valette, and Vilheyna gratefully acknowledges to him 'the ready help of my provident friends' before he reminds him that 'I have been so long a stranger at Malta' that perhaps 'you would wish to show me what preparation you have made for the reception of these unchristian villains'. La Valette, addressing him, in strict decorum, as 'my brother', explains that he had first thought of proposing that they take the road together, with Francisco, to the great fortress of Saint Angelo, the citadel of Malta, which 'you will find still in the same place, where it was long since built by our brother, our celebrated Villiers de L'Isle Adam', the hero of Rhodes and the first Grand Master of Malta. 'But I fear the exercise will be rather unsuitable with the injuries you have sustained by this accident.' 'Far from it,' replies Vilheyna, 'I would not have our young knights' think that he was prevented by a shower of stones from mounting his war-horse. Accordingly the skiff of the galley is instantly set afloat, and presently conveys to the shore 'the Grand Master with the aged and juvenile companion[s] of the Order'. When they set foot on the mainland, La Valette's steed is ready at his command, and he leaves some directions with the commander of the post. They then proceed on horseback with their attendants, including, apparently, Ramegas, although he does not appear again until much later.

In the meantime La Valette tells Vilheyna that 'in riding to the convent', meaning Fort St Angelo, 'I will acquaint you with something, of which you cannot yet be informed', thereby linking chapter five in part two of the manuscript with the Pursuivant's earlier information about the origin of the Siege of Malta. For La Valette gives Vilheyna—and, of course, the reader—the necessary information, but remarkably briefly, about the fortifications, soil and troops of Malta and the expected reinforcements of Knights and Spanish regiments from Sicily. Above all, he emphasises that he has ordered the small garrison of Fort St Elmo, guarding the entrance to the Grand Harbour of Malta, that they must 'defend it to the last extremity' to gain time for the reinforcements to come from Sicily, even though it is untenable, and they risk 'the severe penalty of being excluded from quarter, as having protracted by their useless valour the resistance of an untenable place'. Although La Valette has other important information to communicate to Vilheyna with a bearing on the theme of 'changed manners', Scott defers it to the next chapter in order to recapitulate in his own person as narrator[53] the first phase of the Siege of Malta, which has already taken place in Vilheyna's absence on the passage to Malta. The gist of the recapitulation is that a very large army under Mustapha has disembarked from Admiral Piali's warships in the absence of Dragut at Algiers, whence he is, however, daily expected, and that Piali has prevailed on Mustapha and the other leaders to open the siege with an attack on Fort St Elmo as a *seemingly* easy prize but as essential for a safe anchorage for his fleet in the event of the arrival of the reinforcements from Sicily. Although the details of the disembarkation and the subsequent incidents are naturally derived by Scott from Vertot, he *reverses* the roles of Piali and Mustapha in the decision to attack Fort St Elmo, thereby making Piali play a much larger part in the progress of the siege than in Vertot through a series of original incidents, with dialogue, interspersed in the narrative.

More important than this reversal of roles, however, is the *dramatic* exploitation of the rivalry and distrust between the two Turkish leaders, as a continuation and development of the friction first reported to Vilheyna in Spain by the Pursuivant. It comes to the fore at once, immediately after the opening of the siege with the first attack on Fort St Elmo, which is related as part of the recapitulation with all Scott's familiar knowledge of sieges, helped in this instance with information from Vertot. Although the action and weapons of the siege recall *Ivanhoe*, the exploitation of the jealousy and distrust between the Turkish leaders is more of a parallel to the discords and intrigues of the Christian leaders during the Crusades in *The Talisman*. The friction, moreover, between Piali and Mustapha is directly linked with the theme of 'changed manners' in an original scene, which deserves more detailed treatment not only on that account but also to bring out the striking presentation of the 'profound dissimulation' of Mustapha as perhaps one of the best achievements of the novel. The scene occurs after the failure of Piali's first attack on Fort St Elmo, which the Knights

repulse, with heavy loss to the Turks, by flinging burning hoops on the besiegers, whose very inflammable dresses at once catch fire, so that 'the screams
of the wretches, who by these means were literally burned alive, were heard
far above the tremendous noise of the fire on both sides as well as the cries or
groans of the combatants, fighting or dying on both sides'.

This setback to Piali, however, does not make him lose courage, as he pins
his hopes of ultimate success upon the overwhelmingly superior numbers of his
and Mustapha's troops, whom he orders to excavate a trench before Fort St
Elmo in order to storm it. Bearing in mind, however, the Sultan's positive
orders to him and to Mustapha, as already reported to Vilheyna by the Pursuivant, that they are 'to take no measures in the siege without the consent of
Dragut', Piali considers that it is 'safest to postpone the final attempt to storm
till the arrival of the Viceroy'. In the meantime news has reached him that the
garrison of St Elmo 'were already murmuring at the orders which condemned
them to lay down their lives in a task, which could not have an honourable or
a successful issue'. He therefore approaches Mustapha to discuss this subject with
him, although it is notorious that Mustapha 'seldom voluntarily entered upon
state affairs except in answer to the Sultan's personal inquiries, and had an
especial jealousy of the Capitan Pacha', as the Turkish admiral was officially
called, 'and not the less since he adopted the bold measure of commencing the
siege without either Dragut's express approbation or his own'. For Mustapha
has consented to Piali's plan without enthusiam. Piali addresses him as 'my
father', since Mustapha, who is aged sixty-five in Vertot, is deliberately said by
Scott to be eighty. 'This ground of Malta', Piali tells him, 'is as impossible to
the pickaxe and shovel', since, as Scott has already emphasised, it has a very
shallow soil, inimical to trenches. 'The Knights have been thought invulnerable
to the usual animal sensations of danger or of fear; yet, believe me, father, the
time is come when we shall at the same time mine the impenetrable rock of
Malta and impress fear upon the irrefragable courage of the Knights.'

'The better for you, my Lord of the sea,' answers Mustapha laconically and
at the same time astutely, since he neither wishes 'to commit himself by assenting
to the plan of operations before the Viceroy of Algiers was arrived, which might
be interpreted into an express disobedience of their instructions', nor is he
'willing to hazard his own credit with the Sultan by claiming to share the merit
of having been participant of an attempt, the consequence of which was yet
uncertain'. Mustapha, therefore, in strict adherence to the best traditions of
Turkish diplomacy as practised by 'the great favourites at the Porte', observes
'the same policy during the whole discussion', on the one hand, 'preserving the
means of having suggested the attack upon Saint Elmo thus early in their campaign', and sharing the credit for it with Piali, if successful, and, on the other
hand, if unsuccessful, 'resolved to throw the blame upon the Viceroy for not
having come up to assist them with his advice in the very commencement of
their campaign'. For Mustapha is even more jealous of Dragut than of Piali,

since Dragut's 'reputation', in Scott's own words in the earlier recapitulation, 'was the envy of every rais [sea-captain] in the Turkish service'.

Mustapha's jealousy of Dragut, however, is still to come in this dialogue. For the time being he wants to fathom the grounds for Piali's hope of eventual success against Fort St Elmo. But he comes to this obliquely through calculated self-depreciation and flattery. 'I feel myself with greater reason', he tells Piali, 'the infirmities of an old man', which prevent his 'experience of former days ... being ready to his memory as his duty would require or his goodwill would demand of him'. He is therefore 'most happy to find himself yoked with a colleague, whose profound knowledge and military experience can remedy all the deficiencies, which are the necessary consequence of the fourscore years that have [passed] over this old head of mine'. His infirmities have diminished 'my power of revenging the honour of my gracious master, who[se] wish ought to operate as a powerful medicine, restoring our decayed faculties, both of mind and body, when we are honoured with the approbation of our earlier services'. Since, however, 'even the Gran Seignior himself cannot restore to old age the promptitude and the experience of early youth', it is only just that their master should have matched 'a poor veteran' like Mustapha with 'a man like yourself, so far from having passed the time of action'. And as 'the result of your plans promises success, I should esteem myself honoured by your entrusting me with the grounds' on which Piali bases 'the joyous hopes that the garrison of Saint Elmo is likely to surrender or to mutiny' against La Valette, 'their grand vizier', as Mustapha calls him, who 'has enjoined them by positive orders to continue their defence at all risks'.

'The question', answers Piali, echoing precisely what had been said on the theme of 'changed manners' at the first council of war held at Constantinople to determine on the Siege of Malta, 'would seem strange from your Lordship, had I not heard in the counsel of our nation the most honoured tongue[s] and eloquent lips, who are called to the Turkish council, aver repeatedly that our enemies are changed in their manners, and no longer hold themselves bound to fight to the same extremity as they did in the ancient days of Melec-Ric and the other heroes of the days termed of chivalry.' Piali annoys Mustapha with this remark, not because it is untruthful, but because ironically it puts him in the embarrassing position of 'one who finds his own favourite' opinions quoted against him in a piece of dialogue that is technically perhaps Scott's most subtle structural link with the earlier account of the Pursuivant to Vilheyna. In consequence Mustapha, while admitting, with some petulance, that 'I have said that such a change is beginning among the Knights of the Order', denies that it 'has reached the superiors of the Order', represented par excellence by Vilheyna and La Valette at present and by Villiers de L'Isle Adam in the past. 'Look around, my Lord,' he then exclaims in vigorous oratory and in full view of Malta's defences, 'and think of the immense expenses which have called such batteries and fortifications out of the barren rock, which they are meant to defend. Look at your own muster rolls, and number how many thousand[s] of your best forces have fallen before the smallest fort of the whole, which it is our duty to make ourselves masters of, and say if the Christians, who have defended themselves desperately against such extreme odds, are in [any] respect changed from the countrymen of Melec-Ric.'

'I can only answer to your Lordship', replies Piali, again echoing Mustapha's own words on this subject to the Sultan Suleman in the Pursuivant's account to Vilheyna, 'that gold is found as powerful among the Christian knights and soldiers as in every other country.' Denying this suggestion that the Knights have become 'the slaves of gold' and therefore degenerate in comparison with their ancestors, Mustapha challenges Piali to send an ultimatum to the defenders of St Elmo. 'If you rely upon the slaves of gold,' he tells him, 'for such are seen everywhere, being so much alarmed as to shrink from the clang of your trumpets and the clash of your sabres, send your summons before you', that the Knights of St Elmo 'may know at what risk they constitute themselves defenders of it till the last gasp'. 'The laws of war everywhere forbid [the] bestowing of quarter upon men who exposed themselves in such bravado to the defence of a post which cannot be termed tenable.'

'Reverend my master,' answers Piali, 'your counsel shall be obeyed, and many thanks to you for honouring us with the fruits of your sage experience.' But before explaining how he proposes to follow up Mustapha's advice, he returns to the reported discontent among the defenders of Fort St Elmo, which, he informs Mustapha, has resulted in the Grand Master's having decided to send 'a commission of three persons, from whom he hoped to procure an opinion to vindicate his desperate plan of still defend[ing] this feeble' fort to the last. Piali, therefore, proposes that they 'send into St Elmo an embassy, which, arriving at the same time with those from their Mufti or grand vizier, may instruct them at what risk they will attempt to execute his desperate pleasure, and incline them to a capitulation, of which, if such be your pleasure, we can afterwards modify the terms'. Mustapha, while slyly professing that 'I will not certainly dissent from anything necessary in your opinion to the success of your undertaking, in which I take as much interest as I should in a device of my own or of the Viceroy's', reminds Piali that 'Dragut, I think, will be with us presently'. 'Ought we not to wait a day for his arrival?' But Piali dissents on the ground that 'the active operations have commenced'. Although 'it might have been prudent to have suspended these on account of Dragut's absence', to do so now would 'ensure a great addition to the loss of the faithful', meaning, of course, their own soldiers, who are 'so dissatisfied with that which has already taken place'.

At this point at last, but again obliquely, or rather, by innuendo and mystification, Mustapha is made by Scott to throw out the first hint of his jealousy and suspicion of Dragut. 'Nay, assuredly,' he answers Piali, 'the having determined on the siege of St Elmo without consulting Dragut renders it unnecessary to suspend' operations now. 'Be it said too among ourselves that Dragut is peculiarly interested in those measures which embrace the safety of Algiers, an attempt upon which has been threatened by the Spanish Emperor or part of his forces. So Dragut, if he be again lucky, may appear at our council with the appearance of a conqueror, as a falcon never stoops so proudly to his master as when he has his prey in his clutch.' With this apt image from a field sport that Scott knew so well, Mustapha takes his leave of Piali, and in doing so, 'they exchanged a peculiar smile, which seemed to announce them as putting upon what Mustapha said a mystical and singular interpretation understood by both'. Piali explains to Mustapha, 'with the air of a person who suddenly recollects himself', that whereas the troops under his charge are encamped on 'the eminence called Sceberras', corresponding to modern Valletta, 'yours are disposed in the neighbour[hood] of the Grand Master's country-house called Saint Antonio', which, of course, was non-existent during the siege, but which Scott had come to know well during his own visit to Malta as the temporary residence, in the Governor's absence in England, of John Hookham Frere.54 He therefore allows himself the first of many anachronisms in the novel.

Piali admits that Saint Antonio 'is by much the more healthy of the two' sites, but he tells Mustapha that 'I would ask if we were safe in lying at too great a distance separate,' particularly as 'these Christians are sufficiently enterprising'. 'Having lain thus since we landed,' answers Mustapha, 'I do not imagine that we shall increase the hazard of attack, if we delayed joining till Dragut shall arrive to arrange our posts when he has taken order for that of Algiers.' Piali's only reply is 'a smile as before, when the arrival of Dragut had been mentioned', as a hint that his confidence is not great 'either in the certainty of his speedy arrival or his decisive ability when he should at length appear'. If Mustapha's belief is the same as Piali's, he takes the greatest care not to reveal it in view of his master Suleman's contrary opinion. So he does not even share Piali's smile at the end of the scene, although elsewhere Scott invests him with a smile as a mark of his sardonic humour.

There is nothing like this scene in Vertot, for Scott is creatively using history to enrich the 'original story' of his novel. In sharp contrast to this dialogue, but closely linked to it by the theme of 'changed manners', particularly in the light of Piali's disclosure to Mustapha about La Valette's appointment of three commissioners to report about the situation of the defenders of Fort St Elmo, is the next chapter, which is number six, in the same part two of the manuscript. It returns to Vilheyna riding with La Valette towards Fort St Angelo, and having 'a confidential communication on the same subject', although initially, as Vilheyna is Spanish, it is set in a literary context typical of Scott as a lover of Cervantes. Indeed, in one passage he seems to identify himself with the Spanish author, although in another, as has already been suggested in a previous chapter,55 it is with Don Quixote that he associates some of his most prized ideals. First he emphasises that Vilheyna and La Valette differ from Piali and Mustapha in that 'the reliance of the two Christian knights on the skill and prudence, which each imputed to the other, had long been tried' and vindicated, whereas that between the two pachas 'was faithless and marked with much falsehood and rivalry, each having at heart his own advancement and the depreciation of his colleague in the opinion of their common master'. Nevertheless their conversation is also domin-ated by the situation in Fort St Elmo with reference to the change that 'was about to take place in the Order of Malta and among Christians in general res-pecting the principles upon which they acted' as Knights and gentlemen. Vilheyna deplores not only that 'we should have relinquished or at least aban-doned the dictates of honour and chivalry' but also that 'these infidel miscreants should have had acuteness to perceive it'. Instances abounded of 'the opinions of our fathers' being held up 'to the ridicule of their descendants, and with such success that he is a dull man who would not, when almost dying, listen and laugh at the history of Don Quixote'.

'I have read part of that book you mention,' answers La Valette, but 'the emergency of these times, which leave[s] a Grand Master of the Order little time for such studies', has prevented him from finishing it. Unable to applaud enough 'the genius of the author', Vilheyna explains that, being lately at the court of King Philip of Spain, 'I studied to find the author, and bring him out with me to this siege of Malta, that Miguel de Cervantes, who has the merit of having written a work so incomparable'. Moreover, Cervantes has 'served against the Moors with good reputation' in Charles V's army, so that Vilheyna is about to add that he would have been no misfit in Malta, when La Valette politely questions whether he 'would be useful to us at such a time', although 'I am certainly willing to doubt my own good judgement' in deference to Don Manuel's. Then, admitting that, although 'our business here is rather of a grave and melancholy cast', a person such as Cervantes 'could turn our mourning into mirth', he asks Vilheyna why he did not bring him to Malta. Vilheyna's answer is exactly that given by Scott himself in his journal when he had been offered a seat on the Scottish bench in his financial ruin, but had declined it on the ground that 'I will not seek *ex elemosyna* a place which, had I turned my studies that way, I might have aspired to long ago *ex meritis*'.[56] 'Alas,' Vilheyna exclaims to La Valette, 'Fortune deals her favours with strange partiality, that she has afflicted with the iron gripe of poverty this same Cervantes, whom in other respects she has gifted so highly, and what is worse, has given him a soul [so] delicate that it would be difficult to [per]suade him to accept that bread as elymosynary which he would think he was incapable of toiling to earn.'

Besides, Cervantes—and here Scott allows himself a second anachronism—has lost his right hand 'at the battle of Lepanto', so that Vilheyna considers him 'unfit for further service in action'. Nevertheless 'he is a poet as well as a romancer, and, although his most celebrated work has turned upon ridiculing the *extravagances* of chivalry', but not chivalry itself, 'yet no man in Spain is more capable of impelling his countrymen' to the call of patriotism or of honour, 'like others of the same talents in Greece or other countries'. For that reason it 'would be graceful in our sovereign to extend his bounty to such a well-deserving gentleman', particularly as King Philip II is himself not ignorant of Cervantes' merit, as proved by an anecdote recollected by Vilheyna to La Valette, which is really a variant of the anecdote that Scott had himself heard from Lockhart, on the eve of his departure from Abbotsford for Malta, about Cervantes' last journey to Madrid in a coach with a student, who was later enraptured at discovering that he had been riding with the author of Don Quixote.[57] For Vilheyna tells La Valette that King Philip, on observing a man walking near his palace and making 'the most extravagant gesture[s] and yielding to irresistible bursts of laughing . . . declared that the man must be either mad or reading Don Quixote'. The man, who was a student, 'was found actually engaged with the celebrated romance of Cervantes'.

In view of his loyalty and personal obligations to King Philip, Vilheyna relates this anecdote to La Valette with regret, for he does not share King Philip's implied view that Don Quixote is a madman, or that it was Cervantes' design to represent him as such. On the contrary, 'all in Don Quixote's temper, which springs from his own sentiments and his own heart, is brave, just, generous and disinterested, which, while our author's wit must excite many a smile, still makes clear to us amid all his [Don Quixote's] weaknesses as being the real model of an accomplished gentleman'. Vilheyna, therefore, appeals to La Valette not to do Cervantes 'the wrong to regard him as an enemy to chivalry, although he had taste enough to point out the extravagant mode of composition, which was fashionable in setting it forth'.

'I will believe it to be as you say,' answers La Valette, on the point of leading from this literary preamble to the key issue raised by the defenders of Fort St Elmo, 'yet I could wish that the author had spared his satire instead of striking at maxims and opinions, which are not so common' in the light of the 'changed manners' that have come into fashion. 'Something of the bad effects', he adds to Vilheyna, of this practice of holding up ancient manners and ideals, particularly chivalry, to ridicule, 'I see even now, and you shall know how I suffer under them.' Repeating, therefore, that 'one of my desires [is] to maintain as long as possible the defence of this Fort St Elmo' to deny entrance into Malta harbour to 'the infidel fleet', he declares that 'hitherto it has been enough for the Grand Master to say to a knight, wherever appointed, "This is your post, my brother, stand fast in its defence to the last, and merit your share of paradise by obeying the command of your superior and fighting to the last in the post assigned you."' Far be it from him to 'misrepresent the knights of the convent, as it now exists', by suggesting that 'the mere fear of death' will ever cause one of them to abandon his post. 'But it is not sufficient that they have the order of their Grand Master to discharge this piece of duty. It is not only necessary that I give my orders. I must also reason upon them, and prove to the satisfaction of those, to whom I commit the task, that their executing my charge is absolutely necessary, and unless I can shew them, which they may not find it easy to admit, that their holding it out to the last is necessary to the defence of the island, I cannot be certain that they will not be tempted to deliver it up by capitulation, and reserve their lives for some crisis of their own heads, which scorn to own inferiority to that of the Grand Master.'

It is precisely 'in this crisis', La Valette concludes to Vilheyna, that 'we are tomorrow about to stand', when the report of the three commissioners and a petition from the defenders of Fort St Elmo will be considered by a full Council of the Order. 'Let me have your advice, my brother, for tomorrow,' he therefore asks Vilheyna, who at once answers that 'rely on it, my noble friend, you shall not want my best support' in defence of 'the obedience we swore to grant' as the first of the three vows that every Knight has taken. 'Sad must seem the times,' Vilheyna reflects, 'which approach the Order, when the suppport of one individual shall be necessary to enforce a vow, on the observation of which its very existence depends.'

On this sombre note as a prelude to the crisis to be dramatised in the next chapter Scott concludes the dialogue between the two leaders, for he then takes them, with their attendants, at the end of their ride, into 'the citadel of Saint Angelo', where Vilheyna finds 'a splendid lodging prepared for him in the mansion of the Grand Master himself, who solicited his company as a guest, expressing his hope they would be in society to each other as much as the duties of both would permit'. La Valette then leads the way into a small apartment, 'graced, as is the custom of Malta, with a belvedere or projecting balcony', that had so caught the eye of Scott himself during his own visit.58 The belvedere commands the fortifications of St Angelo and the whole harbour. Fort St Elmo is across the harbour in the distance, and its resistance—as La Valette has already informed Vilheyna, and as even Piali, in his dialogue with Mustapha, has admitted—has hitherto been protracted so successfully largely through La Valette's policy of replacing those Knights who fall to the Turks in daylight with a small fresh supply by night from Fort St Angelo.

Without going to the belvedere, La Valette sounds a silver bell, which is on the table, and a domestic appears, bearing two large silver goblets. La Valette bows with 'a grave and yet hospitable air' to Vilheyna, and drinks his cup of liquor, his 'sleeping drink', as he calls it. Vilheyna follows his example, but neither of them retires immediately to his bed-chamber. Scott keeps them on the scene a little longer to round off chapter six, which began on a note of contrast, with a special technique of parallelism, to be practised again in other chapters. Scott wants, moreover, to repeat those effects of pathos mixed with heroism in the context of a war of religion, that he has practised in the parting scene in Spain between Vilheyna and Angelica. So he presents La Valette's nephew, although not in person for the time being, as a parallel to Francisco in relation to Vilheyna. Accordingly La Valette says to Vilheyna, 'I ought here to bid thee "goodnight, my brother", but I cannot commit thee to rest without imparting to you what most of all sits heavy on my soul concerning the event of tomorrow.

You have often heard of my nephew, who has risen high in the Order, perhaps the higher out of goodwill to me, as I [imagine] respecting a similar case in your family.' His name is Guargogin, although elsewhere Scott, following Vertot, gives it as Henry. Although La Valette is sure that Vilheyna shares his joy in the advancement of Guargogin, 'it will grieve you to hear that in pitching on the supply to be sent to St Elmo, the fatal lot has been drawn by my own darling nephew'. 'It was no doubt easy', he continues, 'to have changed his destination, but with what face could I have urged others to send their children and nephews to a post from which I withdrew my own by authority?'

Vilheyna at first says nothing, but presses his friend's hand. 'I must see the young man tomorrow,' he then says, 'ere he goes upon this perilous duty.' 'Yes,' replies La Valette firmly, 'for it is even heaven to earth if you should after tomorrow have another opportunity to do his father's relative such a courtesy.' The two old men then take a silent leave of each other for the night in 'tears such as heroes weep'. Turning again with ceremony, 'they signed towards each other the blessed cross, and in that sign of hope and consolation wished good night to each other' on the eve of the central scene in *The Siege of Malta*.

It opens, in chapter seven, after a night that has been heavy 'over all the defences of Malta, but especially upon the fort of St Elmo', whence a skiff carries back the three commissioners with their report to the Grand Master, together with a petition from 'fifty of the youngest and stoutest' Knights, who have been condemned 'to lose their lives without fame excepting the consciousness of having done their duty'. The petition is phrased in the appropriate formal style and 'in a tone profferring the most absolute obedience to the Grand Master, if upon consideration he should think it best to insist upon it'. The petitioners assure him that 'we are incapable of such meanness as seeking to evade our oaths, particularly at this moment when we are almost sure to exchange earth for paradise'. 'Let us but know', is all they ask of him, 'that the defence of the Island depends on our fighting to the last' in Fort St Elmo, 'and you shall find bold hearts and determined hands, who shall execute your commands with no less readiness than our predecessors at the command of Villiers de L'Isle Adam.' Given that assurance, there will then be no 'further appeal from your venerable order' until 'the wild cries of the Moors shall announce to your reverence the devoted inferiors have fulfilled their feat and closed by their death the trial of their obedience'. Nevertheless even two of the three commissioners 'appointed by your reverence['s] fraternity' have thought it their duty 'to present a petition of the same purport as the present, praying your Lordship that you shall see it unnecessary that we lay down our lives like men of honour an[d] knights of our holy order'.

La Valette sees the skiff making for Fort St Angelo and bearing, in addition to the commissioners, seven Knights selected out of the fifty to 'add anything farther that may be necessary to explain the present petition'. Convinced that its purpose is 'an appeal from his decision' to the Council of the Order, he resolves 'to meet the opposition as boldly as he could'. Accordingly he orders 'the great bell of the church of Saint John' to sound for a general meeting in the chapter-house attached to the cathedral, for which Scott had conceived such a passion on his visit to Malta.59 The meeting is summoned amid rumours of 'treachery never heard of in the annals of the Order, and the very thought of which called for tears from the old Knights' of the rank and traditions of Vilheyna, 'who avowed that, if such a scandalous dereliction of principle [took place], they would think every drop of life too little to wipe away the disgrace'. At the sound of the great bell the Knights 'put on their vestments', although some, 'who expected to be soon ordered in action', remain in armour. The rest wear 'their habit of peace', which seemed to Scott, on the evidence of what he had himself seen in Malta, to be a dress 'much resembling that of a judge of the present day', complete with a full periwig. All the Knights enter 'the body of the great church (one of the finest in Europe)', and divide themselves according to the seven nationalities or 'langues' of the Order from Western Europe, which had included the English branch until it had been 'broken up in consequence of the heresy of Henry VIII'. The way to the chapter-house extends over 'a train of funeral aisles, carved with ornaments of lapis lazuli, malachite and other precious stones'.

La Valette, as 'the president, or rather the Prince of the Order', ranking as such even among the princes of Europe, including those 'far more powerful and wealthy than himself', sits more elevated in the midst of 'the memorials of his dead predecessors, bearing on their tombs the memory of their bold deeds and of the faith and valour for which they had been renowned in their day'.

> The roof of this magnificent chapter-house was also itself full of history of the past times of the Religion, as the Order was emphatically termed, and reminded the Knights who now occupied [it] that their predecessors had, as they themselves were called upon to do, been called upon to make their choice between [life and] their vows of obedience, poverty and chastity, had chosen the better part, and had their reward. The portraits of the fathers of the Order were delineated upon, dressed in other garments than those which still accompany them to the grave. Their swords are gliding from their extenuated forms and their armour falls to earth as that for which they have no longer any use, and their faces are turned upwards with the expressions of those whose heavenly recompense is about to be paid them. It is a fine illustration of the lines of Coleridge:
> > The good knights are dust,
> > And their bright swords are rust,
> > Their souls are with the saints, we trust.'
> The face of John de Valette, feeling the pressure of a charge at least as weighty as had oppressed any of those whose deeds he was called upon to imitate, sate looking upwards so as to direct the looks

of the knights in the same direction, and listened with a doubtful
expression to the petition of the younger knights, whose less firmness
of temper he seemed to compare with that of their predecessors in
the like circumstances. This was no sooner finished than the Grand
Master, sensible of the benefit of decision in such cases, [began]:
"My brethren, it is scarce necessary to say that every proposal
from our younger brethren, especially if it differs from and craves
an alteration from our own, or which we have ourselves felt it
our duty to adopt, must be heard by us with every indulgence as
to meaning and motive. The subscribers to this petition are the
youngest Knights, the whole hopes, as it were, of the Order, and
feeling and hoping them to be the portion of the Order in which its
future fame must rest, we have thought it just and honourable to
them to assign to them that part of the defence which, if left to
themselves, would, in the idea we have of the increased opportunity
of acquiring fame, have been themselves their choice. And
notwithstanding the petition we have heard just communicated,
we cannot and will not ascribe their remonstrances to any motive
approaching to personal reluctance or consideration of danger.
Our brethren are high-born gentlemen and incapable of so mean a
thought—the[y] are Christian Knights, and would die before they
gave it utterance. But we ourselves may have easily erred in this
manner in supposing that a course, which would have [been]
thought justifiable in the time of Villiers de L'Isle Adam, may be
also justified under a grand master of less experience and judgment.
If it be so, I will at least hope that I am not considered as obstinate
in my errors, and I will presently show you how willing, nay
eagerly desirous, I am to repair my error. We had imposed upon
you the dangerous task of defending to the very last the fort of
St Elmo, because it seems that in sending older brothers of the
Order, we should have [sent] men less capable of the bodily exertion
necessary in such service, and perhaps more capable, by length of
years, of discerning what mode of defence may be adopted with
success when the defenders of St Elmo are cut off. We therefore, my
brethren, have resolved that the Grand Master himself with a list of
the brethren the most experienced in the Order shall be sent upon
their own proposal to the defence of St Elmo in exchange of those
who were last ordered, and although perhaps we are older than is
convenient for such active service, we trust in our patron saint that
he will make supple and vigorous the joints which have grown stiff
in his service, and we rejoice that we may look to have our place[s]
supplied when the time shall [come] by our brethren, who now
decline to occupy it in the first place. It is therefore the peremptory

will of the reverend meeting that, instead of the Knights formerly named, the number of sixty Knights, the highest official persons and of the longest services in the Order, shall take upon them the relief of the Fort of St Elmo, which they shall defend to the last in the stead of those appointed by the last order of the venerable convent."

Whereas the older Knights hear this proposal with great interest, the petitioners feel that, in accepting it, 'they should in plain terms make themselves guilty of the crime of breaking their vow of obedience'. In consequence 'their words were embarrassed, their looks were discomposed, their reply to the Grand Master was uncertain, as they endeavoured to retreat from their petition, and they wished they had never presented it'. At length one of them—'the most general favourite'—openly admits their error, and detests 'the selfishness, which must have made us guilty of parricide by throwing upon our elders, our worthiers and our betters a task of danger more justly destined to ourselves'. 'Let therefore our names stand for service as it did formerly,' exclaims the young man, who is 'joined by the prayers and tears of the assembly, and those thick sobs, both from old and young, which on such occasions say more of wounded pride, conscious remorse and sense of error' than can be expressed in any other or less passionate manner. For a short time the scene in the chapter-house is one of emotion until it is broken by the entrance of an officer representing 'the inhabitants of Malta and Gozo' as 'vassals of the Order', who 'prayed of the kindness of the Grand Meeting' to be admitted to address the Knights, as in the past, in the crisis confronting their island. La Valette readily agrees to do so— 'so soon as the meeting should have done its proper business'—considering that his attention to them, 'in respect of defence of their families [and] distribution of provisions, had made such impression upon them as left him nothing to fear from anything which they might wish to communicate'.

Despite the petitioners' repentance he again entreats 'that the order of service should still stand altered as far as concerns the Grand Master, and that he be permitted to take his fate with the brave men who are to defend Saint Elmo'. But his proposal is received with a general cry of dissent from every quarter on the ground that 'this would, in fact, be to refuse those, who have been guilty of a passing error, the privilege of retreating from it'. 'On the contrary,' says a young, fiery Spaniard called Ludovick de Garcia, whose name Scott appears to have adapted from that of the Viceroy of Sicily in Vertot, 'I propose that Guargogin de La Valette, nephew and presumptive heir of our venerable Grand Master, be removed from the Fort of St Elmo, and transferred, with his uncle's permission, to the citadel of Saint Angelo.' If in this way 'we should save to the Grand Master a moment of anxiety, which affects his own honourable family, let us think it but a small part of the debt which we owe him, whose whole thoughts are given to the public'. A general applause follows this proposal. La Valette, in another example on Scott's part of a touch of pathos injected into a scene of heroism and stoicism, replies, 'with the drops thickening in his aged eyes', that 'to refuse to accept what you intend as [a] mark of your regard would seem dull and ill accommodated to our circumstances', but he must remind them that 'if it should be ordained that my nephew shall die in his harness, it is neither your direction or mine can alter his destination'. There is little merit in saying with resignation 'God's will be done, since by God's will it must be finally decided'. Wiping his watery eyes, he adds, in a more cheerful tone: 'We must hear our vassals of Malta. This is no moment to affront any set of men, and I believe their intentions towards us to be most faithful.'

Accordingly they are admitted to complete Scott's transformation of this whole episode from Vertot, who, besides placing it much later in the siege, draws La Valette as somewhat harsh and calculating, and treats the Maltese vassals very perfunctorily. Scott, on the contrary, enlarges on them and elevates them to fit into his mediaeval ideal of feudal order, based on a happy relationship between masters and their dependants.[60] Thus they present themselves before the Knights 'with that appearance of awe and submissive respect, with which feudal dependants at that period spoke to the[ir] superiors'. Sun-burned and curly-haired and skilled in the 'hardy' exercises of agriculture, fishing and wine-making, they are dressed up by Scott not without some Highland touches, for they appear with 'their carabines, daggers and pistols' as 'a familiar part of their dress', and as 'constantly habituated with their weapons' so as to constitute 'a body of sharpshooters . . . incapable of being excelled'. They speak 'a species of Arabic, which was understood by those of the Order who resided in the island', and they first declare themselves 'perfectly satisfied with the provisions' made by La Valette for their security.

"One thing alone, which prevails upon us to take the liberty of now intruding upon your councils, is a general report current among the defenders of the[se] islands that in this next defence of the fortress of St Elmo the person of our mutual father, the Grand Master himself, is to be exposed like that of a common soldier, although it is well known that the barbarity of the infidel Bachaw Piali is such as to threaten no quarters upon this occasion. Your vassals and petitioners do not pretend to instruct your Lordships in affairs [of] battle, which have been your profession, but you as well [as] they know the sacred authority which tells that, when God permits the sheep to be scattered, he scatters the shepherd as what must produce that natural consequence. Now no natives ever enjoyed a prince or director to whom they [were] more attached at that time as to the present Grand Master, and they can only say that, if the risk of exposing his venerable person can be rendered unnecessary by exposing thereof any proportion of less consequence, the Maltese regiments are desirous of having the honour of supplying whatever force may be necessary to defend the Fort of St Elmo to the last, whether it be a company, a regiment or a yet larger

division of the inhabitants. Their wives and families join in the
same request, willing as they to expose the[ir] husbands and sons
to death itself rather than they should perish at once by a blow
so irretrievable as the death of the Grand [Master]. Give your
orders for the numbers which may be wanted, and you shall see your
vassals of Malta, Comino and Gozo, every man of them, eager to
have their share in a conflict so honourable as that which will
protect our noble master's safety in exchange for our own."

La Valette returns the most cordial thanks for 'their animation for the public
defence', and accepts their offer of a 'company or two' from the Maltese regiments for the defence of Fort St Elmo, which in the last attack has suffered
considerably from the superiority of the Turkish sharp-shooters. 'To these pagan
dogs', therefore, 'we find an adequate opposition in a party of these vassals of
Malta, than whom none meet the infidels better at their own weapon.' As to
La Valette's own safety, the vassals can rest assured of no reluctance on his part
'to expose himself as became his honourable seat among his brethren', but the
general opinion of the meeting is that 'the defence of Saint Elmo was not
sufficiently important to risk exposing the standard of the Religion and the
person of the Grand Master'. The point has not yet come when all must take an
equal share; when it comes, if such is God's pleasure, he has no doubt that he
will 'fight at the head of every brave man, Knight or vassal, whom heaven
should so far honour as to reserve him to die in the last ditch of their defences'.

The Maltese retire from the meeting with a 'gallant expression of countenance' in contrast to the embarrassed looks of the younger Knights, who
observe that Vilheyna's eyes 'were bent upon them with a frowning and
severe' expression. 'Nothing irritates a noble feeling more', is Scott's acute gen-
eralization, by way of comment on Vilheyna's gesture, '[than] that the consequence of being twitted with error by friends to whose better reasoning they
have resigned' their own. Even La Valette himself, although he has solicited
Vilheyna's support for this meeting the night before, at the end of their ride to
Fort St Angelo, is now alarmed 'lest the obstinate character of Don Manuel de
Vilheyna, stubborn in all points of discipline, should [revive] a debate, which had
been so happily settled with assent on either side'. As the meeting is breaking up,
Vilheyna speaks out with 'a deep firm voice', remarking that it is fortunate 'to
our young brethren that their petition was settled before the entrance of the
peasants, our vassals of Malta'. 'A fine blot,' he continues sharply, 'it would make
in the page of our annals to have read that, when the brethren of our Order,
young knights of the longest descent and best blood, which their several
countries produced, had refused a point of duty imposed on the part of the Grand
Master', the next page 'showed that our vassals, men whose wives and families
depend upon their lives, crave permission to expose themselves freely rather
than their Grand Master should be placed or exposed to danger'.

La Valette now really fears that Vilheyna's taunt will 'awaken into anger' the debate about the defence of St Elmo, seeing that 'Don Manuel would have proceeded in the same tone' of censure, more severely indeed than he had treated 'the presuming Pursuivant' in Spain. La Valette therefore politely interrupts him by observing that 'it is an inconvenience, which we are to find from the non-residence at the convent of some of our wisest members, that they lose recollection of the rules of debate' laid down by the Order. 'It grieves me that, as the business of the day is settled unanimously to the satisfaction of all present, I cannot suffer it to be again awakened even by our respected friend, the Commander of Vilheyna and Aldea Bella.' The gallant, even if quick-tempered, Don Manuel at once defers to the Grand Master by answering that 'if my memory be less perfect than it has been, it shall awake at the least sound of my respected friend's voice, and I am silent as to what I intended to say'. His gesture elicits one of those scenes of magnanimity inseparable from Scott's treatment of chivalry. For Vilheyna is approached by his fellow-countryman, Ludovick de Garcia, who has already proposed, even if without securing the Grand Master's assent, that La Valette's nephew be removed from his post of danger in Fort St Elmo. Garcia can only take it upon him to say, he tells Vilheyna, that he regrets 'our petition this day may have given the Commander an opportunity of judging by his own experienced eyes how far his honoured age is dishonoured by the young companions'. 'Forgive me, noble youth,' answers Vilheyna, taking him by the hand, 'and hear me renounce all that my petulance may have let fall, tending to depreciate the gallant Don Garcia de Cordova and his friends.' The young Spaniard, 'whose bold and hasty temper was mixed with a generous frankness of disposition', at once accepts the aged commander's apology and clasps 'his offered hand with the utmost cordiality'.

La Valette, delighted 'to behold brethren to dwell together in amity', quotes a variant of the celebrated line of Horace, *dulce et decorum est pro patria mori*, which Scott had learned at school as part of the eighteenth-century classical heritage. La Valette particularly welcomes this demonstration of unity among the Knights as 'the sword of the enemy hangs over this house'; for another attack on Fort St Elmo is impending. In fact, he concludes the meeting with 'a word concerning the honour of today's battle', of which he suspects that Mustapha and Piali have got wind through their spies, including perhaps the Pursuivant, Dhalistan, as if in vindication of the suspicion of the fisherman of Aldea Bella that Dhalistan is 'in the disguise of the infidels'. 'I cannot prove it,' says La Valette, 'but our presuming pursuivant, who was said to [have] be[en] created a herald at some college of arms, appears to me, if not already corrupted by the Moors, to be on the point of becoming so.' 'Accordingly I conceive you keep a watchful eye upon him,' answers Vilheyna, to whom La Valette explains that 'we only hold him as a security for the safety of an old friend, who has long surprised us with most curious and accurate intelligence'. If the 'old friend', whose name is given as Hadja Hassan, pays with his head for his treachery, then 'the young aspirant of chivalry is likely to find his own head undertake a flight without his body'. 'So be it,' remarks an anonymous Knight, who apparently disapproves of this system of espionage as 'a bad sign either of Christian or heathen'.

La Valette then breaks the news that 'after so much bragging Dragut is come up at length' from Algiers, 'leading a squadron of his best Algerian corsairs with fifteen [hundred] land forces at the least'. 'His lieutenant Ulichiali', another famous corsair, of whom Vilheyna has already heard from the Pursuivant as one of the leaders against Malta in the earlier attack of 1551, has brought an additional land force of 900 men. 'Great things are expected from this blaspheming villain,' continues La Valette in allusion to Dragut's notoriously loose temper, particularly under the influence of wine—strictly 'a forbidden beverage' under Moslemite law—when he is in the habit, as again Vilheyna has heard from the Pursuivant in Spain, of uttering threats against the Knights. La Valette, therefore, remarks of him that he 'may be said to threaten both God and men, for the burden of his song is the general slaughter of the Knights of Malta, and the special object of his malice is the valorous Commander of Vilheyna, his neighbour on the other side of the strait[s] of Gibraltar'. 'I am honoured by his preference;' says Don Manuel, 'has he been seen as yet in the field?' 'He has visited the various works, they say,' answers La Valette, 'but he only slightly approves of the conduct of the siege' as put into operation so far by Piali with Mustapha's grudging consent. 'How can it be otherwise,' continues La Valette, 'since this great Viceroy or King of Tunis not only did not conduct the siege himself but the works have been approved by the Grand Seignior in person, and therefore [they are] to be criticized with [impunity].' Vilheyna's reply to this is a sneering remark in an apparently incomplete or faded sentence at the end of chapter seven, which also concludes part two of the manuscript.

Part Three

Chapter eight has several opening pages missing from the manuscript,* but their text can be supplied from the 1932 typescript, including the motto from one of Scott's favourite anonymous old songs. The pages describe Piali's second attempt to storm Fort St Elmo from the trench that he has ordered to be excavated in front of its outer defences. The action starts at daybreak in weather 'such as is common in Malta at the beginning of the spring, before the excessive heats of summer are to be apprehended, and the occasional modification of a northerly breeze appeases the burning ardour of a climate so extremely southerly and remarkable for the proportion it contains of the torrid zone'. All the mercenary soldiers in the pay of the Knights 'were got under arms and repaired to their alarm posts' in 'offensive or defensive armour', which Scott, with his superior knowledge of this subject over Vertot, spells out in explaining how 'the higher soldiers', in keeping with 'the fashion of the period', generally 'carried muskets and swords, but no bayonets, that weapon not being yet invented or in general

* But see Appendix C, p. 195.

use among Europeans'. Their steel head-piece and the corslet defending their trunks with a strong coat of iron, 'which was welded of proof', are 'all that was retained of the armour which formerly covered the soldier from top to toe'. The Knights themselves 'retained in many instances the complete armour of their rank, especially when they held commissions as officers among the hired soldiers'; otherwise they lay aside their complete armour, 'feeling it so oppressive as to be ponderously heavy, and so cumbrous as to counterbalance the advantage of the protection which it afforded'.

By contrast, La Valette and other superior officers, including Vilheyna, have remained firmly of the opinion of Henry IV of France—about whom Scott, in this particular instance, probably knew much more than Vertot, even though the latter was Henry's compatriot—that 'the protection afforded by the armour was the means of saving many of the men of rank who were entitled to wear it'. Consequently, 'observing that it always produced an effect upon the enemy', La Valette 'used to say in his orders that he should know which of his nobility loved him best by their obeying his commands concerning wearing their armour in battle'. The objection to doing so on the part of his dissenting nobles is that, besides its cumbrousness, armour 'was supposed to render any wound mortal by carrying a fragment of the armour into the flesh'.

As to the principle on which the Knights mix with 'the ordinary soldiers', it varies according to circumstances. 'Sometimes a certain number of Knights were nominated to particular positions, where they formed a third rank behind the hired soldiers in order to support them during the assault. Each pitched his individual pennant before him, which struck terror into the enemy's ranks.' At the same time 'those musketeers who did not wear swords, were usually accoutred for close combat with weapons capable of thrusting, carried in their hands or within their reach'. Some of the weapons 'were twisted round with combustibles which could be set on fire in an instant, and created nearly the same confusion among the Turks as the hoops or circles of fire' thrown by the defenders to repulse Piali's earlier attack on Fort St Elmo. The names of the combustibles—in a typical piece of elaboration by Scott on Vertot—are given as ' "halberds of fire", "fiery martens", and such like, according to the name of the original implement which formed their composition'.

La Valette and Vilheyna occupy an upper tower of Fort St Angelo, from which they can overlook 'every vicissitude' of Piali's attack, 'and direct from time to time succours as circumstances might render necessary'. In this situation, 'their splendid armour and the magnificence of the plumes, which waved over their helmets, summoned to them the attention of the Moorish artillery, who directed many guns against the tower, where they observed such persons of importance to be stationed, conjecturing them naturally to be the principal leaders of the besieged, on whose fall the event of the siege must in a great measure depend'. The trenches of the besiegers and the posts, into which they have forced their cannon to batter the works of the besieged, 'were filled with

Moors of every description, some celebrated for their skill in shots'. Among them are janissaries—the *élite* corps of the Turkish army—'brandishing their long fusees and crying their exclamation of "Allah, Illah, Allah, Mahomed Resoul Illah—there is no god but our god, and Mahomed is his prophet"'. Nevertheless their shout does not burst from 'them with the enthusiasm' generally characterising them on such occasions; for they are 'conscious of the serious danger, which they must incur in engaging with the Knights, grenadiers and others—the *élite* of the Christians—' who are protected by an outer fortification —technically called a cavalier—which has already caused heavy loss to Piali's troops in the first attack.

From this cavalier the fire of the Knights commands the entrenchments of the Turks, while the mercenary soldiers can fling hand grenades, and others the flaming hoops, so that the Turks 'must be exposed to be swept off, at least at the beginning of the engagement, almost without resistance' unless their works 'were made of such height as to exceed the cavalier'. As the fatal shots of the musketeers become thicker and thicker, 'the cries on either side added their exultation to each successful discharge, which came from their own side of the disputed barrier'. Many 'a desperate besieger feared not to expose himself in the trenches, so that, at the risk of giving the enemy the opportunity of aiming at his own person, he might have the chance of bringing down a well approved Knight or Christian soldier'. The flaming hoops, having been thrown among the crowded Turks, who are 'wrapped in their "caftans" or long cotton dresses', spread such fire among them that they are doomed to 'a most horrible death unless they had the means of plunging themselves into the water' surrounding Fort St Elmo.

In this attack upon 'a small fortification by a force to the amount of at least four or five thousand men', Piali is indefatigable in driving them up to the cavalier 'like flocks of sheep', and compelling them 'to labour in wrenching down palisades and pulling down mason work of gigantic solidity'. At length, however, he perceives that 'as often as he led the Turks forward and set them a most inspiring example of toil, patience and facing death, so often was he driven back, in spite of his blows amongst them with his sabre or his *tchabouk*, as well as the shower of sequins which he flung among his ranks'. All his exertions 'ended by their giving place to the Christians and being forced out of the trenches with only one third of the number with which they had entered at the point of the sabre'. For the Knights—as Scott explains in touches of psychological analysis that are not found in Vertot—'had the usual pride which annexes itself to high birth, great reputation and long practice in arms'. This 'made death, however painful, preferable a hundred times to the least slur on reputation'. Moreover, 'the effect of what might still be termed their chivalrous courage extended itself among the ordinary soldiers, who felt the honour of sharing in their ranks and mounting to danger under their guidance', so that they 'resolutely adopted the same alternative of a successful resistance or an honourable death, crowned with the praises of all Europe and the blessing of the Holy Powers whom it wor-shipped'.

Even 'the very women of the garrison'—in keeping with the late professions made on their behalf by the Maltese delegates to La Valette in the Council scene —'assisted in manning the cavalier and casting down heavy stones, artificial fire-works of different kinds, and supplying their own friends with food, medicine, and assistance to leave the works when so wounded as to be unable to continue their defence of them any longer'. Although their resistance 'seemed scarce natural to their sex', they are encouraged in it by 'the enthusiasm of the moment', which forces Piali to sound the retreat at sunset in recognition of failure to exhaust the resolution of the besieged 'by dint of mere force and comparative strength of numbers'. Nevertheless the Moors begin to toil incessantly 'to renew the attack upon a different and more hopeful principle'. Piali 'ransacked his experience to recall to memory the various ingenious stratagems' of engineering 'at a period when the science was by no means very precise nor distinctly understood by those who pursued it or endeavoured to extend its limits'.

Eventually he hits upon a device, which is really of Scott's invention, as again it is not found in Vertot, and it might have been suggested to Scott by the 'ingenious' new 'sort of carriage' for 'the great guns' of the *Barham* that he had observed on the passage to Malta.[61] For the device—as he explains in a part of the manuscript[62] marking perhaps the best improvement in his hand at Naples —consists precisely of a sliding carriage for a cannon, that 'would be elevated to a height, by which the muzzle of the piece would clear the embrasures of the cavalier'. This would 'enable the artillery men appointed for its service to point the missile—despite all defences—at those who defended the cavalier, and de-prive them of that security [by] which they had hitherto made a defence so fatal'. The utmost care is taken 'to observe the secret of this new mode of attack', and Piali is 'not a little pleased with the device and the applause which his engineers anticipated when it should be carried into practice'. 'The skilful arti-sans', who have constructed it, 'enjoyed a distribution of food and wine, which was made them at their general's command'. In addition, he allows them 'a brief space of repose, while he himself hastened to make ready for a fresh attack' on a point of the fortifications of St Elmo 'which had not yet been assailed, and where he hoped to force his way, even if his attack on the cavalier should prove less successful than he was encouraged to hope'.

Accordingly he takes a skiff with muffled oars, in another original scene, to survey the promontory commanded by the fort, the environs of which Scott takes pains to outline 'to ensure our preserving intelligibility', although, in effect, his outline is not without clouded writing. Nevertheless it serves as a structural link with his earlier descriptions of the fortifications, including 'the species of citadel'—meaning Fort St Angelo—'where we described the Grand Master La Valette and the Commander de Vilheyna as taking their stand to observe the progress of the first attack directed by the redoubtable Piali'. The outline, moreover, draws a personal intervention corresponding to the eighteenth-century tradition of novel-writing to which Scott belonged; for, in a direct address to the reader, he explains that 'I might describe the style of the fortifications' in contradistinction to their situation, 'but it would only serve to embarrass my pages with hard names'. Having, therefore, underlined the need to distinguish the original fortifications from the later additions by pointing out, from personal knowledge acquired on the spot, that 'what Malta was during this celebrated siege . . . has been greatly altered since that period', he returns—in improved style and in a hand that remains clear—to Piali's nocturnal reconnaissance by water.

Piali sees with pleasure that 'the sentinels, exhausted by the repeated attacks which they have sustained, and by the very damp atmosphere of a Maltese night in the beginning of May, now slept heavily'. He is therefore hopeful of surprising them in the next attack by 'a party of chosen rais or sea-captains', who look to him for preferment. 'To give some vent to the anticipations of his swelling bosom', he commands his crew, 'who had hitherto been as silent and cautious in their motions as a spider who lays by a fly', to steer towards the pavilion where Mustapha has pitched his camp from his original position near Saint Antonio. For Piali 'felt the necessity of consulting with a leader so eminent, lest he might incur the Sultan's displeasure', and even though Mustapha, on the morning of the late attack, had sent a messenger to him with 'a complaint of his hereditary malady, the gout, as an apology for not making his appearance in the trenches'. Determined that 'neither the unseasonableness of the hour nor the malady of his colleague should prevent his consulting him that night on the improved plan of attack for tomorrow', Piali, in his haste, imprudently shouts "Give more way, men" to the boatmen, who, on hearing these well-known sounds, burst into an involuntary shout, which itself calls forth another half-suppressed shout. The consequence is a burst of fire 'across the waves in pursuit of the knightly wanderer, whose ill-time[d] urgency for haste was so improvidently expressed as to convince all within hearing that a Moorish cruiser had just now [come] within fire of their post'.

Although Piali does not immediately recover from 'the surprise occasioned by his own rashness', he commands the crew to be silent, and makes the circuit of the armed promontory 'under a heavy fire, which sputtered around him, though at no certain aim'. Besides, the defenders of St Elmo have 'directions so far to be sparing of their ammunition as to reserve their fire for a decisive aim, which the skiff of Piali did not on this occasion afford them'. This annoyance, therefore, ceases as he turns the point of St Elmo towards 'an uncouth eminence covered with large stones and brushwood and intersected by pools of water', on which Mustapha, after moving a large part of his army, has 'established the tents belonging to himself, his officers and the principal persons of his household'. Although his immediate troops are asleep, their arms are ready for instant service, 'if commanded at first peep of dawn'. The light of a fire conspicuous on a height points to Mustapha's tent, 'which had been a present from the Sultan to the husband of a near relation of the Ottoman royal family'. For Mustapha is married to an aunt of Suleman called Zulma, whom Scott at this point of the novel brings into the 'original story' as a character entirely of his own invention, conceived from a mere hint in Vertot that *Piali*, but not Mustapha, was a favourite of the Sultan's, to whom he was related by marriage. In other words, Scott again *reverses* the account of Vertot.

Accordingly, in preparation for Zulma's introduction in person in a scene of oriental splendour in the manner of *The Talisman*, followed by another notable dialogue between Mustapha and Piali, Scott suspends the narrative about Piali very briefly to explain that Mustapha's marriage to Zulma 'had been the commencement of his good fortune', and that, 'although he had rather incurred envy than applause by effecting the conquest of Rhodes, yet the Sultan, if he did not love him, affected to venerate him and would not, it was thought, attempt to meditate any evil against him while Malta remained unconquered, considering him, notwithstanding his advanced age, as the only person capable of performing the task which Suleman had most at heart in the world'. Mustapha, moreover, has 'another uncommon advantage' as the husband of Zulma in that his wife is 'so different from the females of the Ottoman family in general, who, like most eastern ladies, held their rank in the highest estimation, and despised their husbands for their inferiority in birth, and perpetually were engaged in quarrels', sometimes culminating in their husbands' downfall. Zulma, on the contrary, is 'a person of such excellent parts that she was capable of understanding her husband's politics, of comprehending the rules of his procedure, and, possessing very principal interest with her nephew, employed it with great dexterity in supporting at the Porte the interest of her husband', which she truly considers to be identical with her own.

Mustapha, for his part, 'observed towards his princely wife an appearance of obedience, which those of his rank were often ashamed of, and, contented with performing the office of a lieutenant of a general, resigned the charge of his household of almost every description, even including his harem, of which she was an exclusive governess'. For despite his advanced age 'his harem as an eastern luxury of the most distinguished kind was filled by the most beautiful women', and 'Zulma was praised for nothing so much as for her attention to her husband's dignity in this particular, held so important in the East'. Zulma is herself now of advanced age, and to this Scott as narrator is inclined to attribute 'this happy agreement' between the couple.

He then resumes the narrative about Piali, whose skiff approaches the watch-fire regularly kept at Mustapha's pavilion from sunset to sunrise. His crew are instantly challenged 'in the usual military fashion', and on the answer being given that Piali is come to inquire after Mustapha and 'to consult what was to be done tomorrow', the troops under arms wade in the water and bear him on shore to the watch-fire, where they request him to wait till the news of his coming is communicated to Mustapha. After a few minutes two of Mustapha's principal officers, 'richly dressed', appear and prostrate themselves at Piali's feet before taking him respectfully by both arms to conduct him up a path from the beach to 'the front of the splendid pavilion, which was pitched in eastern magnificence' on the edge of a hill overlooking 'the lagoon', as Scott commonly calls the Grand Harbour of Malta. The brilliant colours of the pavilion—crimson mingled with purple and yellow—sparkle with gold, silver and precious gems. Its entrance is guarded by a black Nubian slave, and there Piali's two escorts marshal him to 'the principal officer of the Seraglio', who bears a mace of silver 'most curiously cut upon inlaid steel'. He in turn shows Piali out of a large council tent into 'the woman's apartment, to which Mustapha had retired for the evening'.

When the Capitan beheld himself before the door of partition from this peculiarly sacred part of a Moslemah's tent, and saw at the same time, from the slippers of the master, placed at the threshold, the appropriate mark that the master was there in person, he intimated by the most respectful gestures his unwillingness to proceed in a manner so uncommon to the fashions of his country. But the Officer of the Seraglio in a low tone of [respect] intimated that he was sent on purpose to conduct the Capitan Pacha into the apartment, before which he now stood, for neither gout or any other indisposition should prevent him for a moment from seeing and consulting with his noble colleague, who sought now to consult with him on the business of His Royal Highness. To this dutiful message Piali intimated [h]is respectful acquiescence, and was admitted through an outer room or two to an inner apartment, where he found the Bachaw by the light of a lamp, which spread a luxurious twilight through a small apartment richly fitted up. His seat was a splendid carpet of silk and gold, and he had as companion a female [who] was a Lady, apparently having attained an advanced stage in life, but whose features retained the appearance of much intelligence and the remains of what once [had] been beauty. Two young and beautiful female slaves looked with profound respect both on Mustapha and Zulma, to serve whom with the most humble duty appeared to be the purpose of their atten[dance] in the apartment.

Mustapha, for his part, suspects Piali of 'a design to cut him out of the credit, which [he] had long enjoyed of being supposed the only man capable of bringing to an end the siege of Malta, as he had on a former occasion compelled the same fraternity to evacuate the island of Rhodes'. Addressing Piali 'in the mildest and most flattering terms', he affects great regret at having 'from his malady to secure to himself so little share in executing the commission of the Grand Seignior'. On the other hand, he is 'peculiarly happy' that his 'magnanimous master' has joined Mustapha's 'frozen age with the resolute and fiery manhood' of Piali, who, if he and another leader like him had the whole charge of the siege without 'the trouble of consulting a poor, low-spirited and decayed old man', would have 'at once sealed the fate of the besieged'. Piali is equally flattering in answering that, far from being 'the superannuated person of whom you speak, I am sure our princely master regards you as the same conquering hero, to whom the renowned Villiers de L'Isle Adam surrendered the well-fortified island of Rhodes, and I am convinced that it is to your conquering skill [to] which he also trusts for the keys of this robbers' nest, which they call Malta'. 'If I am looked to [to] assist the Grand Seignior,' Piali continues, 'it is only that he may have the unanimous shout of his whole people to surrender power to merit, and place the truncheon of the Grand Vizier into these hands where by common consent it ought long since to have been lodged.'

Brushing this flattery aside, Mustapha tells Piali that 'it is time we should give up our exchange of compliments', and instead exchange ideas upon the progress of the siege, which is precisely what Piali wishes to do in order to insist that they adhere to their original decision 'to expel the Nazarenes from this post or redoubt of St Elmo' despite 'the obstinate character of these unbelieving dogs' resistance'. 'It would ill become me', interposes Zulma, who has hitherto remained beside her husband and the admiral, 'to suppose that a female's ear is fitted to entertain matters of such importance' as are under discussion by Mustapha and Piali. She therefore orders her female attendants to arise and follow her, 'but, although she arose and assumed the appearance of one about to withdraw, yet in earnest she had Mustapha's orders to do no such thing, and it was without surprise that she heard her Bashaw say that "the laws even of the Koran itself were not made for the blood of Othman" '.

Bowing low to 'the relative of the Emperor', Piali intimates his agreement to 'hold his consultation upon the siege in any company, which Mustapha judged politic or advisable'. Accordingly he sets out to him in Zulma's hearing the three measures that he corsiders necessary to capture St Elmo, including the device of 'raising a cannon at the time of firing to a high point of aim' so as to be itself immune to the guns in the bastion or cavalier in front of St Elmo. He also refers to the projected 'attack to be made on water as well as land by a large body of captains and mariners, who have volunteered their services for that duty'. To these proposals 'the astucious old pacha' makes polite objections, 'less from the general rules of the science' of war 'than from peculiarities belonging to this accursed island', particularly its shallow soil, which makes not only trenches but also mine-laying (Piali's third proposal) impracticable. As to Piali's proposed attack by sea, 'the Christians have two regiments of Maltese, trained to swim and work in the waters almost during their whole lives, and who I greatly suspect will be found superior to your raises and sailors in the very trade in which you trust to them'.

Mortified at hearing Mustapha's objections, Piali asks him if they imply that 'my poor thoughts are unlikely to succeed'. 'Far from it,' answers Mustapha, 'but we have already had an immeasureable loss', and ought therefore not to commit themselves to his plan 'without being certain of obtaining a proportional advantage to balance our disadvantages'. 'I should nevertheless be willing to incur a great risk' to the Sultan's forces 'were it not for the terms of our commission, which command us to act in conjunction with the Viceroy of Tunis', with whom they have so far had no opportunity to consult owing to Dragut's absence. In 'a suppressed spirit of displeasure' Piali answers him that 'unless I am much misinformed, Dragut arrived at Malta this evening, and has had the unpleasing surprise to find his ancient enemy, Don Manuel de Aldea Bella y Vilheyna, arrive just a cannon shot before him, and escape him, though watching for him, by just the same distance of time'. Knowing Dragut's temper, Piali has no doubt that 'he will be cursing to the pit of darkness the small space of time, by which he has lost so important a hazard'.

On hearing the sound of trumpets in the distance, accompanied by cymbals, 'such as usually announce the approach of oriental persons of regal rank', Mustapha holds up his finger as if to impose silence, and remarks ironically that Dragut, who has risen to viceroy from 'the ordinary service' of a corsair, is at length come 'to instruct on the subject of their duty the fools' such as Mustapha himself and Piali, 'whose rise in the wars of the Sublime Porte' has been through much more respectable channels. 'He will soon give his assistance to those who[m] the Grand Seignior esteems to stand in so much need, and whom his Excellence esteems to stand in so much need of it.' Gladly catching at Mustapha's tone of displeasure, Piali suggests that 'the Viceroy Dragut did indeed for a man of so much talent set rather too much store by what was after all only a substitute authority'. But Mustapha, fully understanding the drift of Piali's remark, retracts his earlier bitter observation, and reminds him that the Sultan, as 'the commander of the faithful' followers of the Prophet, 'is invest[ed] in the direction of his kingdom with the power of selecting those agents who are the fittest for his purpose, in which you as well as I are far from making an exception of the renowned Dragut, to whom we are directed by our commission to submit our own judgement on this occasion'. 'Unquestionably,' replies Piali, perceiving that 'the wily old vizier' is not disposed to make common cause with him against Dragut, 'or indeed in any respect to throw aside that mask of profound dissimulation, which he was considered as having worn during the greater part of his long life'.

Piali therefore rises to leave, saying that, as they cannot yet know whether Dragut will approve of the altered plan for tomorrow, he will retire to his quarters to see if all is in smooth preparation, or, in the event of Dragut's disapprobation, to make such changes 'as his opinion might render necessary'. He then mentions where he can be found at any hour that evening, should Mustapha summon him to a council. Mustapha exchanges an adieu with him so respectful 'as to amount almost to prostration', but, as soon as he is gone, he tells Zulma, 'in the privacy of his matrimonial tent', that Piali 'is but a youth in comparison, yet dreams in betraying me into a confidence, which might, were I dull enough to rush into it, cost me my Pachalik and my life'. 'Rely upon it, Zulma, he desires to represent me to thy most serene kinsman as having united with him in the hazardous and precarious attack, which he proposes for to-morrow,' whereas 'I knew nothing that such a plan was proposed, or that the Viceroy of Tunis was arrived, until the night-watch'. Zulma assures him that 'I can bear witness to the reality of Piali's conduct respecting his plan, which he has just proposed, and if my nephew applies to me for information, the sage Mustapha's conduct on this occasion is not like to be falsely represented'. 'Zulma, thou art one of those excellent women to whom heaven of old intrusted the direction of their husbands, when they intended to raise them to high achievements. We will be watches tonight, Zulma, for I think Dragut will hardly venture to delay consulting with me, and it behoves me as soon as possible to discover the humour he is in, lest this seaman should make a friend and ally of the viceroy, since the mariners are in general friends to a leader of their own profession.'

Mustapha's speech concludes chapter eight, after which the opening paragraph of chapter nine is missing from the manuscript, but can be supplied from the 1932 typescript. The chapter shifts the scene back to La Valette and Vilheyna on the eve of Piali's third attack on Fort St Elmo in what is perhaps the most imaginatively conceived episode in the novel. In other words, the consultation with Dragut, who, though at first demurring, eventually falls in with Piali's plan, is deferred to a retrospective chapter on its own after the attack itself, which is preceded by a dialogue between La Valette and Vilheyna, who have remained on the battlement of Fort St Angelo as the best vantage-point for surveying the harbour and the more distant fortifications. In the meantime they have received confirmation of Dragut's arrival, with 'a considerable reinforcement of select soldiers', made up of 'crews from his galleys, janissaries and others', and all sharing 'the burning resentment which he nourished against the Christian men and the Knights of Malta as so celebrated a community of that religion'.

The dialogue between La Valette and Vilheyna can only be described as pure Scott, for it introduces that element of 'superstition' inseparable from his novels in the form of strange sounds heard by La Valette and Vilheyna under a general belief of 'a desperate and pitiless battle' about to take place, 'which in a war so particularly of a devotional [kind] was considered as a step from earth to a better world'. The sounds come from tall belfries in a somewhat 'Gothic' setting of shadows of towers and trees in the darkness 'amidst the confused and half-seen landscape of the town and fortifications by midnight' on 'a cloudless southern summer night, tempered by an occasional sirocco', such as Scott might himself have experienced while performing quarantine in Fort Manoel opposite Fort St Elmo.[63] At first Vilheyna interprets 'these imperfect sounds'—to quote his own words to La Valette—as 'a voice from heaven to tell us that this shall be a busy day tomorrow both for Christian and infidel', similar, in other words, to 'the ancient signal, which, it is said by the fathers of the Order, presaged the bloody carnage of Roncesvalles', famous in history for the defeat of Charlemagne and the death of Roland. La Valette,[64] however, while respecting Vilheyna's belief in 'the traditions of our fathers', and without 'in the least less believing in the thickness of the slaughter tomorrow', points out that these sounds 'are not produced by the agency of heavenly spirits but are the devout serving chaplains of the Order', performing divine service in the town adjoining Fort St Angelo. They also come, suggests Vilheyna, from 'the wild cries of the Moors so well known to all Knights of our Order as the *tecbir* or war-cry of the Saracens'. 'It is indeed the war-cry of these infidels, extorted from them by injunctions and blows, for without some such wild means of keeping themselves awake these barbarians, in spite of the impending danger, would betake themselves to rest before the day breaks.' Vilheyna and La Valette then hear 'a scattered report from the seaward batteries', corresponding to that burst of fire which had nearly cost Piali his life while reconnoitring Fort St Elmo. At first La Valette is inclined to attribute it to 'Dragut's arrival', but, on again hearing 'the clamour of the bells', accompanied with 'vocal mus[ic]', he is sure that it is the serving chaplains of the Order, singing a hymn specially composed to 'summon the protection of the immortal shepherd for the sheep-fold when beset by the wolf, to which the present bears too close a resemblance'. On listening with more attention, they hear voices coming from the church of St John 'in solemn chorus from one quarter to another', and they respond with 'the devotional feeling, which it is the peculiar property of so many of the hymns of the Catholic Church to impart'.

When the music has completely died away after undulating 'through the Gothic aisles and complicated labyrinths of the church', the Knights 'once more looked abroad from the battlements and around the horizon, so far as visible, to mark whether any change had yet taken place in it, announcing the arrival of day, which promised to give signal for a combat' so dreadful on the neutral ground before Fort St Elmo. The brave hearts of the Knights, watching for dawn, 'longed yet trembled at the thoughts of mingling in such contest for the last time'. At length 'a very slight and faint tincturing of a dapple colour in the eastern sky' announces the distant break of day. 'There is the first faint tinge of a sun, which the heart of many shall throb to see arise, but few indeed shall survive to see set,' says La Valette to Vilheyna. 'It becomes me to ride or pass by boat round the several posts. Would you, my brother, choose to accompany me?' Vilheyna answers that he will not leave his side. La Vallette expresses his thanks with a cordial squeeze of the hand, and they proceed to inspect the points of defence, attended, in Vilheyna's case, by his squire, Juan Ramegas. All the time they think of St Elmo as 'destined for the most efficient struggle' of the day's onset. La Valette then takes his post on the most advanced part of the fortifications of Fort St Angelo, and Vilheyna displays his own family pennon on a turret. So does the Grand Master, as 'a signal that they overlooked the defenders of St Elmo, whose steadiness had been held a matter of such consequence', when they last drove back Piali's assault.

On beholding the colours of the two leaders—'so renowned for their experience in war'—raised against 'the eastern dawning', the garrison of St Elmo interpret this as an assurance that the Grand Master will not fail to send them a fresh relief 'when they should reach the hour of need'. The feeling within them, as 'men of the most consummate bravery', at the hour when 'the storm, which had loured for the whole night, was approaching near to the moment in which it was generally believed to burst in all its terrors', is, on Scott's own admission as narrator, beyond the power of words: it 'passes show'. So he tries to suggest the tension by means of a long anecdote, in rather involved syntax, about an intrepid British officer 'in the midst of the tremendous fire of Bunker's Hill' during the American War of Independence. Like the officer, the garrison of St Elmo endeavour 'by every exertion of a personal nature' to remove from their minds 'the awful scene of contemplation' presented by their situation. 'Some soldiers are observed to whistle, to sing, to dance, if the nature of the service' permits them, while 'such among them as were of the order of knighthood'— in contradistinction to the foreign mercenaries and Maltese soldiers—imitate the example of the Grand Master and Vilheyna, and display 'their own peculiar pennons and their knightly arms' along 'the three-fold line, which they defended upon the cavalier', so that 'each might make himself individually visible to the eye of the grand master, while prepared to sacrifice themselves, if required, at his orders and under his eye'.

No sooner has this arrangement been made, however, than La Valette observes to his surprise his nephew's pennon 'carried forward into the upper part of the cavalier, and placed close to the place where it crossed at right angles with the line of the hollow way, by which the infidels hoped to possess themselves of that work, which must determine the fate of the fortress'. The purpose of pitching the pennon in so conspicuous a place is plainly to draw the Grand Master's attention to 'the danger which might be incurred in particular by his own nephew', who, armed in plain black armour, raises himself above the crowd that fills the cavalier, and addresses those near him with considerable animation before he carries back the pennon to its original position in the third line of the cavalier below the rows of halberds, pikes and spears shaking their points as they wave over the battlements in a scene already admirably suggested by Scott, at the opening of the chapter, through the motto from one of Byrons' *Turkish Tales*, which Scott had reread with delight in H.M.S. *Barham* on the passage to Malta.[65] Vilheyna 'looked on with great deliberation to guess, if possible, the object of a change so extraordinary at such a time and place'. But the Grand Master at once understands it. 'My nephew', he says, 'is a noble boy —he has moved his pennon, because to place [it] in the point of danger might be supposed to imply that his own life was dearer in my eyes than that of the other brave knights, who share with him in his honourable danger. . . . Gallant boy! Some must be preserved. I hope it is not too selfish in my situation to hope that thou might be preserved to see this bloody day out.' Vilheyna, in another example of parallelism on Scott's part, feels that he stands 'in the same condition' as that of his friend on account of Francisco. Observing, therefore, 'an unwilling and hesitating tear slowly escape' from La Valette's eye, 'and trickle unregarded down his deep-furrowed and weather-beaten cheek, he felt that Nature, like the powerful rod of the prophet, was at work [to] compel the same tear from the same cause down his own cheek'.

The moment, however, that young La Valette steps back to change the position of his pennon the Turkish fusiliers open fire on him. Some four or five bullets rattle against his corslet but without inflicting a wound. Waving his hand with an air of triumph at his escape from their aim, and at the same time springing into the first line, he seizes a musket from a soldier and fires back 'with fatal effect' at 'a person of importance', for 'the Christians shouted and the Moors yelled in a barbarous manner' as battle is joined for the cavalier of St Elmo. 'The Moors therefore accompanied the fierce and wild sound, which they termed their lelies[66] or war-cries and esteemed their passport to Heaven and the doom of those of the opposite faith to the contrary region. The Christians, according to the different country in which they had birth, or the services in which they had been trained, accompanied their exertions with cries of onset and rally, which mingled in an hundred accents, and were answered by a thousand echoes, which hitherto remained silent and now only started, as [it] seemed awakened from slumber.' Although Piali has crowded in the trenches as many men as they can possibly hold, they are unable to take proper aim at the Christians on account of the height of the cavalier, which moreover enables the defenders to harass and reduce the numbers of the besiegers with 'every discharge of musketry'. In consequence Piali is convinced that his new device of raising a huge cannon on a sliding gun-carriage must be put in force speedily. Accordingly he orders the trenches to be cleared, and filled instead by 'a great body of Arabian soldiers, who in point of determination held the lowest rank among the national troops of the Sultan'. These in turn are slaughtered by the defenders, who, as they see them writhing in the trenches—'some wounded, some with crushed bones, some breathing their last'—incautiously leave their positions in the cavalier to pursue them 'without greatly observing that they placed themselves in respect of the enemy in the same disadvantageous situation in which the Moors had so lately stood in respect of them'.

The instant, therefore, that they are in hot pursuit of the Arabians, Piali's voice is heard clear and strong, commanding the working party, who have constructed the elevating carriage for the cannon, to raise it to as great a height as it is capable of being heaved into the air, and, having loaded it with shot, to fire it into the cavalier. 'The slaughter was as great as might have been expected', amounting, besides the wounded, to 'nearly one third of the numbers who had made that morning's imprudent sally from the cavalier'. But 'an odd accident' takes place 'to prevent this menacing and near approaching danger'. And the 'accident' provides Scott with an opportunity to bring Juan Ramegas back into the action of the 'original story', and to conclude both chapter nine[67] and part three of the manuscript of *The Siege of Malta* with an exploit of personal courage and resourcefulness. For Ramegas has been watching, by Vilheyna's and La Valette's side 'with anxious perturbation' the effect made 'upon the fortune of the siege' by Piali's skilful invention. And being practical and religious, he exclaims to La Valette: 'It cannot be but the Gracious must inspire into some Christian head the manner of baffling an invention, which otherwise must cost so many worthy lives without a possibility of counteractions that I can devise. Sure am I that, knowing the axe and saw on such occasions as well as my early youth has taught me, I must have addressed myself to our blessed patron St James with somewhat of a colder spirit than became the occasion.' 'Bend thy mind to it with due earnestness now,' answers La Valette, 'and may St James[68] be your speed.'

'I will,' replies Ramegas, and he asks to be allowed six pioneers with working tools, 'and I will vouch that you shall see wonders.' La Valette tells him that he will be guided in this matter by the opinion of one 'who knows you better than I'. Vilheyna therefore promptly explains that he has known Ramegas for forty years as 'a worthy Castilian, who during that time has been uniformly by my side at sea and war', and that he has 'rapid and luminous ideas of device, as if St James had himself inspired them for the benefit of his selected people'. 'Besides,' adds Vilheyna, 'such of my followers as are in St Elmo are well accustomed to obey his commands, which may be a matter of consequence in such a dubious assault as the present threatens to prove.'

As soon as La Valette hears Vilheyna assent to Ramegas's proposal he points to a skiff moored under Fort St Angelo, and Ramegas, accompanied by a small number of men, rushes to the water-side, taking care 'not to attract the attention of the Moors, who were busied in again loading Piali's newly contrived [weapon], and obtaining a new successful discharge into the cavalier, where everyone now sought some temporary shelter from the fatal fire'. The Turkish musketeers, moreover, 'perceiving themselves so admirably seconded' by Piali's cannon, which has 'revised the situation of the parties', have recovered heart and begun to rely again on their superior numbers.

Ramegas runs his skiff aground in the shallow part of the shore of St Elmo, where he is spied by Piali, as he dashes into the water. Piali commands a Turkish officer to press as near Ramegas and his party of pioneers as possible, 'and send to the infernal regions announced by the prophet that band of miscreant artificers' dispatched to St Elmo by the Grand Master 'for some special commission undoubtedly'. Although the officer answers that 'their death is written upon their forehead', Ramegas and his comrades screen themselves with planks of wood and manage to get into the cavalier. There Ramegas observes an old culverin, placed, when mounted and raised to its utmost height, nearly opposite

Piali's cannon. He therefore sets about clearing it of the rubbish which has blocked it up, assisted by, among others, 'a tall, black sailor', who is none other than Boniface, the Maltese boatman of Vilheyna's *speronaro*, who had lost his son in 'Don Manuel's perilous disembarkation' at Malta. Like his fellow-assistants, Boniface is accustomed to such 'desperate devices' of Ramegas, and and they look upon them as 'something of a superior order of beings' without taking it upon themselves to pronounce whether his expedients are good or bad. All of them are aware that the security of this particular measure is dependent on its secrecy, and 'seldom has it been seen that the old culverin, being of that kind termed a fire-drake, was with so little noise cleared out and prepared for the reception of its old tenant'. 'But, noble Don Ramegas,' asks Boniface, 'how shall we avoid discovery by these sable hell-hounds, when we shall be obliged to strip away from the very outside the trash of leaves and wet straw and withered branches, which form, as it were, its outward covering?' 'I would be [angry] with thee, my old friend, for interfering with thy captain. Thy business is at present to labour and be silent: before the day is over, thou shalt have shouting [at] thy feet. Wait my orders concerning that dry rubbish, and take care to keep what is fit for burning. I will give you the word when it must set all on a blaze together.'

Waving his hand in a triumphant gesture, Boniface wishes that his son were with him, 'for he would have born[e] his hand at the work, whether Turks or devils against us'. His old face then settles into a cold, inflexible expression, while he gradually removes the rubbish from the embrasure of the cavalier 'with a touch that seemed invisible' yet with an arm that is 'superhumanly strong', moving with the 'caution of a cat when desirous of surprising her prey before it had caught the alarm of her presence'. The sense of his recent misfortune as 'a deep and inco[nso]lable' calamity adds to the unvaried expression of his countenance. At length the time arrives when he dares no longer proceed in arranging the combustible material which has been taken out of the embrasure, and consigning it with the utmost caution to a ditch between the cavalier of the Christians and the approaches of the Turks. For he hears the harsh tones of Piali's cannon being raised to fire into the cavalier for the seventh time since the assault has begun. Both Moors and Christians have become accustomed to its sound, the former expecting its discharge as 'a signal to repeat the attempt to advance, in which on each occasion they had proved more successful than at first, though they had not yet been able to make good their [advantage] in any part of the cavalier'. At the seventh discharge, however, 'which as before put to silence several Christians', an unexpected sight appals the Moors, who at first do not know what they are to expect from 'its sudden apparition'. For Boniface has set fire to the combustibles placed precisely between Piali's cannon and the embrasure of the cavalier where Ramegas has pitched the culverin as 'his death-hawk'. At first Piali, who is astonished at so great an appearance of fire from the cavalier, suspects that it comes from a counter-battery, but he is soon put right when the cloud of thick, black smoke between the two cannons, on which either party relies, clears up, and, at a signal from Ramegas, the Christians exert all their strength to wheel the culverin back to prevent any risk of its taking fire and exploding of itself, and then they wheel it forwards into the embrasure and discharge it right against Piali's cannon. Being loaded with balls of iron, stone and chain-shot, it damages the gun-carriage's equilibrium so much that 'it put an end to the invention of Piali'.

Part Four

Its destruction is watched not only by Piali himself but also by Dragut, who at last is brought on the scene in person by Scott in chapter ten, which opens part four of the manuscript with a motto drawn from Byron's description, in *Don Juan*, of the siege of Ismail in Turkey by the Russian army. The chapter, the first page of which is missing from the manuscript, but can be supplied from the 1932 typescript, is the longest in the whole novel, and contains perhaps the most fluent writing as the story moves to a climax through a series of exciting battle-scenes. Scott, in other words, focuses increasingly on the drama and heroism of the siege at the expense of the 'original' characters, thereby explaining why he had initially called the novel 'The Knight of Malta' and then changed the title to 'The Siege of Malta'. In consequence, Vilheyna, Francisco and Boniface suffer the same fate as that already incurred by Angelica and Morayma, in that they never reappear in the story, although it is conceivable that they might have been brought back into it if Scott had not been seized with a fever to leave Naples for home via Rome and Corfu.[69] Indeed that was precisely what he claimed from Naples that he could 'easily' have done, if necessary.[70] In the light of his earlier novels, however, their disappearance serves but to confirm his somewhat hap-hazard method of composition, as best described by himself in his journal with reference to *Woodstock*. 'I never could lay down a plan—or, having laid it down, I never could adhere to it; the action of composition always dilated some passages, and abridged or omitted others; and personages were rendered important or insignificant, not according to their agency in the original conception of the plan, but according to the success or otherwise with which I was able to bring them out. I only tried to make that which I was actually writing diverting and interesting, leaving the rest to fate.'[71]

In consequence of this method of composition the reader never learns whether Francisco is reunited with Angelica, and whether Angelica herself spends the rest of her life in a nunnery. Even Vilheyna's ruling desire of 'one good blow at my old enemy Dragut' remains undeveloped. Only Ramegas and Zulma remain in part four of the manuscript. and the former survives only in a minor capacity compared with Dragut, Mustapha and the newly arrived corsair, Ulichiali, for all of whom Scott contrives a series of original incidents, either entirely of his own creation or based on hints from Vertot. Moreover, he analyses Dragut's character with special reference to 'his indomitable courage' and 'violence of temper', which is compared to 'the volcanic fires' of Mounts Stromboli and Vesuvius, as Scott had seen them for himself on and after the passage to Naples.[72]

The first of the original incidents is the retrospective dialogue between Piali and Dragut before the late attack on St Elmo, in which the former defends himself and his strategy against Dragut's initial and haughty strictures after resolving that his best policy is 'to seem to offer all informa[tion] and cooperation in his power to Dragut, for he despaired of making any efficient alliance with Mustapha, whose cold and crafty character was too dangerous to encounter'. Besides, as Mustapha has himself lately observed to Zulma, Piali looks upon Dragut as 'like himself a sailor born and educated'. His policy pays off, for he secures Dragut's approval for his hitherto untried plan for an attack on Fort St Elmo by sea as well as by land. Dragut, moreover, pledges that 'all the men, who have followed me hitherto from Tunis, picked and tried as every individual among them has been, shall risk their fame and their glory upon this adventure'. Piali is delighted to find that 'he had struck a flint at last, which had effectually returned'. As he tries to elaborate on the anticipated advantages of his plan, he is interrupted by Dragut 'with a burst of enthusiasm to which he seldom gave way', and is treated to 'an adventure of my child[hood]', which serves to confirm at once all that has already been said about Dragut's vindictive threats against the Knights. It also proves to be Scott's most dramatic anecdote, originating perhaps from 'the severe annoyance from vermin' that he had himself complained of as 'the only real hardship' of his quarantine in Malta.[73] For he makes Dragut tell Piali how his bedroom in his father's cottage 'was infected by scorpions, and both I and my faithful dog were repeatedly bitten and suffered loss of sleep and pain'.

> "My father gave me leave and commission to avenge myself on the bitter insect, that has a sting like these Malta Christians. The instinct of revenge acted in my bosom. I swept as many of them together as I could into a small heap and, surrounding them with a ring of charcoal glowing hot, approached it to them nearer and more nearby. They felt the desperation of their situation, and gave way to it by plunging their stings into themselves and each other, a sight which afforded me the greatest delight. I never before dreamed I should have such injuries to revenge or experience such delight in revenging them. But the stings of the scorpions were beds of rosebuds compared to the Christians, and all the miseries I have in my life experienced in the course of a long life were mere jests when compared with the suffering of a Moslemah in the dungeons of Genoa, where I was detained for so many years."

Pleased to see Dragut in this mood, Piali offers to escort him to Mustapha's pavilion to inform him of their agreement regarding the siege. But Dragut immediately urges caution upon him, for 'the cold blood[ed] and wily Mustapha has no right to [be] too early or too fully put into my secrets'. Dragut will tell Mustapha no more than 'is necessary to set the operations a-going': the rest he will reveal only in due time and season. 'Nay, by the Koran, I could almost think of renouncing a campaign, which will increase my honour, immortalize my name, and even glut my vengeance, when I recollect that Mustapha must needs divide with me the reward of my victory.' Piali in consequence adopts a cool attitude when they reach Mustapha's pavilion, where Dragut regrets the heavy loss so far sustained by the army under Mustapha for so few gains. Afraid to contradict him in public, and 'leaving him to renounce his opinion in his own time and manner', Mustapha briefly defends the present operations before suggesting that, if Dragut wishes to change them, they can still do so. Dragut, however, considers, as Piali has argued before him to Mustapha, that the operations have now gone too far to admit of a change 'without committing the glory' of the Sultan and discouraging the troops. It is therefore agreed unanimously to use the whole force of the army to push forward the siege with the utmost vigour.

Dragut, from this point onwards, emerges as an inspired and inspiring leader, although he has a foreboding that 'there is something darkly dealing with my spirit, which impresses on me that I am not very likely to have an opportunity of enlarging the blessed faith of the Moslemahs and chastising the blasphemers of the infidels'. Nevertheless both he and his Tunisian troops are ready at every point, and, forgetting what he has just said to Piali about Mustapha—in another typical gesture of magnanimity on Scott's part as 'heroic' narrator—he walks across the floor of Mustapha's pavilion, and, setting himself beneath the latter's cushion, addresses him as 'noble Bashaw of Egypt', and pleads that, although 'we have been on different occasions less friendly than became two principal servants of the same great prince, this has gone too far; let it end here'. Even Mustapha is affected by such frankness, springing as it does from a desire 'to vindicate himself from the suspicion of party spirit, low-born envy and the malignity common to those who have long been envious of the favour of the same prince'. In consequence Mustapha is temporarily 'ashamed of preserving an animosity against one, who for the time at least sacrificed every feeling of personal interest to the general interest of the army and the progress of the siege'. Accordingly Mustapha feels a revival of the 'high spirit, which had distinguished his youth, and had not yet entirely deserted his old age, though repressed by the cold-blooded sagacity and long-breathed malignity of courtly opposition' as a product of later years.

Even his gout seems to have 'vanished from his recollection', and Zulma herself 'endured a frown beneath which she shrank as she attempted to remind him of the cautious frailty' of his constitution as an invalid. Other leaders besides him and Dragut seem to pride themselves 'on assuming a degree of intrepid bravery, which had not been on former occasions their supposed characteristics'. Piali is among them, for, although an ambitious man and certainly distinguished in the past for courage as 'the only way by which a Turkish general could force himself to rank and wealth', he has hitherto not been supposed to have quite 'the air of loving danger for its own sake', that distinguishes Dragut. Another general of the same calibre and 'a good deal spoken of among the soldiers' is Ulichiali, commonly called 'the Greek' from his birthplace in one of the Greek islands. 'A renegade by religion', it is emphasised by Scott as narrator, in a hint of an impending original scene for Ulichiali of brilliant tension and drama, that he 'still trembled when he thought upon the true [faith] in which in his younger days he had once pitched his better hope'. In consequence, although, in 'bestirring himself where dangers were thickest', he labours in the trenches like a common miner to advance the cause of Mahomet, 'he petitioned from a more holy power to avert the damage which the explosion might occasion'.

Kindled to 'a degree of energy' by their leaders, of which they have not themselves supposed that they are capable, the Turkish officers and soldiers of all ranks receive as a 'mark of infallible success the apparent concord, which seemed to knit the band of unity between their generals'. No less firm in confidence, however, are the Christian defenders, including the officers of the mercenaries, who have 'brought their own bravery to support the celebrated Knights of the military religion'. Both parties 'cast an anxious eye' upon the neutral ground before Fort St Elmo, where Piali has unsuccessfully tried to destroy the cavalier with his cannon. It is precisely the spot where Dragut resolves to renew the attack, supported at the same time by a bombardment by sea. For two or three days he has employed himself so incessantly that he 'seemed to multiply himself in the eyes both of Turk and Christian'. Mustapha and Piali attend him like mere *aides-de-camp*. On the eve of what is intended to be the final assault he takes the best survey he can of the neutral ground, covered as it is with 'the scarred and wounded corpses of men' who have fallen in attacking or defending it. 'The fragments of timber, bronze and iron, the remains of the military engines, still showed with what success the strip' has been maintained, and to what extremity it has held out. Each party has endeavoured to creep as far forward as they dare on the enemy's position, although an irresistible feeling of drowsiness has seized a number of soldiers on both sides 'from the weary and desperate nature of the conflict'.

'Here is but cold watch,' says Dragut aloud, on coming upon a slumbering Moorish sentinel, who, on awaking, starts at the 'splendid scarlet dress and superb green turban' of the speaker, and falls on his knees, as if 'to deprecate the consequence of being found asleep on his post by this severe disciplinarian'. Dragut, however, has 'smoothed down the ferocity of his temper', and only says, 'It is well for you, friend, that you do not belong to my bands; if you had, you should not have told a story of my laxity of discipline'. He then warns him, in the event of another fit of drowsiness, 'to awaken before your Christian friend, who snores on the other side of the half-burned beam there'; otherwise 'you are happy enough to be saved from punishment by having your throat cut'. The sentinel begs him 'to remain here to see how sleepy dogs awake, where the first thing to do upon their waking is to fall a-fighting'. But Dragut proceeds with Piali to a skiff in order to cross the harbour to inspect the newly mounted battery that is to bombard Fort St Elmo from a point that Scott as narrator recalls from personal experience, as it is very close to where he had performed quarantine on his visit to Malta.[74] The battery has been raised by picked Algerian gunners from Dragut's galleys.

In the meantime many more Knights have assembled in Sicily for Malta, and the Spanish Viceroy of that island has 'received them with a great affectation of interest, and pretended the greatest possible earnestness' to assist them with shipping. La Valette is most anxious to have them, for even the smallest reinforcement is of importance to him at such a crisis. He has therefore promised every exertion on his part to bring them over in the teeth of Piali's and Dragut's cruisers. But 'the private intention' of the Viceroy of Sicily is to leave the defence of Malta for some time to La Valette's own forces before 'taking that duty upon the strong shoulders' of King Philip II. He will only raise the siege at the last moment, thereby saving his master troops and money. Nevertheless small bands of Knights and adventurers have crossed from time to time in *speronari*, and in Malta there are almost daily reports of 'great succours' on the way from Messina, so that 'the hopes of such a relief and the fear that it might prove sufficient to raise the siege' render it the topic of the day, 'to which the attention of Moor and Christian was turned with equal anxiety'.

In this state of expectancy and suspense the troops on both sides again hear 'the morning bells salute the light of dawn from the steeple of Saint John's Church in the fortress of Saint Angelo' as a signal for the attack by sea and land on Fort St Elmo. Mustering their advanced parties by land, the Turks spy a neglected post in a low embrasure of the cavalier of St Elmo, and no sooner is this reported to Ulichiali than he orders a large body of janissaries—armed with 'sharpened sabres and the long fusees'—to scale it. As they do so, they join the name of Ulichiali as their immediate commander to their shouts and cries of onset.

> The Greek's pulse beat in an almost suffocating rapidity at hearing the cries of the Moors, while their effect[s] upon the defendants were expressed by loud cries of fear and surprise, groans of the wounded and screams of those who looked for refuge, and could meet with no shelter which promised assurance of any; and such were the impulses of the Grecian's natural feeling that he became more and more confused as the sounds of the defence seemed to increase while those of the assault fiercely mingled with [them] without being able to overcome them. The first instinct of what was expected from him as a commander ranked with others, the most distinguished men of his time, had hurried him on to the attack as far as the foot of the cavalier, towards which the janissaries pressed by files, and up which they pressed their wear[y] way, entering at

the embrasure. A dismal union of shouts and groans with a close
fire of musketry was accompanied by the throbs of Ulichiali's
heart, beating as if it would have throbbed itself to pieces against
the iron folds of its breastplate, while it no longer permitted him
strength or courage to press forward, as had been his original
intention. Had not the soldiers themselves had their own attention
very much occupied, Ulichiali must have caught the attention of the
steady old janissaries, as he stood trembling and shaking at the bottom
of the embrasure, as if about to ascend in his turn but successively
giving way to every private soldier as he pushed by him in his turn.

   In this state of immobility from irresolution to retreat and terror of advancing,
he suddenly finds himself beaten to the ground by two large Turks, who have
fallen from the rampart in a general repulse of the assailants under a charge by
a party of Spanish Knights and soldiers, including Ramegas. The party have
charged under the national war-cry of 'Saint Iago and close Spain', which has
hitherto not been heard in the battle, so that the Turks first mistakenly conclude
that the expected reinforcement has come from Sicily. At the same time the
defenders shower fireworks from the battlements, which reach the two strug-
gling soldiers holding fast on the ground to Ulichiali. 'His terror had during
this assault assumed various shapes, but these now settled into perhaps the most
serious terror which a man can be acted upon—by that, namely, of being burned'
alive. Appalled at the increasing yells from the sharers of his misfortune, he
extricates himself from a mass of blazing cotton in order to retreat from the
trench to the side of the cavalier adjoining the sea, but he hears 'the stern voice
of a Turkish general', who is none other than Mustapha, stemming and thun-
dering back to the assault a crowd of janissaries. The appearance of his blazing
garments serves as 'a signal to the poor soldiers, whose original alarm was half
again renewed', so that Mustapha, on seeing his timid colleague, throws himself
into the retreating janissaries, and, 'using indifferently the flat, the point, and edge
of the sabre' upon the singed Ulichiali, beats him to the ground with his baton,
while exclaiming, 'Turn, thou dog, turn! Durst show the staff, which the Sultan
gave thee, in leading his soldiers to flight instead of victory.' Wrenching Ulichiali's baton from his grasp, Mustapha orders a bucket to be thrown over him,
adding: 'The foulest you can find is fitted for his deserts.' Mustapha then presses
forwards, leaving Ulichiali 'half-stupefied to shame and half-choking with the
foul water employed to quench his flames'.

   Urged by Mustapha and their zealous leaders, the Turks throw themselves
resolutely into the cavalier in the knowledge that no help has yet come from
Sicily, and that the only reinforcements to reach Fort St Elmo are the small
supplies 'successively sent over by the attentive vigilance of the Grand Master'.
Their effect is like that of a powerful medicine, which, 'although it cannot
recall the patient's exhausted powers of nature', can nevertheless renew from
time to time 'an extraordinary temporary impulse'. In fact, 'the stupendous

exertions made by the infidels would scarce have been successful in carrying Saint Elmo' if the fort had been larger and capable of accommodating a more numerous garrison. The spirit of the present garrison, however, 'though in the most perilous circumstance, continued totally unabated since the time of the last Great Council, at which La Vallette had inspired them with his self-denial and undaunted personal courage'. Not only does no one now intimate the least desire to be recalled from St Elmo but two renowned Knights, whom La Valette has required 'to return from that slaughter-house' on account of their old age and personal infirmity, continue to exert 'the last remains of their faded strength' together with their younger brothers in arms, including an intimate friend of La Valette's nephew, who, being shot through the body, refuses young La Valette's offer to carry him to the infirmary on the ground that 'your cares will be better bestow[ed] upon such of our brethren as may have sustained some injury which is not irreparable'.⁷⁵

This 'extremely sanguinary' method of conducting the siege and defence excites 'mutual fear' about the final outcome in both La Valette and Mustapha, the former of whom dispatches a fresh message to the Viceroy of Sicily for an immediate reinforcement in addition to the promised larger expedition. Mustapha, whose losses are overwhelmingly greater than La Valette's, summons a council of war, attended by Piali and a crestfallen Ulichiali, but not by Dragut, who, being renowned for his skill in artillery, has taken personal command of the battery bombarding Fort St Elmo. His absence is a deliberate departure on Scott's part as narrator from the account in Vertot not only to elaborate a special scene for Dragut at the climax of part four of the manuscript of *The Siege of Malta* but also to employ again his technique of parallelism for Mustapha in another original, even theatrical, scene and to combine it with a device hitherto unused by him, namely, oriental fatalism. For Mustapha, having fumed that 'he should be now in his old age stopped by a paltry turret, hardly the strength of a henroost', and having consequently sworn to 'make these Christians suffer' in such a manner that 'the very name of Saint Elmo shall become a sound of terror' to all obstinate defenders, is suddenly struck to the ground by a roof-beam that has been carried away by a Christian bullet. His attendants, at the sight of blood streaming from his nose, mouth and ears, look upon it as 'a[n] evil omen to the siege which, in the opinion of most of the besiegers, he alone was capable of conducting', but the wounded pacha assures them that 'I am not lost to you, though the blow was a stunning one'. He will yet live to see the effect of the combined attack on St Elmo, which, with 'the continued pressure from the ravelin', will soon bring about 'the consummation of our labours'. 'Fling a cloak over me, and bear me for a moment to my pavilion, where a few minutes' rest will recruit my strength and allow me again to be spectator of your courageous efforts.'

The Pacha was, according to his orders, removed to his own pavilion, where his wife Zulma the Princess, as she was usually called, received, with an unsuccessful attempt to preserve her composure, her husband in a condition to which she had never beheld him reduced. Her tears, which she vainly attempted to repress, were not indeed accompanied by lamentations but fell thick and [fast] in silence in the face of the wounded warrior. "Wherefore, Zulma, why disturb me by these tears when by the undaunted blood of Othman, which blend[s] firmly in your veins, you ought rather to supply [me] with the force to discharge my duty, which this accident hath impaired?" "Alas, noble Pacha," said the Princess in a voice broken with sobs, "When did I ever see thee thus? When had ever wave or bullet the time to compel thee to retreat from battle? I fear, I fear this is an intimation of fate, gallant Mustapha. Thy star, long so powerful, is now verging to its setting, and after all thou hast schemed and done, the haughty Dragut will reap the reward of all thy wisdom."

"Not so, Zulma, not so, I say, Princess," replied the wounded warrior. "This stroke is not the stroke of death. I am assured of it by him who never betrayed me. Neither, Lady, shall Dragut reap the crop which he has not sown. His course will not be a long one, and his race draws near the goal even now perhaps, at this moment perhaps."

At this, as if in fulfilment of Mustapha's prediction, and indeed of Dragut's own earlier intuition, 'a mingled chorus of terror, rage and agony' is heard swelling above the shrieks and yells from St Elmo, which itself 'seemed on fire with the report of cannon from every quarter', and then suddenly the terror is followed by a hush 'as by some magic spell'.

"Hark!" said the Pacha of Egypt, raising himself on his couch, "that strange and sudden silence announces that an accident has happened to someone of distinction. Perhaps Dragut, invulnerable in so many feuds, has in this at length proved himself of the race of mortals. Send out a messenger with charges to return on the instant as he values his life, and bring me word what has happened."

Zulma goes into the next apartment to select a daring man to satisfy his inquiries, but before she finds one, 'a wild and general swell of lamentation was heard from the corner of the harbour where Dragut had established' his battery as a fresh menace to the fort's defenders. Listening intently 'by using his feeble hand so expanded as by catching the sound to succeed in making it audible', Mustapha tells Zulma: 'I was right by Heaven. The people lament for that ambitious renegade, and by Heaven they do well to lament him—all save myself; but he ever more stood in my path, nor could I get the just reward due to my services to the Porte while he had the boldness to act as my enemy.' Observing the parallel between the 'means which lately endangered my own life' and the blow that has struck Dragut, he rejoices that 'with him my soul tells me the damage is irreparable', and, although he will do Dragut justice in death by acknowledging that he 'was an incomparable commander of artillery', it is time 'to supply his place, and that few can do but myself'.

> "Order my litter, Zulma; I think I can endure the motion well enough—and let me have men to bear me who do not fear a gun-shot, since they are going so thick this day." "Noble Mustapha," answered his wife, still unable to overcome the extreme terror with which her husband's wound had affected her nerves, "Consider! do you do well in thus exposing yourself?" "Silence, woman," answered the old Pacha, "is it for me to begin at this time of day to fear the crackers of these infidels, which I have braved for eighty years? Yes," he said, "forty years have the pachas been the pillars of the Empire, and this morning Soliman lost one of the bravest of them, besides which it is only a minute past since I snatched a baton from the unworthy hand of another as he set an example to the soldiers of flight instead of advance. Think [you] that I will follow the brave example of the base slave whom I was forced to chastise? No, by Allah, I hated Dragut. I was opposed to him. I rejoice at his death—but it is because I can myself supply his loss at this moment of extreme necessity both to the prince and the state. Order my litter," he said, clapping his hands, "Let me forth to my duty—and the rather conduct thyself like the woman whom thou hast shown thyself in a hundred battles." So saying, the Pacha ascended the litter, which bore him to the thick of the battle, and enabled him to perform the desperate duty of rushing in person to the charge and the rally, as had ever been his universal custom while in entire possession of his strength.

Meanwhile Dragut languishes with a fatal wound caused partly by his 'constant insensibility to danger', which in this instance he has carried to 'temerity' by advancing beyond the cover of the trenches, and partly by his prominent dress, which has drawn the attention of a gunner in a high tower of Fort St Angelo. A shot from the gunner has struck a large fragment of freestone, which, 'by a species of similarity in fate singularly resembling the peril' that has just threatened his rival's life, has rebounded in splinters on Dragut, causing him to fall and discharge blood copiously from mouth and nose. His dress as a contributing factor to his fate is a typical Scott addition to the version in Vertot, although it is but a detail in the context of his transformation of this episode. For he brings in Dragut's son-in-law, Hassan Barbarossa, precisely at this moment whereas in Vertot he appears later, after Dragut's death. Hassan 'saw what had happened, rushed from the trenches, and, placing the fallen chief on his shoulders, proceeded to drag him, tottering under his burden, within the covert trenches, which he had so imprudently abandoned'. Dragut, preserving a bold and confident look, though incapable of expressing himself by speech, makes signs for a cloak to be cast over his body and for himself to be borne to his pavilion. But first, having heard of Mustapha's similar accident, he inquires if he has been carried to his tent, and, on Hassan's answering in the affirmative, he manages to say half-intelligibly but much more magnanimously than his rival: 'Then need no one be ashamed to follow' Mustapha's example. 'Think of me as only a heap of dust; and do thou, in particu[lar], Hassan, abide by thy duty.' Hassan, who is in tears, turns back from Dragut after leaving him in charge of six strong slaves to bear him to the pavilion.

The slaves pursue their way by the safest paths they can find, as another general attack is mounted on Fort St Elmo, preceded by a battering from Piali's galleys. On land hundreds of archers and musketeers advance to the sound of their war-cries and 'barbaric instruments' against the threefold line of Knights and adventurers defending the breaches made by the batteries. The storming parties and the defenders fight fierce hand-to-hand engagements with every weapon available, including, in the defenders' case, their fireworks, 'which were repeatedly found to strike so much terror among the infidels', especially from 'the huge cavalier, which had so long defied the utmost force' of the batteries. Eventually after a six-hour assault Mustapha sounds the retreat, to the 'shouts of exultation' from the defenders of the other forts, including St Angelo, across the harbour. Mustapha, being now in sole charge of the siege, changes his tactics from battery of the cavalier to open storm, for which purpose he packs the trenches with resolute men, only to find that La Valette, 'with his usual prudence', has not failed to send a fresh supply, small but just enough to prolong the defence from day to day. Mustapha therefore decides to cut off these supplies by investing all the fortified places of Malta, including Fort St Angelo, as Dragut would have wished him and Piali to have done in the first instance on starting the siege. This spells the doom of Fort St Elmo, for, although La Valette attempts to break through the blockade with boatloads of Knights, they are driven back. No more remains therefore for what is left of the unfortunate garrison than to prepare to end their days 'like good Christians and with the religious rites prescribed by their church'.

After confessing themselves to such priests as they had among them, and after dressing their wounds, they again hear 'the clash and clang of the martial music' of the Turks, launching their final assault and advancing with confidence 'to a victory, which no one now remained to dispute with them'. Or rather, to be exact, only sixty men are left to defend the breaches, which in a desperate resistance they hold for four hours until Mustapha, to deceive them, sounds a general retreat, and they rush forward in full pursuit of the janissaries, who counter-charge and at last capture the cavalier whence they mow the defenders down with their fire at the conclusion of part four of the manuscript of The Siege of Malta, which coincides, but for two additional paragraphs, with the end of chapter ten.

Parts Five and Six

Mustapha, in keeping with his vow to revenge himself upon the obstinate enemy and to strike terror into the garrisons of the other forts, orders the bodies of those Knights who are still expiring to be disembowelled and fastened to planks of wood and thrown into the harbour to float towards Fort St Angelo. At seeing this barbarous act, La Valette is first filled with grief and indignation, but then retaliates in a manner which Scott, as a humane narrator in contrast to the less scrupulous Vertot, describes as 'not quite worthy of Jean de La Valette', but as 'at least justified by the barbarity of the offence'. For La Valette orders the heads of his Turkish prisoners to be cut off and put into the cannons of Fort St Angelo and then fired into the lines and batteries of the enemy. The shower of heads, thus thundered into Mustapha's entrenchments, denotes that 'the war was to continue on the same relentless principle' after the fall of Fort St Elmo, which coincides with Dragut's death, thereby providing scope for an original scene at the opening of chapter eleven in part five of the manuscript. The scene is in contrast to the mere sentence about Dragut's death in Vertot.

Mustapha considers it sound policy to communicate the news of the fort's fall to Dragut in order to represent it later to the Sultan as part of a plan approved by his colleague. So he takes one or two of his principal officers with him to Dragut's pavilion, where they find him 'stretched upon some Christian ensigns, which had be[en] taken at St Elmo'. His son-in-law, Hassan, sits cross-legged beside him. Incapable of 'making any gesture of welcome', Dragut points to Hassan, as if recommending him to Mustapha's protection. Mustapha professes grief at seeing him in this state, and then, pointing to the ensigns, says, 'I see that you are prepared, like the lion, to die amid the trophies, which you have been the principal cause of gaining'. Cutting him short, Dragut replies that 'this is no time for ceremony', and repeats his earlier gesture of reconciliation. 'We have been long enemies, but that is ended.' After thanking heaven for permitting him 'to see the commencement of the fall of the[se] works', which he brands as a 'nest of inveterate enemies', he again recommends Hassan to Mustapha's patronage 'in his pretensions to my offices'. Hassan will make 'an undaunted commander' to Dragut's Algerian and Tunisian followers, besides being 'a gallant and faithful servant' of the Sultan, to whose 'exclusive service' Dragut claims that he has dedicated his utmost exertions when living and his last breath when dying. Having made an effort to sit upright while finishing 'a dying speech of the character which had dictated his actions during life', he falls back with a deep groan and without the power of again rousing himself.

> Abdul Hassan started up, and looking on his father's bed, and listening to the deep groan which concluded his last speech to Mustapha, suddenly took up the subject where the dying Viceroy had left it off, and addressed the Pacha of Egypt with an energy which seemed to rejoice at finding himself relieved from the necessity of

practising hypocrisy towards the man whom he hated. His swarthy countenance, like a kindling brand, lighted up into an ardent glow, and fixing a look of dislike and passion on the aged Pacha, he addressed him in these uncompromising words: "Pacha of Egypt, thou wert my father's hated enemy, nor was he less yours. Neither were scrupulous of the mode and occasion you took to injure each other. Nor did my father by the last words expect to accomplish any change of our relations by each other. I should think it [un]worthy of me to mendicate for thy friendship. Such as we have been hitherto such will we continue while the earth holds us both, nor is there a land which can bring us to peace. I only desire it shall be written on my monument: "Here lies Abdul Hassan, the son-in-law of Dragut, Viceroy of Tunis. He hated the enemy of his great predecessor, Mustapha the wise and powerful enemy of Dragut, but he did not fear to proclaim his enmity in open council. At least, therefore, he was no hypocrite."

'It cannot be said with equal certainty that he was no fool,' answers Mustapha, who has had full time 'to collect his ready art' of reply. 'Young man, you may repent this before thou art much older.' Hassan later looks at the ruins of Fort St Elmo, and describes it as a place 'so paltry' that, if the Sultan had commanded him and his brave Algerians to assault it, they would have reduced it 'in a week' without any great exertion. Mustapha carefully stores this boast in his memory. He is hardly gone from Dragut's tent half an hour when a cry of lamentation, spreading among the soldiers, announces to the camp 'the death of that cele-brated leader'. Mustapha confers with Piali about Hassan's appointment as Dragut's successor. Piali approves it with pleasure as 'calculated to conciliate the Algerines or such of them at least as [follow] the fool Hassan, who is said openly to have expressed his hatred towards your Lordship'. 'His hatred?' answers Mustapha, 'alas, what is such a sentiment on the part of the young man to me? "When an enemy is avowed," says the sage, "he is disarmed; and a snake at liberty in the chamber is more dangerous than when hidden among the flowers." '

Meanwhile Hassan takes Dragut's body to 'Tunis or Algiers' for burial, and Mustapha begins the siege of Fort St Angelo. When Hassan returns, he brings 5,000 men with him, former followers of Dragut, and commanded by another Greek renegade, an old corsair called Candelissa, whom Dragut had praised for 'the most undaunted courage, as indeed he was easily imposed upon by men whose courage lay chiefly in a bold, wordy way of talking'. Mustapha is anxious that 'Hassan should learn from experience how the blades of the Knights cut'. He therefore calls a council of war, and receives Hassan 'if not with cordiality, at least as if he had entirely forgotten the open defiance, with which the young man had ventured to reply to the civilities which he had addressed to him'. The council having sat late, Mustapha returns at sunset to his pavilion, where he is received by Zulma. 'He looked on her with a smile and an eye that betokened he had something to say to her', but not to the other women in her apartment, who therefore withdraw. 'What thinkest thou is the meaning of this smile on my brow?' he then asks her. 'When an old man smiles,' Zulma replies, 'he foresees or has secured conquest over his enemies.' 'Thou has said it, Zulma; I need not ask thee if thou dost remember the insult with which that rash, hot-brained boy Hassan received with anger and insolence my offers of friendship.' 'Could I merit the affection thou has honoured me with and forget it, Mustapha—may I now ask of thee, it is avenged?' Mustapha answers that so far it *is*, for, although the fool Hassan has had 'the simplicity to ask and take at my hand the character of the doughty Ulichiali, whom I disarmed as a traitor, a coward and a bullying fool', Hassan has made Ulichiali lieutenant-general of one of his bands of Algerian bravoes besides taking Candelissa into his favour. 'With such officers heaven knows how long' Hassan will continue to hold Dragut's title. Zulma remarks that she has heard Candelissa 'termed brave'. 'By himself or by his friends,' answers Mustapha. 'Wait till tomorrow is over, and we shall see with what reputation the boys discharge themselves of the day's duty.'

Having given vent to his feelings, he turns his mind to 'the order of fight for tomorrow', giving way to an occasional sneer, short but expressive, 'at various names, which were marked as destined to stand high in command' of a Turkish assault against a post adjoining Fort Saint Angelo, which he has himself already unsuccessfully failed to capture. Then looking steadily at Zulma, he strikes a more tender note, 'I see, my good princess, that you long seriously to ask me my reasons' for not giving 'my whole genius to tomorrow's battle, which I should probably win, and thereby win my royal cousin's good grace for ever', whereas by leaving the outcome to 'thes[e] young fools, [I] quit the chance of conciliating his favour, since the old corsair Candelissa and the trai[tor] Ulichiali are likely to run away, and will be made to answer for it at the head of the whole army'. 'I will tell thee at once, Zulma', and again he cannot express himself better than by using one of Scott's field-sport images. 'This island', he tells her in confidence, rounded off with a touch of pathos, 'is to me as a wolf to a huntsman, when he neither dare hold him fast or let him go. If [I] take it, I free thy royal cousin out of his greatest fear', but 'having done the greatest service required of me, I will be no longer preserved' in office, however much he may be feared for his 'crabbed temper'. 'Without much ceremony the old hand may be hung up for his last exertions in his master's favour.' 'It is an unhappy state, my Zulma, in which we slaves stand with our masters,' for 'we give them our youth, strength and vigour', but when 'we can supply talent no longer as quick as it is called for, the voice of the Sultan, who envies us, to the viziers, who hate us, is "to the devil with the old man, who is no longer worth the bread he eats"'.

This rather notable piece of dialogue, at the end of chapter eleven, may be said to mark the exhaustion of Scott's creative powers in *The Siege of Malta*, for after it there are no more original scenes. Even Zulma disappears. Indeed, even

before her dialogue with Mustapha, the novel is well on the way towards becoming, as has already been explained,[76] a chronicle derived from Vertot. The
chronicle itself narrates how Hassan and Candelissa are humiliated, exactly as
Mustapha has predicted, and how Mustapha is defeated by La Valette and the
Knights in one attempt after another to capture the defence posts near Fort
St Angelo until at last, in chapter thirteen, he is compelled to raise the siege in
disorder and sail back to Constantinople, when the long-awaited relief force
from Sicily lands at Malta and prepares to give battle to what is left of his army.
The leaders of the relief force are then welcomed by La Valette, although they
are shocked to find Malta in ruins and to see with their own eyes the losses and
suffering endured by the defenders. All Christendom rejoices at La Valette's
victory in 'a siege which attracted the attention of two great divisions of the
world, and seemed not unlikely to decide its fate'. At Constantinople, on the
other hand, there is anger on the Sultan's part against Mustapha and Piali,
particularly the former, although the failure of the expedition is concealed from
the public and is accompanied with threats—indeed preparations—to send
another and larger one commanded by Suleman in person. The fleet that is to
transport it, however, is destroyed by fire long after La Valette has communicated to the sovereigns of Europe his grand design of building a new city on the
site marked at one end by Fort St Elmo. All the sovereigns contribute gener-
ously, and the city, named after La Valette, becomes, in Scott's own words at
the conclusion of *The Siege of Malta*, 'perhaps one of the most singular in
Europe', with *auberges* or hotels for the resident Knights resembling 'modern
clubrooms', and with buildings abounding in 'belvederes, turrets, battlements
and projections of all kinds', which may seem wasteful by 'modern economy',
but which nevertheless are pleasant on aesthetic grounds. The harbours of the
city 'are perhaps the finest in the world', including one for vessels performing
quarantine, on which account 'the author of these sheets' of *The Siege of Malta*
was 'lodged in the house of an ancient Spanish grand master, which pre-
dominates nearly over the spot famous for the death of Dragut'.

    The chronicle itself, which, in general, is fluent and full of incidents, is not a
total plagiarism from Vertot, as Scott selects, rearranges and condenses the
material, and here and there makes significant alterations and additions, as when,
for instance, he amends Vertot in order to continue representing Mustapha as
jealous of his colleagues and bent on securing for himself the title of 'conqueror
of Malta'. Again Scott continues to contrive those 'modes of resistance' connected with sieges almost right till the end, so that he incorporates another one
of them into a description by Vertot of how the Knights beat off an assault by
Mustapha. Scott, moreover, *humanises* Vertot in a passage relating how a Knight
surprises and slaughters the sick and wounded of the Turks to frustrate a
dangerous attack by Mustapha. Vertot positively gloats over the incident,
whereas Scott apologetically attributes it to 'the spirit of the times resembling
too much that which prevailed between those of two opposite religions'. Fin-

ally, in describing how La Valette's nephew meets a hero's death in battle, and how 'the elder Valette' endures the distressful event, Scott precedes Vertot's account of it with a reference to the old man's countenance as bearing 'a stern solemnity and gravity of carriage, by which an ancient Roman might have been distinguished on a similar occasion'. In other words, he invests La Valette with his favourite brand of stoicism, derived more immediately from his kinsmen of 'the old Sandy-Know[e] breed', as he calls them in his journal.[77]

As to the plagiarism itself, it ought to be borne in mind that such borrowing was common in Scott's age, so much so that he had himself remarked, in a significant journal entry about his many imitators as a historical novelist, that his great advantage over them was that 'they steal too openly', as when, for instance, Horace Smith 'inserted in *Brambletye House* whole pages from Defoe's *Fire and Plague of London*'. In contrast to them, he claimed that he did not steal but '*convey* an incident or so', and when he did so, 'I am [at] as much pains to avoid detection as if the offence could be indicted in literal fact at the Old Bailey'.[78] While it cannot be said that in the last two chapters of *The Siege of Malta* he succeeds in avoiding detection, since the borrowing from Vertot is too obvious, and since Vertot was himself already well known to English readers from numerous editions in translation, several of them published in Edinburgh, his remarks serve to put this question of plagiarism in the proper historical perspective. It would also be in perspective to bear in mind that in *The Siege of Malta* the plagiarism comes towards the end of the novel (and so many of Scott's novels have weak endings) after numerous scenes of his own invention, which were written after he had already suffered three strokes, and when he was abroad without an amanuensis.

Finally, the determining, practical factor behind the plagiarism might well have been, as has already been hinted,[79] the increasing pressure upon Scott to honour his advance commitment with Cadell to send him the whole of *The Siege of Malta* from Naples by the spring of 1832 for publication as the last novel in 'the magnum'.[80] The pressure might account for the general impression of *rapid* writing conveyed by Scott's hand in the last two chapters of the manuscript. On realising that, contrary to his earlier, confident expectations, he was running a real risk of not achieving the deadline agreed on with Cadell, perhaps if he continued with time-consuming original scenes, and, moreover, as the pressure upon him mounted with the impending termination of the lease of his *palazzo* at Naples, combined with his feverish urge to depart from Naples for home, he might, in a weak moment, and in the knowledge that literary borrowing, especially from foreign authors, was common practice, have resorted to Vertot as a quick, practical resolution of his predicament. Even allowing this, however, *The Siege of Malta* does not emerge, on balance, as the work of shame that it has hitherto been given out to the world to be. On the contrary, it evokes admiration for Scott's character: an admiration exactly like that attributed by Lockhart to Laidlaw as Scott's amanuensis at Abbotsford at the time that

Laidlaw, as explained at the beginning of this book,[81] had been listening to Scott dictating *Count Robert of Paris* to him between three strokes. It is in that 'prevalent feeling of admiration, this time evoked by *The Siege of Malta*, that the foregoing long description of its contents has been written in the hope that, despite Lockhart's wish that the manuscript would never 'see the light',[82] and despite John Buchan's warning to 'any literary resurrectionist' against 'the crime of giving *The Siege of Malta* to the world', it will be seen that the kind of resurrection attempted in this book is justified.

References for Chapter 6

1. MS 5317, f. 108.
2. Cf. Ch. IV, p. 64.
3. Cf. ibid, & pp. 66, 68.
4. Cf. ibid, p. 80. Cf. also p. 71.
5. Ibid, p. 88; Ch. V, p. 107.
6. Cf. Ch. IV, pp. 80, 88.
7. Ibid, p. 79.
8. ff. 111A–112.
9. ff. 23, 24, 48. Folio 24 is missing from the MS, but Scott's direction is given in the 1878 copy.
10. f. 48.
11. Cf. Ch. IV, p. 80.
12. E.g., ff. 4–5, 79–80, 144–45.
13. Cf. Ch. IV, p. 64.
14. f. 24.
15. Nov. 2–7, 1932. Royal Malta Library, Valletta, Malta.
16. Berg 64B4878–79.
17. ff. 6, 21.
18. f. 122.
19. f. 24.
20. *The Scotsman*, Aug. 1–2, 4, 1871.
21. Cf. Ch. V, p. 104.
22. f. 52.
23. f. 21.
24. *Letters*, vi, 444–45.
25. Cf. Ch. V, p. 109.
26. Cf. Ch. IV, p. 88.
27. Cf. E. Johnson, *The Great Unknown*, 1972, ii, 1270; W. E. K. Anderson, *The Journal of Sir W. Scott*, 1972, xlvi.
28. Sept. 29, 1928, p. 10, col. 6.
29. *Sir W. Scott*, 1906, p. 240.
30. Cf. Ch. IV, p. 80.
31. Scott files, departmental records, Department of MSS, National Library of Scotland, July 5, 1944.
32. Cf. Ch. I, p. 10.
33. Charles S. Frendo, 'Sir W. Scott's *Siege of Malta*' in *Malta Chronicle*, Nov. 2, 1932.
34. Nov. 2–7, 1932.
35. Nov. 18, 1932, p. 13, col. 7. The 'Chase National Bank', New York, where the MS of *The Siege of Malta* was stated by Frendo to have originally been deposited by G. Wells for safety, was confused in *The Glasgow Herald* with 'The National Bank of Valetta'.
36. J. Buchan, *Sir W. Scott*, 1932, p. 331.
37. pp. 38–47.
38. p. 12.
39. p. 46.
40. Cf. Ch. IV, pp. 68, 70–71.
41. Scott files, departmental records, Department of MSS, National Library of Scotland, July 5, 1944.
42. Cf. Ch. II, p. 33; Ch. IV, pp. 38, 71.
43. S. Fowler Wright, *The Siege of Malta*, 1942, pp. 1–2.
44. Scott files, departmental records, Department of MSS, National Library of Scotland, July 5, 1944.
45. Cf. Ch. II, p. 33.
46. Cf. Ch. IV, p. 68.
47. Cf. Ch. II, p. 32.
48. There is no textual warrant at all for putting this observation of the Pursuivant, together with an anecdote, about the sacking of Gozo in a *footnote*, and closing Ch. II at f. 22 instead

of at f. 23 of the MS, as appears to have been done in the 1878 version and 1932 typescript (p. 33) of the MS. When Scott wanted to have a footnote, he indicated it unmistakably. (See ff. 117a, 119a.) That Ch. II ends not at f. 22 but at f. 23 is clear from the *sense* of the text, which explicitly states that 'the Herald of the Order had made an end' of his speech, and, on being invited by Vilheyna to 'proceed', he resumes the conversation only to say that 'it becomes [me] to be silent' at the end of the chapter. See also next note.

49. This *technical* point appears to have been missed in the 1878 and 1932 versions of the MS, as a result of which a whole page of MS (f. 48), marking the opening of Ch. III, and intended to be a kind of summary by Scott as narrator, is represented in the typescript (pp. 35–36) as a continuation of the Pursuivant's speech, complete with inverted commas (which are spurious), whereas at the end of the summary or recapitulation (f. 49, l. 3 of MS) it is stated that 'we [i.e., Scott as narrator] have detailed at some length the information. . . .' The error, as reflected in the typescript (pp. 35–36), largely stems from the unwarranted creation of a footnote (see previous note) in order to close Ch. II at that point (f. 22) instead of at f. 23. See also 53n.

50. Cf. ff. 51–53, 64–67.

51. Lockhart x, 138.

52. Cf. Ch. II, p. 36.

53. Cf. similar technique of recapitulation at opening of Ch. III, ff. 48–49.

54. Cf. Ch. III, pp. 39, 44–45, 50.

55. Cf. Ch. IV, pp. 79–80.

56. *Journal* 80.

57. Cf. Ch. I, pp. 9, 18.

58. Cf. Ch. III, p. 50.

59. Cf. ibid, p. 45.

60. Cf. Ch. IV, pp. 76–77.

61. Cf. Ch. II, p. 30.

62. f. 29.

63. Cf. Ch. III, pp. 38–40.

64. In the text (f. 39, l. 5) Scott appears to have inadvertently written 'the Commander' (i.e., Vilheyna) for 'the Grand Master' (i.e., La Valette) as the speaker of this reply.

65. Cf. Ch. II, p. 30.

66. In *The Siege of Malta* Scott uses *lelie* and *tecbir* rather indifferently for the war-cry of the Saracens.

67. Ch. IX ends with four lines on the inset to f. 47 of MS.

68. In the 1932 typescript (p. 135, l. 7) 'St James' is altered to 'St John', but Ramegas, a Castilian, and La Valette are referring to St James as the patron saint of Spain.

69. Cf. Ch. IV, pp. 73, 81–82, 86.

70. Cf. ibid, p. 88.

71. *Journal* 86. See also ibid 215.

72. Cf. Ch. IV, pp. 54, 56, 74, 83.

73. *Journal* 684.

74. Cf. Ch. III, p. 42.

75. Young La Valette is not in Vertot's account of this scene. Scott, moreover, deepens its pathos by enlarging somewhat on the wounded Knight's direct speech.

76. Ch. IV, p. 88.

77. *Journal* 57.

78. Ibid 215.

79. Cf. Ch. IV, p. 88.

80. Cf. Ch. III, pp. 41, 51; Ch. IV, pp. 55 67, 72.

81. Ch. I, p. 8.

82. Lockhart x, 148.

Appendices

While this book was going through the press, the author's attention was kindly drawn to two documents by Dr James Corson. As they provide supplementary evidence of facts related in the book, they are reproduced here as appendices.

Appendix A is a copy of the financial statement drawn up in Edinburgh by Scott's publisher, Robert Cadell, in reply to two letters from Malta, in which Scott informed Cadell that he was writing *The Siege of Malta*, which he wished that Lockhart would revise when completed, and leaving it to Cadell to decide on the method of publication. This financial statement, therefore, which Cadell called 'A View of The Siege of Malta', supplements his letter to Scott, to which reference is made on p. 55 of this book. The relevant pages relating to Scott's two letters to Cadell are 31, 41, 47. This document provides further confirmation of the point made on p. 109, that Lockhart was inaccurate and misleading in stating that Scott wrote *The Siege of Malta* 'in spite of all remonstrances'.

Appendix B is a copy of the bill for Scott's board and lodging at Beverley's Hotel in Malta. The relevant pages in the book relating to it are 48, 50, 54.

Appendix A

19 December 1831

View of
    The Siege of Malta   3 vols post octavo
             by the Author of Waverley

5000 copies	
Printing say 42 Sheets @ £5 - 15	£241 - 10 -
Alterations etc very numerous	120
Paper say 47 Reams	587 - 10 -
Advertising	150
Author	2000
Mr Lockhart's revising	105
	————
	£3204

```
5000 Books
 200 over
5,200 @ 21/3            £5525
                   off    225
                        _____
                         5,300
America & France          120
                        £5,420
                        _____
```

(The manuscript is now in the National Library: MS 6080)

Appendix B

Malta 12th December 1831

£70
Three weeks after date pay to Thomas Beverley Hotel
keeper Malta this my *second* of exchange for the sum of
seventy pounds the first being unpaid without farther
advice from

Your obedient Servant
Walter Scott

Messrs Coutts & Co
Bankers Strand London

(The original manuscript is in Selkirk Public Library.
Only the signature is in Scott's hand. The bill itself
is in the hand of Beverley or a clerk.)

Appendix C

Just as this book was about to be published its author succeeded in tracing one
of the missing pages of the manuscript of *The Siege of Malta*, reference to
which is made in Chapter VI, p. 162, ll. 27–8. The page in question, which
corresponds to f. 28 of the manuscript, lies in the Brotherton Collection of
rare books and manuscripts, University of Leeds, and a facsimile of it can be
seen in *Some Unpublished Letters of Sir Walter Scott, from the Collection in the
Brotherton Library*, compiled by J. Alexander Symington (Oxford, 1932), p. 168.
A transcription of the missing page is also printed in the same book (pp. 167–
168), and, although it is not perfectly accurate, it is incomparably superior
to the version in the 1932 typescript of *The Siege of Malta*, which is based on
the 1878 copy of the manuscript. A collation of Symington's version, in fact,
and of the 1932 typescript serves to provide further confirmation of the radical
editing of the manuscript by the 1878 copyist. (See p. 126 of this book.)

Bibliography

Manuscripts

National Library of Scotland, Edinburgh
MS 1752	(*Scott Letters, 1831–32*)
1553–54	(*Letters of Anne Scott, 1831–32*)
1554	(*Scott Family Letters*)
1614 & 917	(*Journal and Letters of Charles Scott, 1831–32*)
921	(*William Laidlaw's Account of Scott's Last Days at Abbotsford*)
3389	(*Mrs J. Davy's Malta Diary, 1831*)
5317	(*Letters to Scott, 1831–32*)
3009	(*Album of Draycott House*)
2617ff. 65–76	(*Letters of Mrs E. Fletcher to Allan Cunningham, 1820–34*)
138	(*Letters from Scott to his Family, 1788–1822*)
786	(*Correspondence of Thomas Thomson relating to Scott, 1832*)
2890	(*Miscellaneous Scott correspondence, 1823–31*)
MSS 855, 860	(*Letters to W. Laidlaw, 1831–32*)
3919, 5317	(*Letters from R. Cadell to Sir W. Scott, 1831–32*)
Acc. 5188	(*Cadell MSS, 1830–35*)
MS Acc. 5131	(*Scott Letters, vol. V, 1831–32*)

New York Public Library

Berg Collection 339591B (*MS of 'The Siege of Malta'*)
Berg Collection 64B4879 (*MS copy (1878) of 'The Siege of Malta'*)
Berg Collection 64B4878 (*Typescript (1932) of 1878 MS copy of 'The Siege of Malta'*)

Public Record Office, London

ADM 51/3082 (*Log of the Proceedings of H.M. Ship, Barham, Hugh Pigot Captain, 1831*)

Hughenden Archives, High Wycombe

Box 122, B/XXI/C/240 (Letters from J. Clay to Benjamin Disraeli from Venice with a reference to Scott in Malta)

Stamford, Lincolnshire

Family Letters of John Hookham Frere and Susan
Frere with references to Scott's Visit to Malta:
Oct., 1831–Jan., 1832.

Scott: Works

Letters, ed. Sir H. Grierson (1932–35).
The Journal, ed. W. E. K. Anderson (1972).
The Novels and Poetry.
The Life of Bonaparte.
Lives of the Novelists.
Paul's Letters to his Kinsfolk.
Seventeenth-Century (Private) Letters, ed. D. Grant (1947).

Printed Sources

ALIBONE, S. A.: *A Critical Dictionary of British and American Authors* (1870),
vol. II. [For Washington Irving and Scott.]
AMBROSE, MARY, E.: 'The First Italian Translations of Scott' in *Modern Language
Review*, January 1972, 74–82.
ANONYMOUS: *Malta Government Gazette*, 1831–32.
The Caledonian Mercury, Edinburgh, 1831–32.
The Scotsman, Edinburgh, 1831–32.
ASPINALL, A.: 'Some New Scott Letters III' in *Times Literary Supplement*,
24 April 1948.
BALLANTYNE, J.: 'The Last Days of Sir Walter Scott' in *Edinburgh Evening
Courant*, 16 August, 1871.
BLESSINGTON, COUNTESS OF: *The Literary Life and Correspondence*, ed. R. R.
Madden (1890).
BOSIGELIN, P. M.: *Ancient and Modern Malta* (London, 1805).
BOYER, A.: *The History of the Reign of Queen Anne digested into Annals*
(1703).
The Draughts of the Most Remarkable Fortified Towns of Europe (1701).
BRYDONE, P.: *A Tour through Sicily and Malta* (1774).
BUCHAN, J.: *Sir Walter Scott* (1932).
BUNSEN, BARON: *Memoirs*, ed. Frances, Baroness Bunsen (1868).
CARSWELL, D.: *Sir Walter Scott* (1930).
CHAMBERS, R.: *Life of Sir Walter Scott, with Abbotsford Notanda* (1871).
CLAY, EDITH: 'Notes of Sir William Gell to Sir Walter Scott' in *Journal of the
Warburg Courtauld Institute*, vol. 33, 1970, 336–343.

COCHRANE, J. B.: *Catalogue of the Abbotsford Library* (Edinburgh, 1838).

COLE, OWEN B.: 'A Last Memory of Sir Walter Scott' in *Cornhill Magazine*, September 1923, 257–267.

CROKER, J. W.: *Correspondence and Diaries*, ed. L. J. Jennings (1885).

CUMMING, W. F.: *Notes of a Wanderer* (1839).

DAVY, DR J.: *Memoirs of the Life of Sir H. Davy* (1836).
'The New Volcano in the Mediterranean' (Graham Island) in *Philosophical Transactions of Royal Society* for 1832–34.

FERRIER, SUSAN: 'Recollections of Visits to *Ashestiel* and Abbotsford' reprinted in *Marriage*, ed. R. Bentley (1881).
Memoir and Correspondence, ed. J. A. Doyle (1929).

FESTING, G.: *John Hookham Frere and his Friends* (1899).

FRENDO, C. S.: 'Sir W. Scott's *Siege of Malta*' in *Malta Chronicle*, 2–7 Nov., 1932.

FRERE, SIR BARTLE: *Memoir of J. H. Frere* (1874).

GELL, SIR WILLIAM: *Reminiscences of Sir Walter Scott's Residence in Italy, 1832*, ed. J. C. Corson (1957).
Letters to the Society of Dilettanti, 1831–35, ed. Edith Clay, 1976.

GREVILLE, C. C.: *Memoirs* (1874).

GRIERSON, SIR HERBERT: *Sir Walter Scott, Bart.* (1938).

HALL, CAPT. B.: *Fragments of Voyages and Travels, 3rd Series* (1833).

HEMLOW, JOYCE: *Fanny Burney* (1958).

HOGG, J.: *Familiar Anecdotes of Scott*, ed. D. Mack (1972).

HOLLAND, SIR HENRY: *Recollections of a Past Life* (1872).

HOME, J. A.: *Lady Louisa Stuart* (1899).

HUGHES, MRS: *Letters and Recollections of Sir Walter Scott*, ed. H. G. Hutchinson (no date).

JENSEN, J. V.: *Thorvaldsens Portrætbuster* (Copenhagen, 1926).

JOHNSON, E.: *Sir Walter Scott: The Great Unknown* (1970).

KNIGHTON, SIR WILLIAM: *Memoirs*, ed. Lady Knighton (1838).

LANG, A.: *Sir Walter Scott* (1906).

LOCKHART, J. G.: *The Life of Sir Walter Scott* (1839).
Ancient Spanish Ballads (1822).

MACAULAY, T. B.: *Letters*, ed. T. Pinney, vol. II (1974).

MILNES, MONCKTON R. (Lord Houghton): *Life, Letters and Friendships* by T. W. Reid (1890).

MOORE, T.: *Memoirs, Journal and Correspondence*, ed. J. Russell (1854).

MOORMAN, MRS M.: *Wordsworth: The Later Years* (1965).

PARKER, W. M.: 'Scott's Last Journey' in *The Scotsman*, 16 April, 1932.
'Scott in Florence and Venice' in *The Scotsman*, 10 March, 1962.

PECK, W. E.: 'A Publisher's Friendship for Scott' in *Sir Walter Scott Quarterly*, Jan. 1928, vol. I, no. 4.

PLON, E.: *Thorvaldsen: His Life and Works*, tr. Mrs Cashel Holy (1870).

ROGERS, S.: *Recollections* (1859).

RUSSELL, MRS F.: 'Scott's Last Verses' in *The Times*, 19 August, 1932.

SCHETKY, J. H.: *Sketches*, ed. by his daughter (1877).

SHERWOOD, MRS: *Life*, ed. by her daughter, Sophia Kelly (1854).

SKENE, J.: *Memories of Sir Walter Scott* (1909).

SLADE, A.: *Turkey, Greece and Malta* (1837).

SMILES, S.: *A Publisher and his Friends: Memoir and Correspondence of J. Murray* (1890).

SULTANA, D. E.: *Samuel Taylor Coleridge in Malta and Italy* (1969).

SYMINGTON, J. A.: *Some Unpublished Letters of Sir Walter Scott* (1932).

DE VERTOT, ABBÉ: *History of the Knights Hospitallers of St. John*, tr. into English (Edinburgh 1757, 1770).

VINCENT, H. P.: *Letters of Dora Wordsworth* (privately printed, Chicago, 1944).

WARBURTON, E.: *The Crescent and the Cross*, 16th edition, no date.

WARING, G.: *Letters from Malta and Sicily* (1843).

WORDSWORTH, W. and D.: *Letters: The Later Years*, ed. E. de Selincourt (1939).

WRIGHT FOWLER, S.: *The Siege of Malta* (1942).

Maps

1. Europe and North Africa showing places mentioned in connection with Scott's Journey (1831–32)

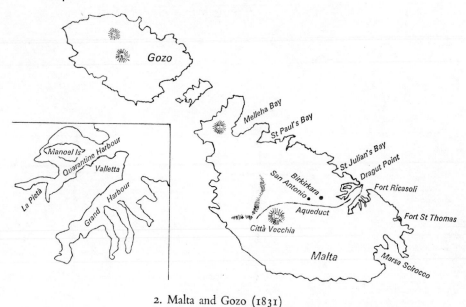

2. Malta and Gozo (1831)

3. Fortifications of Malta and Turkish positions in the Great Siege of 1565

205

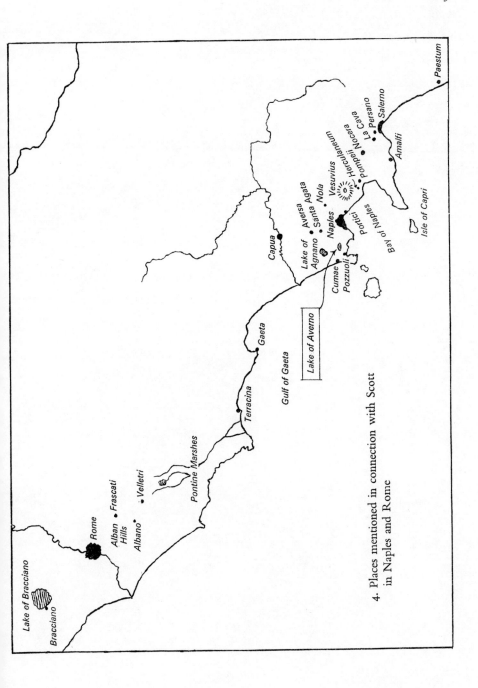

4. Places mentioned in connection with Scott
in Naples and Rome

Paestum

Salerno
La Persano
Nocera
Pompeii
Herculaneum
Vesuvius
Nola
Naples
Portici
Bay of Naples
Santa Agata
Aversa
Lake of Agnano
Cumae
Pozzuoli
Capua
Lake of Averno
Gaeta
Gulf of Gaeta
Terracina
Pontine Marshes
Velletri
Frascati
Alban Hills
Albano
Rome
Lake of Bracciano
Bracciano
Amalfi
Isle of Capri

Index

90, 109; *The Siege of Malta* (*see also* mottoes), 28, 31, 32n^{21}, 33n^{25}, 34nn$^{34,\ 36}$, 35n^{39}, 36nn$^{49,\ 52}$, 39n^{5}, its title, 41; 41n^{17}, 42–3, 45–8, 50–1, 54–5, 59–60, 63–72, 74–76, is dispatched, 79–82, 86–8; 96, 98, 100–2, 107; is not considered publishable, 109–10; misrepresented by Lockhart, 125–6; manuscript described, 64, 122–9; its arrangement of parts and chapters, 88, 122–4; some of it burnt, 71, 80, 122; its missing pages, 124–5, 130, 132, 146, 162, 171, 177; its 'cloudiness', confusions and errors, 59, 68, 80, 86, 107, 126, 131, 135–6, 162; its 'original story', 46–7, 68, 88, 124, 151, 167, 175, 177–8, 189, 191; its theme of changed manners, 68, 79–80, 109, 132, 135, 137, 139, 147, 149–51, 153; its anachronisms, 98, 151–2, 172; its instances of the technique of parallelism, 154–5, 174, 183–4; characters dropped from it, 177, 189; its ending, 125, 191; 1878 manuscript version of it, 123–4, 126–9; 1932 typescript, 47n^{49a}, 124, 127–30, 132, 146, 162, 171, 175n^{68}, 177; purchase of the manuscript, 126–7; *Tales of the Crusaders* (*see also The Talisman*), 10; *Tales of a Grandfather*, 3, 23, 95, 101–2; *Tales of my Landlord* (*see also Castle Dangerous, Count Robert of Paris, The Heart of Midlothian, Old Mortality*), 16, 114; *The Talisman*, 34, 49, 80, 144, 167; *Vision of Don Roderick*, 32; *Waverley*, 95; *Woodstock*, 6, 12, 14, 18–19, 21, 24, 177

Scott, Major Walter, 2–5; is to have free passage to Naples, 6–7; 8, 12–14, 18, is sent north to quell riots, 21–2; 24–5, 28–30, 35, 39, 42; his appearance, 44; his behaviour, 45, 51, 56; presses Scott to leave Malta for Naples, 47; 48, 55, 57, 59–62, has leave extended, 64–5; 66, 69; his return, 71–2, 74, 80; 81–2, 87, 90, 100, 109, 119

Selkirk Public Library, 195

Shakespeare, William, 2, 20, 22, 35, 39, 41, 51, 64, 75, 99, 100, 107, 123

Sheed and Ward, publishers, 126

Sheffield, 4, 8–9, 13

Shelley, Percy Bysshe, 97–8, 103, 107

Sherwood, Mrs, 116n^{97}

Shortreed, Andrew, 46–7, 56–7, 70–2

Sicily, 54, 136, 147, 158, 181–3, 190

Sidmouth, Henry Addington, 1st Viscount, 20–1

The Siege of Malta see Scott, Sir W.: *Works*

Skene, Miss Helen, 67–8, 83

Skene, James, 35n^{44}, 36n^{45}, 38n^{3}, 39n^{5}, 41–3, 46, 48nn$^{54-6}$, 49n^{63}, 51, 54, 57, 71, 80, 103, 107, 119n^{107}

Skene, Lieutenant J. H., 41, 46

Smiles, Samuel, 7n^{30}, 9n^{44}

Smith, Horace, 191

Smollett, Tobias, 8, 13

Southey, Robert, 32

Spain, 31–4, 74, 116, 129–43, 147, 152, 161, 181–2

The Spectator, 117–18

speronari, 143–6, 176, 181

Stafford, Lady, 25, 29

Sterzing, Tyrol, 114

Sticchini, Signor, amanuensis, 64, 68

Stoddart, Sir John, 17, 39, 41–2, 49

Stoddart, J. F., 42

Stoddart, Lady, 39

Stopford, Lady Charlotte, 103

Strachan, Lady, 116

Strahan, Lady, 58, 62, 66, 78

Street, Celia, 12, 17, 51, 74, 105, 110, 115

Stromboli, Italy, 54, 178

Stuart, Prince Charles Edward, 95, 100, 102, 110n^{74}

Stuart, Henry, Cardinal of York, 100–2

Stuart, Sir John, hero of Maida, 95

Stuart, Lady Louisa, 9, 12, 15, 20–1, 23–4, 42, 54, 57, 65, 70, 72, 86, 90

Stuart, Royal House of, 82, 100–2, 113

Stuttgart, 105, 115

Suleman the Magnificent, *pl*; 129, 135–6, 148–50, 162, 167–70, 174, 185, 188–90

Swift, Jonathan, 19, 107

Talbot, Sir George, 78

Talbot, Marianne, 78, 82

Tarentum, Archbishop of, 61–2

Tasso, Torquato, 17, 111

Tegernsee, Germany, 115

Terni, Italy, 110

Terracina, Italy, 95

Thorwaldsen, Bertel, 102–3

The Times, 61n^{36}, 89n^{149}

Times Literary Supplement, 25n^{130}

Titian, 112

Torlonia, Duke and Duchess of, 105, 108

A general view of The Siege of Malta, from one of the
frescoes by Matteo Perez d'Aleccio in the Palace of the
Grand Masters in Valletta, Malta. Scott was given a port
folio of plates of these frescoes by John Hookham Frere